Perl Medic

Perl Medic
Transforming Legacy Code

Peter J. Scott

ADDISON-WESLEY

Boston ♦ San Francisco ♦ New York ♦ Toronto ♦ Montreal
London ♦ Munich ♦ Paris ♦ Madrid
Capetown ♦ Sydney ♦ Tokyo ♦ Singapore ♦ Mexico City

The publisher offers discounts on this book when ordered in quantity for special sales. For more information, please contact:

U.S. Corporate and Government Sales
(800) 382-3419
corpsales@pearsontechgroup.com

For sales outside of the U.S., please contact:

International Sales
(317) 581-3793
international@pearsontechgroup.com

Visit Addison-Wesley on the Web: www.awprofessional.com

Library of Congress Cataloging-in-Publication Data

Scott, Peter (Peter J.), 1961-
    Perl medic : transforming legacy code / Peter Scott.
        p. cm.
    Includes bibliographical references and index.
    ISBN 0-201-79526-4
        1. Perl (Computer program language) I. Title.

QA76.73.P22S395 2004
005.13'3--dc22

                                                    2004041060

Text printed on recycled paper

First printing, February 2004

To my mother, for teaching me to read at a tender age after much begging. One thing led to another…

Table of Contents

Preface

"Worldwide, there are well over 200 billion lines of software that are
fragmented, redundantly defined, hard to decipher, and highly inflexible . . .
organizations run the risk of being mired down by a mountain of legacy code."

— William Ulrich, *Legacy Systems: Transformation Strategies*

Congratulations! Let's say you just graduated with a computer science degree and now, bucking the economic trend, you've landed a job at a prestigious company with a large information technology department. You're going to be replacing Bill, a programmer who won the lottery and was not seen or heard from again, save for a postcard from Puerto Vallarta two weeks later. Your coworkers warn you not to mention the postcard to your supervisor. You sit in Bill's cubicle throwing out pieces of vendor advertising left in the center desk drawer, thinking about how you're going to apply the elegant principles and sublime paradigms that professors inculcated in you at college. Just then, your supervisor arrives and, leaning over your shoulder, taps at your keyboard, bringing up a file.

"This is the last program Bill was working on. We think it's almost finished. We're behind schedule, so see if you can get it done by Thursday at the latest."

As he leaves, you look at the program's tangle of misindented lines and cryptic variable names, searching for comments, but the only ones you can find read, "XXX–Must change" and "Kludge!–But should work." You wonder whether this is a corporate hazing ritual, but your instinct tells you otherwise.

Welcome to the real world.

In the real world, you're lucky if you get to spend all your time developing one new program after another. Much of the time you'll have to deal with someone else's. In the real world, programmers take over responsibility for programs written by people they might not know, like, or agree with. Even if you're fortunate enough to avoid this situation, you'll still have to maintain your own code; and one day you're going to look at something you wrote two years ago and ask, "What idiot wrote this?" Thereby arriving at more or less the same situation as the less fortunate programmers.

This book is about taking over Perl code, whether written by someone else or by yourself at a time when you were less wise about maintainability. Many problems of code inheritance are common to all languages, but I have noticed them especially in Perl.

Why does Perl tend to foster maintenance issues? The answer to this is the dark side of Perl's strength and motto: "There's More Than One Way To Do It" (enshrined in the acronym TMTOWTDI). Perl provides so many ways to do it that someone else quite possibly picked one that wasn't your way, or might have used several different ways all in the same program.

The medical metaphor for this book stems from the rather drastic nature of the work we do as maintenance programmers. Often we must perform triage, deciding what code is worth saving and what is beyond redemption. Frequently we only have time for first aid, applying a field dressing to a ruptured program. We also have a hard time explaining our bills to the client. There may not be a Hippocratic Oath for programming, but it wouldn't hurt to come up with one.

I wrote this book because I kept finding myself telling my students, "I'm going to teach you how to program Perl well, but I'd have to teach you a lot more before you could take over a program that wasn't written well, and you wouldn't appreciate taking that much time away from learning how to write good programs of your own." So I've written a book to fill that need.

Perl is to computer languages as English is to human languages: bursting with irregular verbs, consistent only when it's convenient, borrowing terms from other languages to form a great melting pot of syntax. Most computer languages are described in terms of some kind of functional niche (Pascal: teaching computer languages; FORTRAN: numeric analysis; Prolog: rule-driven expert systems; etc.). Perl's makers simply describe it as "a language for getting your job done." (See the preface to [WALL00].) Perl hosts a fantastic conglomeration of syntactic devices that allow a programmer from virtually any background to find a familiar foothold for learning the language.

The full picture isn't as chaotic as this might imply: Larry Wall and others have done a brilliant job of tying together these eclectic devices into a framework that has an essential beauty. Therefore, just as the British speak of a "BBC English," while many people program Perl with, say, a LISP or C accent, there is something approaching an "accentless Perl" style that leverages the language's features to their best advantages. I will show how you can "speak Perl like a native" in order to optimize the maintainability of your programs.

It's true that you're officially allowed to program Perl in "baby talk" and Perl gurus have promised "not to laugh." (See the same preface.) But by the same token, while aviators call any landing you can walk away from a good one, what I'm doing in this book is helping you avoid having your pilot's license revoked.

Perl is like those people behind the travelers' help desk in airports; it's very good at understanding you no matter how poor your command of their language is. Because there are so many ways to write a Perl program that is not only syntactically correct (Perl makes no objection to running it) but also semantically correct (the program does what it's supposed to—at least in the situations it's been tried in), there is a wide variety of Perl programming styles that you might encounter, ranging from beautiful to what can charitably be described as incomprehensible.

The savvy among you will take that information and ask, "Where do my programs fit on that scale?" Because someone else may end up inheriting your code, and you'd prefer that they not end up sending it to authors like me as bad examples to go in books like this. See Chapter 5 for more advice on avoiding scorn.

If your experience or image of Perl is limited to short, mundane scripts, this book will appear to be overkill. I want you to know that Perl can quite easily accommodate large—as in tens of thousands of lines of code, multiple modules, and multiple programmers—projects. Projects of the size that demand rigorous requirements, documentation, and testing. If you're used to Perl programs escaping that sort of attention, I believe that is partly the result of a misperception of the role and power of Perl.

For example, if a C program is written to fulfill some requirement and turns out to be 1,000 lines long, then the common reaction is, "This must be serious . . . we'd better have code walkthroughs, acceptance testing, operational readiness reviews, and static code analyses. Oh, and don't forget the Help Desk training and documentation."

But if a Perl program *that fulfills exactly the same requirements* weighs in at 100 lines (and 10:1 is a typical compression ratio for C code to Perl), the reaction is more likely to be, "Ah, a simple utility . . . and in a plebeian scripting language to boot. Just plunk it in the delivery directory and get on with the next task."

When a Perl program reaches the 1,000-line mark, however, the honeymoon is probably over. Much of what I have to say addresses large programs. Chapter 3 in particular will show you how to get the respect of development teams who are used to putting everything through regression testing.

Please also see my earlier book with Ed Wright, *Perl Debugged* (Addison-Wesley, 2001) for more advice on good practices for developing and debugging Perl programs.

Perl or perl?

When you read this book and other works about Perl, you'll see an apparent inconsistency in capitalization: sometimes it's written as "Perl", and others as "perl". There's really no inconsistency; the authors are referring to two different things. Perl is the language itself; perl is the program that runs Perl programs. There is only one Perl, but there are many perls (one or more for each type of computer).

Sometimes this distinction gets a bit blurred: For instance, most people will write, "Perl objects to mismatched parentheses" when it is arguably the program that's doing the objecting and not the language. Just don't write "PERL"; Perl isn't an acronym, it doesn't stand for anything.[1] (Well, aside from standing

---

1. "Practical Extraction and Reporting Language" is an ex post facto moniker of convenience. It's a term of endearment, not a formal title. Ditto for "Pathological Eclectic Rubbish Lister."

for diversity of expression, freedom from artificial constraints, and the right to have fun in your work. But we'll get to those later.)

Obtaining Perl

It would be remiss of me to tell you so much about Perl without telling you how to get it, although these days it's hard to avoid; you probably already have it, especially if you have any flavor of UNIX or Linux. The easiest way to find out whether you have it is to get a command prompt and type:

```
perl -v
```

and see if you get a response. If not, try:

```
whereis perl
```

which on a UNIX system or similar will look around for Perl. If that doesn't work for you either, here are brief instructions on how to download and install Perl:

- For Microsoft Windows machines, get the free ActivePerl distribution: `http://www.activeState.com/ActivePerl/download.htm`
- For Macintosh:

  `http://www.cpan.org/ports/index.html#mac`

  (That URL is for pre-X versions of the OS; Perl comes with Mac OS X and builds fine on it, too.)
- For binary distributions for all other machines:

  `http://www.cpan.org/ports/`
- For the source of perl itself:

  `http://www.cpan.org/src/`

The source file you want is called stable.tar.gz. The file devel.tar.gz is for Perl developers or testers only, and the file latest.tar.gz is the same as stable.tar.gz for complex historical reasons. Anything mentioning "Ponie" will be for developers only through 2004 at least, and any perl with a three-number component version with an odd middle number is likewise a development version.

Building Perl from source on a supported UNIX architecture requires just these commands after you download and unpack the right file:

```
./Configure
make
make test
make install
```

The Configure step asks you zillions of questions, and most people won't have a clue what many of those questions are talking about; but the default answers Configure recommends are usually correct.[2]

`www.cpan.org` is the master Comprehensive Perl Archive Network (CPAN) site, mirrored around the world. CPAN is also the official repository of contributed modules (see Section 8.1).

Historical Perl

You're probably not used to seeing instructions on how to obtain an out-of-date version of Perl. But you just might have to do that under some circumstances that will be explored later in this book. (Note: The older the version of Perl, the less likely the references I am about to give will enjoy substantial longevity.) The timeline for all releases of Perl is in the *perlhist* documentation page.

---

2. If you want to let Configure use those recommendations and go on without asking you, you can give it the options -des and it'll churn away happily without your intervention. If you need more platform-specific help, look in the distribution for the README.*platform* file corresponding to your system.

You can get all major versions starting with 5.004_05 from `ftp://ftp.cpan.org/pub/CPAN/src/5.0/`. Earlier versions of Perl 5 (with the exception of 5.004_04, which was widely used) exhibited significant bugs, memory leaks, and security holes and are harder to find. However, you can get what looks like every version of Perl ever released at `http://retroperl.cpan.org/`. Using a perl before version 5.003 is not an activity to be undertaken lightly. You will not receive bug fixes or any other support beyond a terse admonition to leave the Stone Age and upgrade to a real version. I am revealing this source only for cases in which you must use an old perl to verify operation of a legacy program that does not work on a modern perl. If you must get a perl 4 from there, the last and best version of Perl 4 is version 4.0.36.

Retroperl even includes versions 1.0, 1.010, 2.0, 2.001, 3.01. To call these of historical interest only would be an understatement. If you think you need to get one of these perls for any serious work you may be more in need of an archaeologist or a therapist. As an example of nonserious work, however, in 2002 Michael Schwern and others released an upgrade to Perl 1 (bringing it to version 1.0_15) as a birthday present to Perl and Larry Wall, to show that it could still work on modern machines. See `http://dev.perl.org/perl1/`.

Historical versions of modules are under `http://backpan.cpan.org/modules/`, but you'll have to go down the *authors* branch to find what you want.

Who This Book Is For

If you've been working with Perl long enough to have heard terms like *scalar, array,* and *hash,* then you're in the right place. Parts of this book are aimed at early beginners and some parts require more experience to comprehend. Feel free to skip past anything that's over your head and come back to it at a later date.

Typographical Conventions

I use the following conventions in this book:

- Standard text: Times New Roman
- Code examples and URLs: `Courier`
- User input: **`Bold Courier`**

Sometimes my code examples have line breaks where none existed in the original. In places where these line breaks would cause problems or aren't obvious, I've put a backslash (\) at the end of the line to indicate that the line should be joined with the next one.

When I want to show that I typed an end-of-file character in a terminal session, I show it as a Control-D on its own line:

`^D`

even though those characters will normally be overwritten by the next thing to be printed. Substitute whatever the terminal driver on your operating system uses if not a Control-D (e.g., Control-Z, Return on Windows).

When referring to Perl modules, I will often add ".pm" to the end of one-word module names to follow common practice and avoid confusion, but leave it out of module names with multiple components because that is the convention. For example, CGI.pm, but IO::Socket.

Citations are referenced by a tag in square brackets, for example, [SCOTT01], and the details are given in the Bibliography near the end of the book.

I reference many pages that are part of the standard documentation that comes with every Perl; you can type `perldoc` followed by the page name and it will display. I show these in italics: for instance, *perlsub* is the page containing information about subroutines in Perl.

For Further Reference

Visit this book's Web site at `http://www.perlmedic.com`.

Get introductions to Perl programming from the following:

- [SCHWARTZ01]
- [WALL00]
- [CHAPMAN98]
- [JOHNSON99]
- [HALL98]

Perl Versions

In this book, I refer to the latest "stable" version of Perl, which is 5.8.3 as of this writing. The vast majority of what I say works unaltered on older versions of Perl 5, but not Perl 4. If you use any version of Perl older than 5.004_04, you should upgrade for reasons unconnected with features: 5.003 had issues such as security problems and memory leaks. You can find out the version number of your perl by passing it the `-v` flag:

```
% perl -v
This is perl, v5.8.3 built for i586-linux
Copyright 1987-2003, Larry Wall
[...]
```

Perl won't execute a script named on the command line if the `-v` flag is present. A more detailed description of your perl's configuration can be obtained with the `-V` flag; if you use the `perlbug` program that comes with perl to issue a bug report, it automatically includes this information in your report.

A separate development track exists for Perl; you will know if you have one of those versions because the release number either contains an underscore followed by a number of 50 or larger or contains an odd number between two dots. *Nothing is guaranteed to work in such a distribution;* it's intended for testing. If you find you have one and you didn't want it, the person who downloaded your perl probably visited the wrong FTP link. This happens more often than most people would think; take a moment to check your perl if you're not sure.

Perl 6

If you've spent much time in the Perl universe, you've heard about Perl 6. I won't be covering how to port programs to Perl 6 for a very logical reason: It doesn't exist yet.[3]

A stable version of Perl 6 is still a few years away. When it emerges however, it will bear approximately the resemblance to Perl 5 that a Lamborghini Countach does to a Volkswagen Beetle (well, the new one, anyway). (Which is to say, backward compatibility has been prioritized beneath new capability for the first time in Perl development.)

Don't panic. Perl 4 hung around for an indecent time after Perl 5 came out and Perl 5 will be ported, maintained, and improved for many years after Perl 6 emerges. The recently started Ponie[4] project (http://www.poniecode.org) will enable Perl 5 to run on top of the Parrot engine underlying Perl 6. Your Perl 5 programs will quite likely keep working as long as you do.

This book will be applicable in large measure to Perl 6 in any case; most of the Perl 6 magic involves not removing existing features, but adding cool new ones. If you want to find out more about Perl 6 anyway, see [RANDAL03].

---

3. Except for development versions that test some of the features that have been decided on recently.
4. Ponie stands for Perl On New Implementation Engine (even though it isn't capitalized).

Acknowledgments

Elaine Ashton and Jarkko Hietaniemi provided many valuable comments and help that I was happy to incorporate. Thanks also to Allen Wyke, Dan Livingston, and Adam Turoff for thoughtful and comprehensive reviewing. I am extremely grateful to Uri Guttman for the most detailed feedback I have ever seen, and to Uri and his wife Linda for some fun diversions at Perl conferences. Any remaining errors are in no way attributable to any of these reviewers. Ed Wright wrote the FrameMaker styles for typesetting and Carl Miyatake provided a Japanese translation. Ann Palmer did the cover illustration and interior artwork.

I would like to thank Karen McLean at Prentice Hall for her saintly patience, and Mike Henderson at Addison-Wesley for taking on this project in the first place. Anne Garcia and Heather Mullane performed critical production duties; Vanessa Moore spent ages ensuring the excellence of the finished product. I also thank my many students for the valuable lessons they have provided me. Kudos also to my friends at the Jet Propulsion Laboratory who regularly accomplish the spectacular against overwhelming odds. The model question in Chapter 12 appears by permission of its author, Mary Byrne.

Lastly, I would like to thank my wife Grace, for her support, love, and constant help throughout a period much longer than either of us anticipated. Most spouses would have stopped there, but she also toiled tirelessly on the index, proofreading, and copy editing. Greater support an author could not expect.

Chapter 1

Introduction (First Response)

"I hate quotations. Tell me what you know."
— Ralph Waldo Emerson

1.1 First Things First

Let's start with the basics of what to do when you're presented with someone else's code to maintain:

Don't panic!

First, you have a strategic decision to make: Do you want this responsibility or not? Your best if not only chance to reject this assignment—if that is an option at all—with any semblance of honor may be right at the outset, even though you have nowhere near enough information to tell you how arduous it will turn out to be. If you can, stall for time so you can find out more about what this project entails.

Let's assume that you've decided that the best thing you can do for your career right now is to take over this code (even if you think you have no choice in the matter, this is a much more empowering way to view it). Your first duty is:

Find the author!

Only superhuman developers will have left you so many resources for maintaining this code that your job won't be massively eased by personal contact with them. Even if they're in the process of cleaning out their desk while a security guard hovers impatiently nearby, track them down now and ask them:

- Did anyone else work on this code? Who?
- Are there any other files or data that weren't given to you that would be useful?
- Are there any documentation, engineering notebooks, or Post-it® notes stuck to the monitor that pertain to the project? The programmer may be in the process of round-filing them as you speak.

If the developer is not on the verge of being ejected involuntarily from the premises,[1] find out whether they have any time to work with you on taking over this project. Tell your supervisor that "pair programming" is a good thing according to the popular Extreme Programming methodology[2] and this is a golden opportunity to try it out. If all else fails, consider buying the former developer lunch for a week out of your own money. You'll still end up so far ahead of the game with what you learn from them that you'll make it back in compensation or kudos. However, the developer will probably spend some time with you for nothing if you tell them you want their help in learning how they created their code; most people are touched by such flattery.

1.2 Reasons for Inheritance

It's important to know why people inherit code, because you might jump to the wrong conclusion about which one applies in your case. Perhaps:

- The original developer is gone.
- The original developer is bored with the program and wants to be rid of it.
- The original developer is reassigned or otherwise has no time to spare. (Don't give up; this might be more negotiable than it first appears.)
- The responsibility for the function performed by the program has been reassigned from the original developer's group to your group.

---

1. And if they are, take any advice they give you with a grain of salt—the welfare of the company you now represent to them may not be uppermost on their mind.
2. It really is. See [BECK00].

You might also have been brought on board because the program might need to be modified in ways that are within your ability but are beyond the capacity of the original developer:

- The program needs to be ported from one environment to another.
- The performance of the program needs to be improved.
- The program needs a data interface that uses a new protocol or format.
- The program has expanded to the point where it has to be restructured to make further modification cost-effective.
- The program performs operations that are needed by other programs and these are to be collected into object-oriented modules for easy reuse.

Here are some extremely unpleasant but feasible scenarios:

- The program has grown so large that even the original developer cannot figure out how to make a change to it.
- The program lives in a very brittle environment of many dependencies on fragile or operational systems and any change or upgrade is bound to break one of them.
- The program has not been documented and the original developer has been successful at convincing management that such a task is beneath his or her dignity.

There are also a number of unsavory possibilities motivated by politics, such as an attempt to sabotage the reputation of you or your group by giving you an impossible task. Or you might have been given the project simply as something to keep you busy. Sad to say, going into information technology is no way to escape politics.

1.3 What Next?

Take the files that were delivered to you and put them somewhere they can never be changed. Either make a copy of them on read-only media, or check them into a source code control system—preferably both. In your process of modifying these files there will likely come times when you want to see what they contained before some change you have already made. Putting the files under revision control from the start will be a decision you will come to value immensely. Systems that can do that range from the ubiquitous and free but venerable RCS and SCCS (see, e.g., [BOLINGER95]), through the popular CVS (see for example [VESPERMAN03]), to the latest open source project, Subversion (`http://subversion.tigris.org/`). Later on I'll show you how to integrate Perl files with those products.

1.4 Observe the Program in Its Natural Habitat

You need to know as soon as possible that the program actually works. Don't assume that it works just because you're told so! Perhaps you're not in the group that's responsible for the current operation of this program and you're supposed to get it to do something else. Go to the original owners and watch them run the program. Then check that the program they ran is identical to the one you were given.[3] Then figure out how you can run the program yourself without making any modifications. This might not be as easy as it sounds; the program might depend on things like files you're not permitted access to or accounts you don't have. There might not be a test environment that you can try the program out on (more on this in Chapter 3). However, it is vital that you can reproduce the successful operation of the program you have just witnessed with as few modifications as possible.

---

3. This may seem needlessly pedantic, but not if you consider the mind-puddling difficulty of diagnosis that would ensue if the two actually were different.

1.5 Get Personal

Use any personal knowledge that you have of the developer, or find out what you can about how they program. Are they inclined to test and be thorough, or do they frequently make mistakes and goof off? If you don't know anything about them, don't assume they knew what they were doing and then puzzle endlessly over a strange fragment of code. That code might be irrelevant or just wrong, and left in for no good reason. Knowing the habits and level of sophistication of the developer will be invaluable in deciphering the program.

Knowing something about the programming background of the developer could also be helpful. If they have, for instance, much experience in C but little in Perl, their Perl programs may look like C code. Don't spend a lot of time puzzling over why they have neglected efficient mechanisms such as list returns from functions or hashes when the cause is quite probably that they have discovered that they can program Perl "just like C" (or Java, or bash, or . . .)

1.6 Strictness

The most common cause for grief in inheriting a Perl program is the absence of these two magic lines from the beginning of every file:

```
use warnings;
use strict;
```

If the program contains a -w on the #! line, that counts the same as a use warnings in the main program and every module that it uses. Because the use warnings pragma is a relatively recent addition to Perl (version 5.6.0 or later) you're more likely to find the -w flag in inherited programs.

Why these lines are not the default for Perl programs has been the source of much contention between certain people in the Perl community, including me. But they aren't the default, so we're stuck with the situation. Omitting these lines from a Perl program is as close to professional suicide as you can get this side of putting a whoopie cushion on the CEO's boardroom chair. In case you're not aware of how important these lines are, I'll go into more details on their effects in Chapter 5. First let's deal with what you should do if you are handed code that lacks them.

If you have the opportunity and the *chutzpah,* hand the program back to the developer who wrote it, and as politely as you can, ask them to add `use strict` and `use warnings` (or `-w`) to the code, and let you have it back after they have fixed the code so that it runs without errors or warnings. (If the code includes modules written by the developer, each one of them should include a `use strict` at the top, and a `use warnings` if the main program isn't using the `-w` flag.)

This is not the time to tell them that doing this will almost certainly result in dozens of fatal errors, hundreds of warnings, and numerous changes required of the code in order to make it compliant with these new directives.

They will think that your request is a trivial addition. Let them. The changes they make to enforce compliance will make your job immeasurably easier, because the way they choose to resolve each error or warning will be based on understanding of the code that they have and you do not.

If you think this tactic is underhanded, you haven't yet tried to maintain a significant body of code that was developed without `use strict` and `use warnings`. After doing that, you'll be inclined to approve far more stringent forms of punishment for a developer who omits them. The rack, for instance.

1.7 Warnings

The question often arises of whether to leave warnings enabled in production code. Those against doing so say that you don't want the customer seeing "dirty laundry" generated by your program—what if something quite innocuous in your program today turns out to be the subject of a warning added to a later version of Perl?

I prefer to leave the warnings in production programs. My point of view is that warnings are like strictness exceptions, only pickier, and should be treated the same: Either code to avoid the warning, or explicitly disable the warning around code where:

- You know why the warning is being generated; and
- You know that the warning is unlikely to be generated for any other reason; and
- It's clearer to disable the warning than to recode.

If a new warning is added to Perl, the odds are that you'd want to know if you had code that triggered it. Today's warnings could become tomorrow's fatal error if you're using a feature that is being deprecated.

Don't scratch the itch to turn warnings off merely because they are inconvenient. Think of them instead as a programming mentor nagging you to make your code robust. You might respond, "No, I know what I'm doing, so don't complain about this again," by disabling the warning; or you might change the code.

For instance, suppose you are writing code that looks up people in a database by their username and inserts their e-mail address in a message template:

```
if (my $user = $db->lookup_user(username => $username))
{
  my $email = $user->email;
  open MAIL, "|$SENDMAIL" or croak "Mail: $!";
  print MAIL <<"EOMAIL";
To: archive\@listserver,$email
Subject: Your account
[...]
EOMAIL
  close MAIL;
}
```

Testing may go just fine. But suppose one day a user comes along who doesn't have a registered e-mail address, and so the `email()` accessor method returns `undef`. Without warnings, there will be no clue that the user didn't get the message they deserved unless someone inspects the e-mail archive that was copied.

I am *not* saying that the best way to write that e-mail-sending code is to allow the warning facility to catch the case where the address is undefined. It would have been better to have written something like:

```
if (my $user = $db->lookup_user(username => $username))
{
  if (my $email = $user->email)
  {
    open MAIL, "|$SENDMAIL" or croak "Mail: $!";
    print MAIL <<"EOMAIL";
To: archive\@listserver,$email
Subject: Your account
[...]
EOMAIL
    close MAIL;
  }
  else
  {
    # Handle the user not having an email address
  }
}
```

But you don't always have that much foresight. Leaving warnings enabled helps make up for that shortcoming.

I'll go into warnings and strictness in great detail in Chapter 5.

1.7.1 What Were They Doing?

Find out especially what the developer was optimizing their code for. Before you discard a complicated section in favor of something much simpler, find out whether it was written that way to meet performance requirements. Then find out whether it's still necessary to use those optimizations to meet the current requirements.

Code could have been optimized for several different factors, some of which I illustrate here with sample code, each example doing exactly the same thing (as explained by the comment in the first one).

• Maintainability:

```perl
# Print words with an even number of letters, AND even
# number of each vowel, AND even position in the input
OUTER: while (<>)
{
  next if $. % 2;
  chomp;
  next if length() % 2;
  for my $vowel (qw/a e i o u y/)
  {
    my @vowels = /$vowel/g;
    next OUTER if @vowels % 2;
  }
  print "$_\n";
}
```

• Performance:

```perl
while (<>)
{
  next if ($. | (length() - 1)) % 2;
  next if tr/a// % 2;
  next if tr/e// % 2;
  next if tr/i// % 2;
  next if tr/o// % 2;
  next if tr/u// % 2;
  next if tr/y// % 2;
  print;
}
```

• Brevity:

```perl
#!/usr/bin/perl -ln
($x=aeiouy)=~s#.#y/$&//|#g;eval("$x$.|y///c")%2&&next;print
```

• Job security:

```
@i = map { chomp; $x++ %2 ? $_ : () } <>;
while ($i = shift @i)
{
  ord(pack "w/a*", $i) & 1 and next;
  $_ = "$i\n";
  $i =~ s/$_(.*)$_/$1/ for qw/a e i o u y/;
  print unless $i =~ /[aeiouy]/;
}
```

As you can see, the Perl philosophy of "There's More Than One Way To Do It" (TMTOWTDI) can result in radically different code, depending on whether the author wants it to be readable, fast, as short as possible, or incomprehensible, respectively.

Remember that it is the norm for programs to grow by evolution and accretion. The more successful the program was, the more likely it is to have had other functionality grafted onto it in response to requirements creep. Don't spend a long time trying to figure out the design rationale of a program; there may not be one left.

Chapter 2

Surveying the Scene

"What we have inherited from our fathers and mothers is not all that 'walks in us.' There are all sorts of dead ideas and lifeless old beliefs. They have no tangibility, but they haunt us all the same and we can not get rid of them. Whenever I take up a newspaper I seem to see Ghosts gliding between the lines. Ghosts must be all over the country, as thick as the sands of the sea."

— Henrik Ibsen, *Ghosts*

2.1 Versions

It's important to know as soon as possible what version of Perl the program was developed for. This isn't necessarily the same as the version of Perl it may currently be running against, but find that out anyway so you have an upper bound. Again, get this information from the gold source: the original running environment. Type the complete path to perl that appears in the main program's shebang line (see below) followed by the -v argument to find out the version; for example:

```
% /opt/bin/perl -v
This is perl, v5.6.1 built for i386-linux
Copyright 1987-2003, Larry Wall
```

If this output indicates that they're running on a newer perl than the one you have (run the same command on your perl), do whatever you can to upgrade. Although upgrading may be unnecessary, if you have any difficulties getting the code to work, your energy for debugging will be sapped by the nagging fear that the problem is due to a version incompatibility.

One reason upgrading may be unnecessary is that the operating group upgraded their perl after the original program was written, and the program did not trigger any of the forward incompatibilities. A program written for Perl 4 could easily work identically under Perl 5.8.3 and probably would; the Perl developers went to fanatical lengths to preserve backward compatibility across upgrades.

Look at the dates of last modifications of the source files. You may need to visit the original operational system to be able to determine them. Although the dates may be more recent than any significant code changes (due to commenting, or insignificant changes to constants), the earlier the dates are, the more they can bound for you the most recent version of Perl the program was developed for. See the version history in Chapter 7 to find out how to determine that version.

2.2 Part or Whole?

Are you in fact taking over a complete program or a module used by other programs (or both)? Let's see how we can find out.

2.2.1 Shebang-a-Lang-a-Ding-Dong

You can recognize a Perl program file by the fact that the first two characters are:

```
#!
```

and somewhere on the rest of that line the word "perl" appears.[1] Developers call this the shebang line. It is possible to create a Perl program without this line by requiring it to be run explicitly with a command something like

```
% perl program_file_name
```

although it would be strange to receive a main program in this state. Don't depend on the filename ending with an extension like .pl or .plx; this is not necessary on many systems. A .pl extension is commonplace on Windows systems, where the file extension is required to tell the operating system the type of the file; aside from that .pl extensions were often used as a convention for "Perl Library": files containing specialized subroutines. These mostly precede the introduction in Perl 5 of objects, which provide a better paradigm for code reuse.

One time when the extension of a file is guaranteed, however, is for a Perl module; if the filename ends in .pm, then it's a module, intended to be used by another file that's the actual program.

---

1. A Perl program on Windows could get away without this line, because the .pl suffix is sufficient to identify it as a Perl program, but it is good practice to leave the line in on Windows anyway. (The path to Perl isn't important in that case.)

Caveat: Sometimes a .pm file may begin with a shebang; this almost certainly means that someone created a module that contains its own tests so that executing the module as a program also works. If you see a .pm like this, try running it to see what happens. A file that's not a .pm can't be a module, but could still be a dependency rather than the main program. If it begins with a shebang, it could be a library of subroutine or constant definitions that's been endowed with self-testing capabilities. It may not be possible to tell the difference between this type of file and the main program without careful inspection or actual execution if the developer did not comment the file clearly.

It is quite possible that you will have to change the shebang line to refer to a different perl. The previous owners of the program may have located their perl somewhere other than where the one you plan to use is. If the code consists of a lot of files containing that path, here's how you can change them all at once, assuming that /their/path/to/perl is on the original shebang line and /your/path/to/perl is the location of your perl:

```
% perl -pi.bak -e \
  's#/their/path/to/perl#/your/path/to/perl#g' *
```

This command puts the original version of each file—before any changes were made—in a file of the same name but with .bak appended to it. If you've been using a revision control system to store the files in, you don't need to make copies like that. (I told you that would turn out to be a good decision.) Leaving out the .bak:

```
% perl -pi -e 's#/their/path/to/perl#/your/path/to/perl#g' *
```

results in in-place editing; that is, the original files are overwritten with the new contents.

This command assumes that all the files to be changed are in the current directory. If they are contained in multiple subdirectories, you can combine this with the find command like this:

```
% find . -type f -print | xargs perl -pi -e \
's#/their/path/to/perl#/your/path/to/perl#g'
```

Of course, you can use this command for globally changing other strings besides the path to perl, and you might have frequent occasion to do so. Put the command in an alias, like so:

```
% alias gchange "find . -type f -print | xargs \
perl -pi.bak -e '\!1'"
```

the syntax of which may vary depending on which shell you are using. Then you can invoke it thusly:

```
% gchange s,/their/path/to/perl,/your/path/to/perl,g
```

Note that I changed the substitution delimiter from a # to a , : A shell might take the # as a comment-introducing character. Because you might be using this alias to change pieces of code containing characters like $ and ! that can have special meaning to your shell, learn about how your shell does quoting and character escaping so you'll be prepared to handle those situations.

Note also that I put the .bak back. Because otherwise one day, you'll forget to check the files into your version control system first, because the alias isn't called something like *gchange_with_no_backups*.

If you want to develop this concept further, consider turning the alias into a script that checks each file in before altering it.

2.2.2 .ph Files

You may encounter a .ph file. This is a Perl version of a C header (.h) file, generated by the h2ph program that comes with perl. The odds are that you can eliminate the need for this file in rewriting the program. These .ph files have not been commonly used since Perl 4 because the dynamic module loading capability introduced in Perl 5 made it possible, and desirable, for modules to incorporate any header knowledge they required. A private .ph file is probably either a copy of what h2ph would have produced from a system header (but the author lacked the permission to install it in perl's library), or a modified version of the same. Read the .ph file to see what capability it is providing and then research modules that perform the same function.

2.3 Find the Dependencies

Look for documentation that describes everything that needs to exist for this program to work. Complex systems could have dependencies on code written in other languages, on data files produced by other systems, or on network connections with external services. If you can find interface agreements or other documents that describe these dependencies they will make the job of code analysis much easier. Otherwise you will be reduced to a trial-and-error process of copying over the main program and repeatedly running it and identifying missing dependencies until it appears to work.

A common type of dependency is a custom Perl module. Quite possibly the program uses some modules that should have been delivered to you but weren't. Get a list of modules that the program uses in operation and compare it with what you were given and what is in the Perl core. Again, this is easier to do with the currently operating version of the program. First try the simple approach of searching for lines beginning with "use " or "require ". On UNIX, you can use egrep:

```
% egrep '^(use|require) ' files...
```

Remember to search also all the modules that are part of the code you were given. Let's say that I did that and the output was:

```
use strict;
use warnings;
use lib qw(/opt/lib/perl);
use WWW::Mechanize;
```

Can I be certain I've found all the modules the program loads? No. For one thing, there's no law that `use` and `require` have to be at the beginning of a line; in fact I commonly have `require` statements embedded in `do` blocks in conditionals, for instance.

The other reason this search can't be foolproof is that Perl programs are capable of loading modules dynamically based on conditions that are unknown until run time. Although there is no completely foolproof way of finding out all the modules the program *might* use, a pretty close way is to add this code to the program:

```
END {
  print "Directories searched:\n\t",
        join ("\n\t" => @INC),
        "\nModules loaded:\n\t",
        join ("\n\t" => sort values %INC),
        "\n";
}
```

Then run the program. You'll get output looking something like this:

```
Directories searched:
   /opt/lib/perl
   /usr/lib/perl5/5.6.1/i386-linux
   /usr/lib/perl5/5.6.1
   /usr/lib/perl5/site_perl/5.6.1/i386-linux
   /usr/lib/perl5/site_perl/5.6.1
   /usr/lib/perl5/site_perl/5.6.0
   /usr/lib/perl5/site_perl
   /usr/lib/perl5/vendor_perl/5.6.1/i386-linux
   /usr/lib/perl5/vendor_perl/5.6.1
   /usr/lib/perl5/vendor_perl
   .
Modules loaded:
   /usr/lib/perl5/5.6.1/AutoLoader.pm
   /usr/lib/perl5/5.6.1/Carp.pm
   /usr/lib/perl5/5.6.1/Exporter.pm
   /usr/lib/perl5/5.6.1/Exporter/Heavy.pm
   /usr/lib/perl5/5.6.1/Time/Local.pm
```

```
/usr/lib/perl5/5.6.1/i386-linux/Config.pm
/usr/lib/perl5/5.6.1/i386-linux/DynaLoader.pm
/usr/lib/perl5/5.6.1/lib.pm
/usr/lib/perl5/5.6.1/overload.pm
/usr/lib/perl5/5.6.1/strict.pm
/usr/lib/perl5/5.6.1/vars.pm
/usr/lib/perl5/5.6.1/warnings.pm
/usr/lib/perl5/5.6.1/warnings/register.pm
/usr/lib/perl5/site_perl/5.6.1/HTML/Form.pm
/usr/lib/perl5/site_perl/5.6.1/HTTP/Date.pm
/usr/lib/perl5/site_perl/5.6.1/HTTP/Headers.pm
/usr/lib/perl5/site_perl/5.6.1/HTTP/Message.pm
/usr/lib/perl5/site_perl/5.6.1/HTTP/Request.pm
/usr/lib/perl5/site_perl/5.6.1/HTTP/Response.pm
/usr/lib/perl5/site_perl/5.6.1/HTTP/Status.pm
/usr/lib/perl5/site_perl/5.6.1/LWP.pm
/usr/lib/perl5/site_perl/5.6.1/LWP/Debug.pm
/usr/lib/perl5/site_perl/5.6.1/LWP/MemberMixin.pm
/usr/lib/perl5/site_perl/5.6.1/LWP/Protocol.pm
/usr/lib/perl5/site_perl/5.6.1/LWP/UserAgent.pm
/usr/lib/perl5/site_perl/5.6.1/URI.pm
/usr/lib/perl5/site_perl/5.6.1/URI/Escape.pm
/usr/lib/perl5/site_perl/5.6.1/URI/URL.pm
/usr/lib/perl5/site_perl/5.6.1/URI/WithBase.pm
/opt/lib/perl/WWW/Mechanize.pm
/usr/lib/perl5/site_perl/5.6.1/i386-linux/Clone.pm
/usr/lib/perl5/site_perl/5.6.1/i386-linux/HTML/Entities.pm
/usr/lib/perl5/site_perl/5.6.1/i386-linux/HTML/Parser.pm
/usr/lib/perl5/site_perl/5.6.1/i386-linux/HTML/PullParser.pm
/usr/lib/perl5/site_perl/5.6.1/i386-linux/HTML/TokeParser.pm
```

That doesn't mean that the user code loaded 34 modules; in fact, it loaded 3, one of which (WWW::Mechanize) loaded the rest, mostly via other modules that in turn loaded other modules that—well, you get the picture. Now you want to verify that the program isn't somehow loading modules that your egrep command didn't find; so create a program containing just the results of the egrep command and add the END block, like so:

```
use strict;
use warnings;
use lib qw(/opt/lib/perl);
use WWW::Mechanize;

END {
  print "Directories searched:\n\t",
        join ("\n\t" => @INC),
        "\nModules loaded:\n\t",
        join ("\n\t" => sort values %INC),
        "\n";
}
```

Run it. If the output is identical to what you got when you added the END block to the entire program, then egrep almost certainly found all the dependencies. If it isn't, you'll have to dig deeper.

Even if the outputs match, it's conceivable, although unlikely, that you haven't found all the dependencies. Why? Just because one set of modules was loaded by the program the time you ran it with your reporting code doesn't mean it couldn't load another set some other time. You can't be certain the code isn't doing that until you've inspected every eval and require statement in it. For instance, DBI (the DataBase Independent module) decides which DBD driver module it needs depending on part of a string passed to its connect() method. Fortunately, code that complicated is rare.

Now check that the system you need to port the program to contains all the required modules. Take the list output by egrep and prefix each module with -M in a one-liner like so:

```
% perl -Mstrict -Mwarnings -MWWW::Mechanize -e 0
```

This runs a trivial program (0) after loading the required modules. If the modules loaded okay, you won't see any errors. If one or more modules don't exist on this system, you'll see a message starting, "Can't locate *module*.pm in @INC . . . "

That's quite likely what will happen with the preceding one-liner, and the reason is the `use lib` statement in the source. Like `warnings` and `strict`, `lib` is a *pragma,* meaning that it's a module that affects the behavior of the Perl compiler. In this case it was used to add the directory /opt/lib/perl to `@INC`, the list of directories perl searches for modules in. Seeing that in a program you need to port indicates that it uses modules that are not part of the Perl core. It could mean, as it did here, that it is pointing perl toward a non-core Perl module (WWW::Mechanize) that is nevertheless maintained by someone else and downloaded from CPAN. Or it could indicate the location of private modules that were written by the developers of the program you are porting. Find out which case applies: Look on CPAN for any missing modules. The easiest way to do this is to go to `http://search.cpan.org/` and enter the name of each missing module, telling the search engine to search in "modules".[2]

So if we want to write a one-liner that searches the same module directories as the original code, we would have to use Perl's `-I` flag:

```
% perl -Mstrict -Mwarnings -I/opt/lib/perl -MWWW::Mechanize \
  -e 0
```

However, in the new environment you're porting the program to, there may not be a /opt/lib/perl; there may be another location you should install third-party modules to. If possible, install CPAN modules where CPAN.pm wants to put them; that is, in the `@INC` site-specific directory. (Local business policies might prevent this, in which case you put them where local policy specifies and insert `use lib` statements pointing to that location in your programs.)

If you find a missing module on CPAN, see if you can download the same version that is used by the currently operational program—not necessarily the latest version. Remember, you want first of all to re-create the original environment as closely as possible to minimize the number of places you'll have to look for bugs if it doesn't work. Again, if you're dealing with a relatively small, unprepossessing program, this level of caution may not be worth the

---

2. Unless you're faced with a huge list to check, in which case you can script searches using the CPAN.pm module's expand method.

trouble and you will usually spend less time overall if you just run it against the latest version of everything it needs.

To find out what version of a module (Foo::Bar, say) the original program uses, run this command on the operational system:

```
% perl -MFoo::Bar -le 'print $Foo::Bar::VERSION'
0.33
```

Old or poorly written modules may not define a $VERSION package variable, leaving you to decide just how much effort you want to put into finding exactly the same historical version, because you'll have to compare the actual source code texts (unless you have the source your module was installed from and the version number is embedded in the directory name). Don't try getting multiple versions of the same module to coexist in the same perl installation unless you're desperate; this takes considerable expertise.

You can find tools for reporting dependencies in programs and modules in Tom Christiansen's *pmtools* distribution (http://language.perl.com/misc/pmtools-1.00.tar.gz).

2.3.1 Gobbledygook

What if you look at a program and it really makes no sense at all? No indentation, meaningless variable names, line breaks in bizarre places, little or no white space? You're looking at a deliberately obfuscated program, likely one that was created by running a more intelligible program through an obfuscator.[3]

Clearly, you'd prefer to have the more intelligible version. That's the one the developer used; what you've got is something they delivered in an attempt to provide functionality while making it difficult for the customer to make modifications or understand the code. You're now the developer, so you're

---

3. Granted, some programs written by humans can appear obfuscated even when there was no intention that they appear that way. See Section 1.5.

entitled to the original source code; find it. If it's been lost, don't despair; much of the work of reconstructing a usable version of the program can be done by a beautifier, discussed in Section 4.5. A tool specifically designed for helping you in this situation is Joshua ben Jore's module B::Deobfuscate (`http://search.cpan.org/dist/B-Deobfuscate/`).

Chapter 3

Test Now, Test Forever (Diagnosis)

"A crash is when your competitor's program dies. When your program dies, it is an 'idiosyncrasy'. Frequently, crashes are followed with a message like 'ID 02'. 'ID' is an abbreviation for idiosyncrasy and the number that follows indicates how many more months of testing the product should have had."

— Guy Kawasaki

This chapter might appear at first blush to be out of sequence. We're steadily getting more specific in the details of taking over code, and here near the beginning is a chapter on how to do testing. Shouldn't it be near the end?

In a word, no. I am going to describe a philosophy of testing that will revolutionize your development practices if you have not already encountered it. I will show you how to implement it for Perl code and give a detailed example. It is so pivotal to the development process that I want to make sure you see it as soon as possible. So yes, it really should come before everything else.

3.1 Testing Your Patience

Here's the hard part. Creating tests while you're writing the code for the first time is far, far easier than adding them later on. I know it looks like it should be exactly the same amount of work, but the issue is motivation. When robots are invented that can create code, they won't have this problem, and the rest of us can mull over this injustice while we're collecting unemployment pay (except for the guy who invented the robot, who'll be sipping margaritas on a beach somewhere, counting his royalties and hoping that none of the other programmers recognize him).

But we humans don't like creating tests because it's not in our nature; we became programmers to exercise our creativity, but "testing" conjures up images of slack-jawed drones looking for defects in bolts passing by them on a conveyor belt.

The good news is that the Test:: modules make it easy enough to overcome this natural aversion to writing tests at the time you're developing code. The point at which you've just finished a new function is when your antitesting hormones are at their lowest ebb because you want to know whether or not it works. Instead of running a test that gets thrown away, or just staring at the code long enough to convince yourself that it *must* work, you can instead write a real test for it, because it may not require much more effort than typing:

```
is(some_func("some", "inputs"), qr/some outputs/,
  "some_func works");
```

The bad news is that retrofitting tests onto an already complete application requires much more discipline. And if anything could be worse than that, it would be retrofitting tests onto an already complete application that you didn't write.

There's no magic bullet that'll make this problem disappear. The only course of action that'll take more time in the long run than writing tests for your inherited code is not writing them. If you've already discovered the benefits of creating automated tests while writing an application from scratch then at least you're aware of how much they can benefit you. I'll explore one way to make the test writing more palatable in the next chapter.

3.2 Extreme Testing

This testing philosophy is best articulated by the Extreme Programming (XP) methodology, wherein it is fundamental (see [BECK00]). On the subject of testing, XP says:

- Development of tests should precede development of code.
- All requirements should be turned into tests.
- All tests should be automated.
- The software should pass all its tests at the end of every day.
- All bugs should get turned into tests.

If you've not yet applied these principles to the development of a new project, you're in for a life-altering experience when you first give them an honest try. Because your development speed will take off like a termite in a lumberyard.

Perl wholeheartedly embraces this philosophy, thanks largely to the efforts in recent years of a group of people including Michael Schwern, chromatic, and others. Because of their enthusiasm and commitment to the testing process, the number of tests that are run when you build Perl from the source and type "make test" has increased from 5,000 in Perl 5.004_04 (1997) to 70,000 in the current development version of Perl 5.9.0 (2004). That's right, a 14-fold increase.

True to the Perl philosophy, these developers exercised extreme laziness in adding those thousands of tests (see sidebar). To make it easier to create tests for Perl, they created a number of modules that can in fact be used to test anything. We'll take a look at them shortly.

What is it about this technology that brings such joy to the developer's heart? It provides a safety net, that's what. Instead of perennially wondering whether you've accidentally broken some code while working on an unrelated piece, you can make certain at any time. If you want to make a radical change to some interface, you can be sure that you've fixed all the dependencies because every scenario that you care about will have been captured in a test case, and running all the tests is as simple as typing "make test". One month into creating a new system that comprised more than a dozen modules and as many programs, I had built up a test suite that ran nearly 600 tests with that one command, all by adding the tests as I created the code they tested. When I made a radical change to convert one interface from functional to object-oriented, it took only a couple of hours because the tests told me when I was done.

This technique has been around for many years, but under the label *regression testing*, which sounds boring to anyone who can even figure out what it means.[1] However, using that label can be your entrance ticket to respectability when trying to convince managers of large projects that you know what you're talking about.

---

1. It's called regression testing because its purpose is to ensure that no change has caused any part of the program to *regress* back to an earlier, buggier stage of development.

What's this about laziness? Isn't that a pejorative way to describe luminaries of the Perl universe?

Actually, no; they'd take it as a compliment. Larry Wall enumerated three principal virtues of Perl programmers:

1. *Laziness:* "Hard work" sounds, well, hard. If you're faced with a mindless, repetitive task—such as running for public office—then laziness will make you balk at doing the same thing over and over again. Instead of stifling your creative spirit, you'll cultivate it by inventing a process that automates the repetitive task. If the Karate Kid had been a Perl programmer, he'd have abstracted the common factor from "wax on" and "wax off" shortly before fetching an orbital buffer. (Only to get, er, waxed, in the tournament from being out of shape. But I digress.)

2. *Impatience:* There's more than enough work to do in this business. By being impatient to get to the next thing quickly, you'll not spend unnecessary time on the task you're doing; you'll find ways to make it as efficient as possible.

3. *Hubris:* It's not good enough to be lazy and impatient if you're going to take them as an excuse to do lousy work. You need an unreasonable amount of pride in your abilities to carry you past the many causes for discouragement. If you didn't, and you thought about all the things that could go wrong with your code, you'd either never get out of bed in the morning, or just quit and take up potato farming.

So what are these magic modules that facilitate testing?

3.2.1 The Test Module

Test.pm was added in version 5.004 of Perl. By the time Perl 5.6.1 was released it was superseded by the Test::Simple module, which was published to CPAN and included in the Perl 5.8.0 core. Use Test::Simple instead.

If you inherit regression tests written to use Test.pm, it is still included in the Perl core for backward compatibility. You should be able to replace its use with Test::Simple if you want to start modernizing the tests.

3.2.2 The Test::Simple Module

When I say "simple," I mean *simple*. Test::Simple exports precisely one function, ok(). It takes one mandatory argument, and one optional argument. If its first argument evaluates to true, it prints "ok"; otherwise it prints "not ok". In each case it adds a number that starts at one and increases by one for each call to ok(). If a second argument is given, ok() then prints a dash and that argument, which is just a way of annotating a test.

Doesn't exactly sound like rocket science, does it? But on such a humble foundation is the entire Perl regression test suite built. The only other requirement is that we know how many tests we expected to run so we can tell if something caused them to terminate prematurely. That is done by an argument to the use statement:

```
use Test::Simple tests => 5;
```

The output from a test run therefore looks like:

```
1..5
ok 1 - Can make a frobnitz
ok 2 - Can fliggle the frobnitz
not ok 3 - Can grikkle the frobnitz
ok 4 - Can delete the frobnitz
ok 5 - Can't use a deleted frobnitz
```

Note that the first line says how many tests are expected to follow. That makes life easier for code like Test::Harness (see Section 3.2.9) that reads this output in order to summarize it.

3.2.3 The Test::More Module

You knew there couldn't be a module called Test::Simple unless there was something more complicated, right? Here it is. This is the module you'll use for virtually all your testing. It exports many useful functions aside from the same `ok()` as Test::Simple. Some of the most useful ones are:

`is($expression, $value, $description)`
Same as `ok($expression eq $value, $description)`. So why bother? Because `is()` can give you better diagnostics when it fails.

`like($attribute, qr/regex/, $description)`
Tests whether `$attribute` matches the given regular expression.

`is_deeply($struct1, $struct2, $description)`
Tests whether data structures match. Follows references in each and prints out the first discrepancy it finds, if any. Note that it does not compare the packages that any components may be blessed into.

`isa_ok($object, $class)`
Tests whether an object is a member of, or inherits from, a particular class.

`can_ok($object_or_class, @methods)`
Tests whether an object or a class can perform each of the methods listed.

`use_ok($module, @imports)`
Tests whether a module can be loaded (if it contains a syntax error, for instance, this will fail). Wrap this test in a `BEGIN` block to ensure it is run at compile time, viz: `BEGIN {use_ok("My::Module")}`

There's much more. See the Test::More documentation. I won't be using any other functions in this chapter, though.

Caveat: I don't know why you might do this, but if you `fork()` inside the test script, don't run tests from child processes. They won't be recognized by the parent process where the test analyzer is running.

3.2.4 The Test::Exception Module

No, there's no module called Test::EvenMore.[2] But there is a module you'll have to get from CPAN that can test for whether code lives or dies: Test::Exception. It exports these handy functions:

`lives_ok()`
> Passes if code does not die. The first argument is the block of code, the second is an optional tag string. Note there is *no comma* between those arguments (this is a feature of Perl's prototyping mechanism when a code block is the first argument to a subroutine). For example:

```
lives_ok { risky_function() } "risky_function lives!";
```

`dies_ok()`
> Passes if the code *does* die. Use this to check that error-checking code is operating properly. For example:

```
dies_ok { $] / 0 } "division by zero dies!";
```

`throws_ok()`
> For when you want to check the actual text of the exception. For example:

```
throws_ok { some_web_function() } qr/URL not found/,
          "Nonexistent page get fails";
```

The second argument is a regular expression that the exception thrown by the code block in the first argument is tested against. If the match succeeds, so does the test. The optional third argument is the comment tag for the test. Note that there *is* a comma between the second and third arguments.

---

2. Yet. I once promised Mike Schwern a beer if he could come up with an excuse to combine the UNIVERSAL class and an export functionality into UNIVERSAL::exports as a covert tribute to James Bond. He did it. Schwern, I still owe you that beer . . . .

3.2.5 The Test::Builder Module

Did you spot that all these modules have a lot in common? Did you wonder how you'd add a Test:: module of your own, if you wanted to write one?

Then you're already thinking lazily, and the testing guys are ahead of you. That common functionality lives in a superclass module called Test::Builder, seldom seen, but used to take the drudgery out of creating new test modules.

Suppose we want to write a module that checks whether mail messages conform to RFC 822 syntax.[3] We'll call it Test::MailMessage, and it will export a basic function, msg_ok(), that determines whether a message consists of an optional set of header lines, optionally followed by a blank line and any number of lines of text. (Yes, an empty message is legal according to this syntax. Unfortunately, too few people who have nothing to say avail themselves of this option.) Here's the module:

Example 3.1 Using Test::Builder to Create Test::MailMessage

```
1   package Test::MailMessage;
2   use strict;
3   use warnings;
4   use Carp;
5   use Test::Builder;
6   use base qw(Exporter);
7   our @EXPORT = qw(msg_ok);
8
9   my $test = Test::Builder->new;
10
11  sub import
12  {
13    my $self = shift;
14    my $pack = caller;
15
16    $test->exported_to($pack);
17    $test->plan(@_);
```

3. http://www.faqs.org/rfcs/rfc822.html

```
18
19    $self->export_to_level(1, $self, 'msg_ok');
20  }
21
22  sub msg_ok
23  {
24    my $arg = shift;
25    my $tester = _new();
26    eval
27    {
28      if (defined(fileno($arg)))
29      {
30        while (<$arg>)
31        {
32          $tester->_validate($_);
33        }
34      }
35      elsif (ref $arg)
36      {
37        $tester->_validate($_) for @$arg;
38      }
39      else
40      {
41        for ($arg =~ /(.*\n)/g)
42        {
43          $tester->_validate($_);
44        }
45      }
46    };
47    $test->ok(!$@, shift);
48    $test->diag($@) if $@;
49  }
50
51  sub _new
52  {
53    return bless { expect => "header" };
54  }
55
56  sub _validate
57  {
58    my ($self, $line) = @_;
59    return if $self->{expect} eq "body";
```

```
60    if ($self->{expect} eq "header/continuation")
61    {
62       /^\s+\S/ and return;
63    }
64    $self->{expect} = "body", return if /^$/;
65    /^\S+:/ or croak "Invalid header";
66    $self->{expect} = "header/continuation";
67  }
68
69  1;
```

In line 1 we put this module into its own package, and in lines 2 and 3 we set warnings and strictness to help development go smoothly. In lines 4 and 5 we load the Carp module so we can call croak(), and the Test::Builder module so we can create an instance of it. In lines 6 and 7 we declare this to be a subclass of the Exporter module, exporting to the caller the subroutine msg_ok(). (Note that this is *not* a subclass of Test::Builder.)

In line 9 we create a Test::Builder object that will do the boring part of testing for us. Lines 11 through 20 are copied right out of the Test::Builder documentation; the import() routine is what allows us to say how many tests we're going to run when we use the module.

Lines 22 through 49 define the msg_ok() function itself. Its single argument specifies the mail message, either via a scalar containing the message, a reference to an array of lines in the message, or a filehandle from which the message can be read. Rather than read all of the lines from that filehandle into memory, we're going to operate on them one at a time because it's not necessary to have the whole message in memory. That's why we create the object $tester in line 25 to handle each line: it will contain a memory of its current state.

Then we call the _validate() method of $tester with each line of the message. Because that method will croak() if the message is in error, we wrap those loops in an eval block. This allows us easily to skip superfluous scanning of a message after detecting an error.

Finally, we see whether an error occurred; if an exception was thrown by `croak()` inside the `eval` block, `$@` will contain its text; otherwise `$@` will be empty. The `ok()` method of the Test::Builder object we created is the same function we're used to using in Test::Simple; it takes a true or false value, and an optional tag string, which we pass from our caller. If we had an exception, we pass its text to Test::Builder's `diag()` method, which causes it to be output as a comment during testing.

The `_new()` method in lines 50–53 is not called `new()` because it's not really a proper constructor; it's really just creating a state object, which is why we didn't bother to make it inheritable. It starts out in life expecting to see a mail header.

Lines 56–70 validate a line of a message. Because anything goes in a message body, if that's what we're expecting we have nothing to do. Otherwise, if we're expecting a header or header continuation line, then first we check for a continuation line (which starts with white space; this is how a long message header "overflows"). If we have a blank line (line 67), that separates the header from the body, so we switch to expecting body text.

Finally, we must at this point be expecting a header line, and one of those starts with non-white-space characters followed by a colon. If we don't have that, the message is bogus; but if we do, the next line could be either a header line or a continuation of the current header (or the blank line separating headers from the body).

Here's a simple test of the Test::MailMessage module:

```
1   #!/usr/bin/perl
2   use strict;
3   use warnings;
4
5   use lib qw(..);
6   use Test::MailMessage tests => 2;
7
8   msg_ok(<<EOM, "okay");
9   from: ok
```

```
10  subject: whatever
11
12  body
13  EOM
14  msg_ok(\*DATA, "bogus");
15
16  __END__
17  bogus mail
18  message
```

The result of running this is:

```
1..2
ok 1 - okay
not ok 2 - bogus
#      Failed test (./test at line 14)
# Invalid header at ./test line 14
# Looks like you failed 1 tests of 2.
```

Although we only used one Test:: module, we could have used others, for example:

```
use Test::MailMessage tests z=> 2;
use Test::Exception;
use Test::More;
```

Only one of the use statements for Test::Modules should give the number of tests to be run. Do not think that each use statement is supposed to number the tests run by functions of that module; instead, one use statement gives the total number of tests to be run.

brian d foy[4] used Test::Builder to create Test::Pod,[5] which is also worth covering.

---

4. That's not a typo; he likes his name to be spelled, er, rendered that way, thus going one step farther than bell hooks.
5. Now maintained by Andy Lester.

3.2.6 The Test::Pod Module

Documentation in Perl need not be entirely unstructured. The Plain Old Documentation (POD) format for storing documentation in the Perl source code (see the *perlpod* manual page) is a markup language and therefore it is possible to commit syntax errors. So rather than wait until your users try to look at your documentation (okay, play along with me here—imagine that you *have* users who want to read your documentation), and get errors from their POD viewer, you can make sure in advance that the POD is good.

Test::Pod exports a single function, `pod_ok()`, which checks the POD in the file named by its argument. I'll show an example of its use later in this chapter.

3.2.7 Test::Inline

If you're thinking that tests deserve to be inside the code they're testing just as much as documentation does, then you want Test::Inline. This module by Michael Schwern enables you to embed tests in code just like POD, because, in fact, it uses POD for that embedding.

3.2.8 Test::NoWarnings

Fergal Daly's Test::NoWarnings (formerly Test::Warn::None) lets you verify that your code is free of warnings. In its simplest usage, you just use the module, and increment the number of tests you're running, because Test::NoWarnings adds one more. So if your test starts:

```
use Test::More tests => 17;
```

then change it to:

```
use Test::NoWarnings;
use Test::More tests => 18;
```

and the final test will be that no warnings were generated in the running of the other tests.

3.2.9 The Test::Harness Module

Test::Harness is how you combine multiple tests. It predates every other Test:: module, and you'll find it in every version of Perl 5. Test::Harness exports a function, `runtests()`, which runs all the test files whose names are passed to it as arguments and summarizes their results. You won't see one line printed per test; `runtests()` intercepts those lines of output. Rather you'll see one line printed per test *file*, followed by a summary of the results of the tests in that file. Then it prints a global summary line. Here's an example of the output:

```
t/01load....ok
t/02tie.....ok
t/03use.....ok
t/04pod.....ok
All tests successful.
Files=4, Tests=24,  2 wallclock secs ( 1.51 cusr +  0.31 csys =
1.82 CPU)
```

As it runs, before printing "ok" on each line, you'll see a count of the tests being run updating in place, finally to be overwritten by "ok". If any fail, you'll see something appropriate instead of "ok".

You can use Test::Harness quite easily, for instance:

```
% perl -MTest::Harness -e 'runtests(glob "*.t")'
```

but it's seldom necessary even to do that, because a standard Perl module makefile will do it for you. I'll show you how shortly.

Test::Harness turns your regression tests into a full-fledged deliverable. Managers just love to watch the numbers whizzing around.

3.3 An Example Using Test:: Modules

Let's put what we've learned to use in developing an actual application. Say that we want to create a module that can limit the possible indices of an array, a bounds checker if you will. Perl's arrays won't normally do that,[6] so we need a mechanism that intercepts the day-to-day activities of an array and checks the indices being used, throwing an exception if they're outside a specified range. Fortunately, such a mechanism exists in Perl; it's called *tieing,* and pretty powerful it is too.

Because our module will work by letting us tie an array to it, we'll call it Tie::Array::Bounded. We start by letting h2xs do the rote work of creating a new module:

```
% h2xs -AXn Tie::Array::Bounded
Writing Tie/Array/Bounded/Bounded.pm
Writing Tie/Array/Bounded/Makefile.PL
Writing Tie/Array/Bounded/README
Writing Tie/Array/Bounded/test.pl
Writing Tie/Array/Bounded/Changes
Writing Tie/Array/Bounded/MANIFEST
```

That saved a lot of time! h2xs comes with perl, so you already have it. Don't be put off by the name: h2xs was originally intended for creating perl extensions from C header files, a more or less obsolete purpose now, but by dint of copious interface extension, h2xs now enjoys a new lease on life for creating modules. (In Section 8.2.4, I'll look at a more modern alternative to h2xs.)

Don't be confused by the fact that the file Bounded.pm is in the directory Tie/Array/Bounded. It may look like there's an extra directory in there but the hierarchy that h2xs created is really just to help keep your sources straight. Everything you create will be in the bottom directory, so we could *cd* there. For instant gratification we can create a Makefile the way we would with any CPAN module:

---

6. If you're smart enough to bring up $ [, then you're also smart enough to know that you shouldn't be using it.

```
% cd Tie/Array/Bounded
% perl Makefile.PL
Checking if your kit is complete...
Looks good
Writing Makefile for Tie::Array::Bounded
```

and now we can even run a test:

```
% make test
cp Bounded.pm blib/lib/Tie/Array/Bounded.pm
PERL_DL_NONLAZY=1 /usr/local/bin/perl -Iblib/arch -Iblib/lib -
I/usr/lib/perl5/5.6.1/i386-linux -I/usr/lib/perl5/5.6.1 test.pl
1..1
ok 1
```

It even passes! This is courtesy of the file test.pl that h2xs created for us, which contains a basic test that the module skeleton created by h2xs passes. This is very good for building our confidence. Unfortunately, test.pl is not the best way to create tests. We'll see why when we improve on it by moving test.pl into a subdirectory called "t" and rebuilding the Makefile before rerunning "make test":

```
% mkdir t
% mv test.pl t/01load.t
% perl Makefile.PL
Writing Makefile for Tie::Array::Bounded
% make test
PERL_DL_NONLAZY=1 /usr/local/bin/perl -Iblib/arch -Iblib/lib -
I/usr/lib/perl5/5.6.1/i386-linux -I/usr/lib/perl5/5.6.1 -e 'use
Test::Harness qw(&runtests $verbose); $verbose=0; runtests
@ARGV;' t/*.t
t/01load....ok
All tests successful.
Files=1, Tests=1,  0 wallclock secs ( 0.30 cusr +  0.05 csys =
0.35 CPU)
```

The big difference: "make test" knows that it should run Test::Harness over the .t files in the t subdirectory, thereby giving us a summary of the results.

There's only one file in there at the moment, but we can create more if we want instead of having to pack every test into test.pl.

At this point you might want to update the MANIFEST file to remove the line for test.pl now that we have removed that file.

If you're using Perl 5.8.0 or later, then your h2xs has been modernized to create the test in t/1.t; furthermore, it will use Test::More.[7] But if you have a prior version of Perl, you'll find the test.pl file we just moved uses the deprecated Test module, so let's start from scratch and replace the contents of t/01load.t as follows:

```
#!/usr/bin/perl
use strict;
use warnings;

use Test::More tests => 1;
use blib;
BEGIN { use_ok("Tie::Array::Bounded") }
```

The `use blib` statement causes Perl to search in parent directories for a blib directory that contains the Tie/Array/Bounded.pm module created by make. Although we'll usually run our tests by typing "make test" in the parent directory, this structure for a .t file allows us to run tests individually, which will be helpful when isolating failures.

Running this test either stand-alone ("./01load.t") or with "make test" produces the same output as before (plus a note from `use blib` about where it found the blib directory), so let's move on and add some code to Bounded.pm. First, delete some code that h2xs put there; we're not going to export anything, and our code will work on earlier versions of Perl 5, so remove code until the executable part of Bounded.pm looks like this:

---

7. I name my tests with two leading digits so that they will sort properly; I want to run them in a predictable order, and if I have more than nine tests, test 10.t would be run before test 2.t, because of the lexicographic sorting used by the `glob()` function called by "make test". Having done that, I can then add text after the digits so that I can also see what the tests are meant for, winding up with test names such as 01load.t.

```
package Tie::Array::Bounded;
use strict;
use warnings;
our $VERSION = '0.01';
1;
```

Now it's time to add subroutines to implement tieing. `tie` is how to make possessed variables with Perl: Literally anything can happen behind the scenes when the user does the most innocuous thing. A simple expression like `$world_peace++` could end up launching a wave of nuclear missiles, if `$world_peace` happens to be tied to Mutually::Assured::Destruction. (See, you can even use Perl to make covert political statements.)

We need a `TIEARRAY` subroutine; *perltie* tells us so. So let's add an empty one to Bounded.pm:

```
sub TIEARRAY
{
}
```

and add a test to look for it in 01load.t:

```
use Test::More tests => 2;
use blib;
BEGIN { use_ok("Tie::Array::Bounded") }

can_ok("Tie::Array::Bounded", "TIEARRAY");
```

Running "make test" copies the new Bounded.pm into blib and produces:

```
% make test
cp Bounded.pm blib/lib/Tie/Array/Bounded.pm
PERL_DL_NONLAZY=1 /usr/local/bin/perl -Iblib/arch -Iblib/lib -
I/usr/lib/perl5/5.6.1/i386-linux -I/usr/lib/perl5/5.6.1 -e 'use
Test::Harness qw(&runtests $verbose); $verbose=0; runtests
@ARGV;' t/*.t
t/01load....Using /home/peter/perl_Medic/Tie/Array/Bounded/blib
t/01load....ok
All tests successful.
```

```
Files=1, Tests=2,  0 wallclock secs ( 0.29 cusr +  0.02 csys =
0.31 CPU)
```

We have just doubled our number of regression tests!

It may seem as though we're taking ridiculously small steps here. A subroutine that doesn't do anything? What's the point in testing for that? Actually, the first time I ran that test, it failed: I had inadvertently gone into overwrite mode in the editor and made a typo in the routine name. The point in testing every little thing is to build your confidence in the code and catch even the dumbest errors right away.

So let's continue. We should decide on an interface for this module; let's say that when we tie an array we must specify an upper bound for the array indices, and optionally a lower bound. If the user employs an index out of this range, the program will die. For the sake of having small test files, we'll create a new one for this test and call it 02tie.t:

```
#!/usr/bin/perl
use strict;
use warnings;

use Test::More tests => 1;
use blib;
use Tie::Array::Bounded;

my $obj = tie my @array, "Tie::Array::Bounded";
isa_ok($obj, "Tie::Array::Bounded");
```

So far, this just tests that the underlying object from the tie is or inherits from Tie::Array::Bounded. Run this test *before* you even add any code to TIE-ARRAY to make sure that it does indeed *fail:*

```
% ./02tie.t
1..1
Using /home/peter/perl_Medic/Tie/Array/Bounded/t/../blib
not ok 1 - The object isa Tie::Array::Bounded
#     Failed test (./02tie.t at line 10)
```

```
#     The object isn't defined
# Looks like you failed 1 tests of 1.
```

We're not checking that the module can be used or that it has a TIEARRAY method; we already did those things in 01load.t. Now we know that the test routine is working properly. Let's make a near-minimal version of TIEARRAY that will satisfy this test:

```
sub TIEARRAY
{
  my $class = shift;
  my ($upper, $lower);
  return bless { upper => $upper,
                 lower => $lower,
                 array => []
               }, $class;
}
```

Now the test passes. Should we test that the object is a hashref with keys upper, lower, and so on? No—that's part of the private implementation of the object and users, including tests, have no right peeking in there.

Well, it doesn't really do to have a bounded array type if the user doesn't specify any bounds. A default lower bound of 0 is obvious because most bounded arrays will start from there anyway and be limited in how many elements they can contain. It doesn't make sense to have a default upper bound because no guess could be better than any other. We want this module to die if the user doesn't specify an upper bound (italicized code):

```
sub TIEARRAY
{
  my ($class, %arg) = @_;
  my ($upper, $lower) = @arg{qw(upper lower)};
  $lower ||= 0;
  croak "No upper bound for array" unless $upper;
  return bless { upper => $upper,
                 lower => $lower,
                 array => []
               }, $class;
}
```

Note that when we want to die in a module, the proper routine to use is croak(). This results in an error message that identifies the calling line of the code, and not the current line, as the source of the error. This allows the user to locate the place in their program where they made a mistake. croak() comes from the Carp Module, so we added a use Carp statement to Bounded.pm (not shown).

Note also that we set the lower bound to a default of 0. True, if the user didn't specify a lower bound, $lower would be undefined and hence evaluate to 0 in a numeric context. But it's wise to expose our defaults explicitly, and this also avoids warnings about using an uninitialized value. Modify 02tie.t to say:

```
use Test::More tests => 1;
use Test::Exception;
use blib;
use Tie::Array::Bounded;

dies_ok { tie my @array, "Tie::Array::Bounded" }
        "Croak with no bound specified";
```

If you're running 02tie.t as a stand-alone test, remember to run *make* in the parent directory after modifying Bounded.pm so that Bounded.pm gets copied into the blib tree.

Great! Now let's add back in the test that we can create a real object when we tie with the proper calling sequence:

```
my $obj;
lives_ok { $obj = tie my @array, "Tie::Array::Bounded",
            upper => 42
          } "Tied array okay";
isa_ok($obj, "Tie::Array::Bounded");
```

and increase the number of tests to 3. (Notice that there is no comma after the block of code that's the first argument to dies_ok and lives_ok.)

All this testing has gotten us in a pedantic frame of mind. The user shouldn't be allowed to specify an array bound that is negative or not an integer. Let's add a statement to TIEARRAY (in italics):

```
sub TIEARRAY
{
  my ($class, %arg) = @_;
  my ($upper, $lower) = @arg{qw(upper lower)};
  $lower ||= 0;
  croak "No upper bound for array" unless $upper;
  /\D/ and croak "Array bound must be integer"
    for ($upper, $lower);
  return bless { upper => $upper,
                 lower => $lower,
                 array => []
               }, $class;
}
```

and, of course, test it:

```
throws_ok { tie my @array, "Tie::Array::Bounded", upper => -1 }
         qr/must be integer/, "Non-integral bound fails";
```

Now we're not only checking that the code dies, but that it dies with a message matching a particular pattern.

We're really on a roll here! Why don't we batten down the hatches on this interface and let the user know if they gave us an argument we're *not* expecting:

```
sub TIEARRAY
{
  my ($class, %arg) = @_;
  my ($upper, $lower) = delete @arg{qw(upper lower)};
  croak "Illegal arguments in tie" if %arg;
  croak "No upper bound for array" unless $upper;
  $lower ||= 0;
  /\D/ and croak "Array bound must be integer"
    for ($upper, $lower);
```

```
return bless { upper => $upper,
               lower => $lower,
               array => []
             }, $class;
}
```

and the test:

```
throws_ok { tie my @array, "Tie::Array::Bounded", frogs => 10 }
        qr/Illegal arguments/, "Illegal argument fails";
```

The succinctness of our approach depends on the underappreciated *hash slice* and the `delete()` function. Hash slices [GUTTMAN98] are a way to get multiple elements from a hash with a single expression, and the `delete()` function removes those elements while returning their values. Therefore, anything left in the hash must be illegal.

We're nearly done with the pickiness. There's one final test we should apply. Have you guessed what it is? We should make sure that the user doesn't enter a lower bound that's higher than the upper one. Can you imagine what the implementation of bounded arrays would do if we didn't check for this? I can't, because I haven't written it yet, but it might be ugly. Let's head that off at the pass right now:

```
sub TIEARRAY
{
  my ($class, %arg) = @_;
  my ($upper, $lower) = delete @arg{qw(upper lower)};
  croak "Illegal arguments in tie" if %arg;
  $lower ||= 0;
  croak "No upper bound for array" unless $upper;
  /\D/ and croak "Array bound must be integer"
    for ($upper, $lower);
  croak "Upper bound < lower bound" if $upper < $lower;
  return bless { upper => $upper,
                 lower => $lower,
                 array => []
               }, $class;
}
```

and the new test goes at the end of 02tie.t (italicized):

Example 3.2 Final Version of 02tie.t

```perl
#!/usr/bin/perl
use strict;
use warnings;

use Test::More tests => 6;
use Test::Exception;
use blib;
use Tie::Array::Bounded;

dies_ok { tie my @array, "Tie::Array::Bounded" }
        "Croak with no bound specified";

my $obj;
lives_ok { $obj = tie my @array, "Tie::Array::Bounded",
          upper => 42 }
          "Tied array okay";

isa_ok($obj, "Tie::Array::Bounded");

throws_ok { tie my @array, "Tie::Array::Bounded", upper => -1 }
          qr/must be integer/, "Non-integral bound fails";

throws_ok { tie my @array, "Tie::Array::Bounded", frogs => 10 }
          qr/Illegal arguments/, "Illegal argument fails";

throws_ok { tie my @array, "Tie::Array::Bounded",
            lower => 2, upper => 1 }
          qr/Upper bound < lower/, "Wrong bound order fails";
```

Whoopee! We're nearly there. Now we need to make the tied array behave properly, so let's start a new test file for that, called 03use.t:

```perl
#!/usr/bin/perl
use strict;
use warnings;
```

```
use Test::More tests => 1;
use Test::Exception;
use blib;
use Tie::Array::Bounded;

my @array;
tie @array, "Tie::Array::Bounded", upper => 5;

lives_ok { $array[0] = 42 } "Store works";
```

As before, let's ensure that the test fails before we add the code to implement it:

```
% t/03use.t
1..1
Using /home/peter/perl_Medic/Tie/Array/Bounded/blib
not ok 1 - Store works
#     Failed test (t/03use.t at line 13)
# died: Can't locate object method "STORE" via package
"Tie::Array::Bounded" (perhaps you forgot to load
"Tie::Array::Bounded"?) at t/03use.t line 13.
# Looks like you failed 1 tests of 1.
```

How about that. The test even told us what routine we need to write. *perltie* tells us what it should do. So let's add to Bounded.pm:

```
sub STORE
{
  my ($self, $index, $value) = @_;
  $self->_bound_check($index);
  $self->{array}[$index] = $value;
}

sub _bound_check
{
  my ($self, $index) = @_;
  my ($upper, $lower) = @{$self}{qw(upper lower)};
  croak "Index $index out of range [$lower, $upper]"
    if $index < $lower || $index > $upper;
}
```

We've abstracted the bounds checking into a method of its own in anticipation of needing it again. Now 03use.t passes, and we can add another test to make sure that the value we stored in the array can be retrieved:

```
is($array[0], 42, "Fetch works");
```

You might think this would fail for want of the FETCH method, but in fact:

```
ok 1 - Store works
Can't locate object method "FETCHSIZE" via package
"Tie::Array::Bounded" (perhaps you forgot to load
"Tie::Array::Bounded"?) at t/03use.t line 14.
# Looks like you planned 2 tests but only ran 1.
# Looks like your test died just after 1.
```

Back to *perltie* to find out what FETCHSIZE is supposed to do: return the size of the array. Easy enough:

```
sub FETCHSIZE
{
  my $self = shift;
  scalar @{$self->{array}};
}
```

Now the test does indeed fail for want of FETCH, so we'll add that:

```
sub FETCH
{
  my ($self, $index) = @_;
  $self->_bound_check($index);
  $self->{array}[$index];
}
```

Finally we are back in the anodyne land of complete test success. Time to add more tests:

```
throws_ok { $array[6] = "dog" } qr/out of range/,
          "Bounds exception";
is_deeply(\@array, [ 42 ], "Array contents correct");
```

These work immediately. But an ugly truth emerges when we try another simple array operation:

```
lives_ok { push @array, 17 } "Push works";
```

This results in:

```
not ok 5 - Push works
#      Failed test (t/03use.t at line 19)
# died: Can't locate object method "PUSH" via package
"Tie::Array::Bounded" (perhaps you forgot to load
"Tie::Array::Bounded"?) at t/03use.t line 19.
# Looks like you failed 1 tests of 5.
```

Inspecting *perltie* reveals that PUSH is one of several methods it looks like we're going to have to write. Do we really have to write them all? Can't we be lazier than that?

Yes, we can.[8] The Tie::Array core module defines PUSH and friends in terms of a handful of methods we have to write: FETCH, STORE, FETCHSIZE, and STORESIZE. The only one we haven't done yet is STORESIZE:

```
sub STORESIZE
{
  my ($self, $size) = @_;
  $self->_bound_check($size-1);
  $#{$self->{array}} = $size - 1;
}
```

We need to add near the top of Bounded.pm:

---

8. Remember, if you find yourself doing something too rote or boring, look for a way to get the computer to make it easier for you. Top of the list of those ways would be finding code someone else already wrote to solve the problem.

```
use base qw(Tie::Array);
```

to inherit all that array method goodness.

This is a big step to take, and if we didn't have canned tests, we might wonder what sort of unknown havoc could be wrought upon our module by a new base class if we misused it. However, our test suite allows us to determine that, in fact, nothing has broken.

Now we can add to 01load.t the methods FETCH, STORE, FETCHSIZE, and STORESIZE in the can_ok test:

Example 3.3 Final Version of 01load.t

```
#!/usr/bin/perl
use strict;
use warnings;

use Test::More tests => 2;
use blib;
BEGIN { use_ok("Tie::Array::Bounded") }

can_ok("Tie::Array::Bounded", qw(TIEARRAY STORE FETCH STORESIZE
                                 FETCHSIZE));
```

Because our tests pass, let's add as many more as we can to test all the boundary conditions we can think of, leaving us with a final 03use.t file of:

Example 3.4 Final Version of 03use.t

```
#!/usr/bin/perl
use strict;
use warnings;

use Test::More tests => 15;
use Test::Exception;
use blib;
use Tie::Array::Bounded;
```

```perl
my $RANGE_EXCEP = qr/out of range/;

my @array;
tie @array, "Tie::Array::Bounded", upper => 5;
lives_ok { $array[0] = 42 } "Store works";
is($array[0], 42, "Fetch works");

throws_ok { $array[6] = "dog" } $RANGE_EXCEP,
        "Bounds exception";
is_deeply(\@array, [ 42 ], "Array contents correct");

lives_ok { push @array, 17 } "Push works";
is($array[1], 17, "Second array element correct");

lives_ok { push @array, 2, 3 } "Push multiple elements works";
is_deeply(\@array, [ 42, 17, 2, 3 ], "Array contents correct");

lives_ok { splice(@array, 4, 0, qw(apple banana)) }
        "Splice works";
is_deeply(\@array, [ 42, 17, 2, 3, 'apple', 'banana' ],
        "Array contents correct");

throws_ok { push @array, "excessive" } $RANGE_EXCEP,
        "Push bounds exception";
is(scalar @array, 6, "Size of array correct");

tie @array, "Tie::Array::Bounded", lower => 3, upper => 6;

throws_ok { $array[1] = "too small" } $RANGE_EXCEP,
        "Lower bound check failure";

lives_ok { @array[3..6] = 3..6 } "Slice assignment works";
throws_ok { push @array, "too big" } $RANGE_EXCEP,
        "Push bounds exception";
```

Tests are real programs, too. Because we test for the same exception repeatedly, we put its recognition pattern in a variable to be lazy.

Bounded.pm, although not exactly a model of efficiency (our internal array contains unnecessary space allocated to the first $lower elements that will never be used), is now due for documenting, and h2xs filled out some POD stubs already. We'll flesh it out to the final version you can see in the Appendix. I'll go into documentation more in Chapter 10.

Now we create 04pod.t to test that the POD is formatted correctly:

Example 3.5 Final Version of 04pod.t

```perl
#!/usr/bin/perl
use strict;
use warnings;

use Test::Pod tests => 1;
use blib;
use Tie::Array::Bounded;
pod_ok($INC{"Tie/Array/Bounded.pm"});
```

There's just a little trick there to allow us to run this test from any directory, since all the others can be run with the current working directory set to either the parent directory or the t directory. We load the module itself and then get Perl to tell us where it found the file by looking it up in the %INC hash, which tracks such things (see its entry in *perlvar*).

With a final "make test", we're done:

```
Files=4, Tests=24,  2 wallclock secs ( 1.58 cusr +  0.24 csys =
1.82 CPU)
```

We have a whole 24 tests at our fingertips ready to be repeated any time we want.

You can get more help on how to use these modules from the module Test::Tutorial, which despite the module appellation contains no code, only documentation.

With only a bit more work, this module could have been submitted to CPAN. See [TREGAR02] for full instructions.

3.4 Testing Legacy Code

"This is all well and good," I can hear you say, "but I just inherited a swamp of 27 programs and 14 modules and they have no tests. What do I do?"

By now you've learned that it is far more appealing to write tests as you write the code they test, so if you can possibly rewrite this application, do so. But if you're stuck with having to tweak an existing application, then adopt a top-down approach. Start by testing that the application meets its requirements . . . assuming you were given requirements or can figure out what they were. See what a successful run of the program outputs and how it may have changed its environment, then write tests that look for those effects.

3.4.1 A Simple Example

You have an inventory control program for an aquarium, and it produces output files called cetaceans.txt, crustaceans.txt, molluscs.txt, pinnipeds.txt, and so on. Capture the output files from a successful run and put them in a subdirectory called success. Then run this test:

Example 3.6 Demonstration of Testing Program Output

```
1   my @Success_files;
2   BEGIN {
3     @Success_files = glob "success/*.txt";
4   }
5
6   use Test::More tests => 1 + 2 * @Success_files;
7
8   is(system("aquarium"), 0, "Program succeeded");
9
10  for my $success (@Success_files)
11  {
12    (my $output = $success) =~ s#.*/##;
13
14    ok(-e $output, "$output present");
15
```

```
16    is(system("cmp $output $success > /dev/null 2>&1"),
17        0, "$output is valid");
18  }
```

First, we capture the names of the output files in the success subdirectory. We do that in a BEGIN block so that the number of names is available in line 6. In line 8 we run the program and check that it has a successful return code. Then for each of the required output files, in line 14 we test that it is present, and in line 16 we use the UNIX *cmp* utility to check that it matches the saved version. If you don't have a *cmp* program, you can write a Perl subroutine to perform the same test: Just read each file and compare chunks of input until finding a mismatch or hitting the ends of file.

3.4.2 Testing Web Applications

A Common Gateway Interface (CGI) program that hasn't been developed with a view toward automated testing may be a solid block of congealed code with pieces of web interface functionality sprinkled throughout it like raisins in a fruit cake. But you don't need to rip it apart to write a test for it; you can verify that it meets its requirements with an end-to-end test. All you need is a program that pretends to be a user at a web browser and checks that the response to input is correct. It doesn't matter how the CGI program is written because all the testing takes place on a different machine from the one the CGI program is stored on.

The WWW::Mechanize module by Andy Lester comes to your rescue here. It allows you to automate web site interaction by pretending to be a web browser, a function ably pulled off by Gisle Aas' LWP::UserAgent module. WWW::Mechanize goes several steps farther, however (in fact, it is a subclass of LWP::UserAgent), enabling cookie handling by default and providing methods for following hyperlinks and submitting forms easily, including transparent handling of hidden fields.[9]

---

9. If you're thinking, "Hey! I could use this to write an agent that will stuff the ballot box on surveys I want to fix," forget it; it's been done before. Chris Nandor used Perl to cast thousands of votes for his choice for American League All-Star shortstop [GLOBE99]. And this was before WWW::Mechanize was even invented.

Suppose we have an application that provides a login screen. For the usual obscure reasons, the login form, login.html, contains one or more hidden fields in addition to the user-visible input fields, like this:

```
<FORM ACTION="login.cgi" METHOD="POST">
 <INPUT NAME="username" TYPE="text">
 <INPUT NAME="password" TYPE="text">
 <INPUT NAME="fruglido" TYPE="hidden" VALUE="grilku">
 <INPUT TYPE="Submit">
</FORM>
```

On successful login, the response page greets the user with "Welcome, " followed by the user's first name. We can write this test for this login function:

Example 3.7 Using WWW::Mechanize to Test a Web Application

```
1   #!/usr/bin/perl
2   use strict;
3   use warnings;
4
5   use WWW::Mechanize;
6   use Test::More tests => 3;
7
8   my $URL = 'http://localhost/login.html';
9   my $USERNAME = 'peter';
10  my $PASSWORD = 'secret';
11
12  my $ua = WWW::Mechanize->new;
13  ok($ua->get($URL)->is_success, "Got first page")
14    or die $ua->res->message;
15
16  $ua->set_fields(username => $USERNAME,
17                  password => $PASSWORD);
18  ok($ua->submit->is_success, "Submitted form")
19    or die $ua->res->message;
20
21  like($ua->content, qr/Welcome, Peter/, "Logged in okay");
```

In line 12 we create a new WWW::Mechanize user agent to act as a pretend browser, and in line 13 we test to see if it was able to get the login page; the get() method returns a HTTP::Response object that has an is_success() method. If something went wrong with fetching the page the false value will be passed through the ok() function; there's no point in going further so we might as well die() (line 14). We can get at the HTTP::Response object again via the res() method of the user agent to call its message() method, which returns the text of the reason for failure.

In lines 16 and 17 we provide the form inputs by name, and in line 18 the submit() method of the user agent submits the form and reads the response, again returning an HTTP::Response object allowing us to verify success as before. Once we have a response page we check to see whether it looks like what we wanted.

Note that WWW::Mechanize can be used to test interaction with any web application, regardless of where that application is running or what it is written in.

3.4.3 What Next?

The kind of end-to-end testing we have been doing is useful and necessary; it is also a lot easier than the next step. To construct comprehensive tests for a large package, we must include unit tests; that means testing each function and method. However, unless we have descriptions of what each subroutine does, we won't know how to test them without investigative work to find out what they are supposed to do. I'll go into those kinds of techniques later.

3.5 A Final Encouragement

In addition to the more obvious benefits, constructing tests before or contemporaneously with code development encourages good program interface design.

Take, for example, a web-based system incorporating CGI programs and an extensive back end. When writing tests for such a beast it will become rapidly apparent that testing it via the CGI interface is tedious at best. You have to wait for the whole server round trip to happen, and most of that time is occupied by the operation of software and networks you may not be responsible for and don't want to test. By cutting out the fat and calling the back end directly you'll eliminate the tedium. However, you don't want to leave out interface code that should be tested. So you make the CGI programs as small as possible: Gather user inputs, pass them on to interface-independent code, take the outputs of that code and format them for the user. That way you have so little code in the CGI programs that testing them will be a snap. A single call to a CGI program itself will accomplish that, and every other test can concentrate on going directly to the back end.

Congratulations. You've just reinvented the Model-View-Controller pattern (see [GAMMA95]), a device generally recognized to be a pretty good thing.

3.5.1 A Final Caveat

Tests can't replace using your brain. They're only as smart as their creator: If there's a bug that isn't tested for, the tests won't find it. You still have to look at what you write and think about it, or it could harbor a bug that you didn't think to test for. Testing just saves you from having to repeat the same train of thought over and over again.

Chapter 4

Rewriting (Transplants)

"I would rather make my name than inherit it."

— William Makepeace Thackeray

4.1 Strategizing

Perhaps the most important question you will have to answer to begin with is this: To what extent should you rewrite the code? Even if at first it looks far too long to replace, rewriting from scratch is an option you should pursue if at all possible for a host of reasons:

- It allows you to psychologically "own" the code: It's no longer someone else's code; it's yours, because you typed it.

- You'll be far more familiar with the code, because people remember things much better if they've written them instead of merely having read them.

- The code may not need to be that long; the original code may have been accidentally or deliberately overelaborated and maybe there's a slim program in there just waiting to be liberated from the adiposity encasing it.

- You'll be able to create tests incrementally as you write each new function.

- Perhaps the program started as either a prototype or an application designed to handle a much smaller problem, but it became a victim of its own success and accreted new functionality as a hermit crab accumulates barnacles (the difference being that the crab can still get around). You can recode to fit the new, more complete requirements.

- Similarly, the program may contain vestigial code that hasn't been used in years. If you rewrite, you'll automatically exclude it without having to hunt it down.

- You can incorporate the latest technology in the new program. In particular, advanced modules are being created now at a dizzying pace; quite possibly large parts of the original code duplicate functionality that can now be left to the module maintainers.

Remember, it'll almost certainly take longer to figure out the code than you think. Consider whether increasing your estimate of the size of the task changes your mind about whether to rewrite or not.

4.2 Why Are You Doing This?

The goals of rewriting are similar to the goals of developing a program from scratch. You must consider these questions: Who are you writing for? How do the demands on your rewrite differ from the demands placed on the original code?

4.2.1 Who's the Audience?

Who is going to see your code? In some environments, code will be inspected by people who will not be involved in maintaining it, may not work in the same department, or may not even be programmers. But their reactions could nevertheless be influential. Determine before you start whether you are in such an environment and find out what you can about the reviewers' tastes. You may be better off coding to a low degree of sophistication so not to antagonize reviewers who are unable to understand more advanced code constructions.

Even if you're fortunate enough not to be incarcerated in such a politically distorted workplace, you must consider who is going to be maintaining this program. Assuming you're not attempting to ensure job security through creating code so obfuscated that no one else can decipher it, if someone else is going to assume responsibility for your program you will want to minimize the extent to which they have to bug you for help. Therefore, if you know who that person is going to be, you should keep the sophistication of your code to a level that they can assimilate. (Of course, this strategy has its limits; if you're creating an air traffic control system to be maintained by a recent high school graduate, accommodation may not be possible.[1])

---

1. If you're creating an air traffic control system in Perl, please drop me a line. If your system is supposed to be maintained by teenagers, please also include a map of the areas it serves; rest assured I will put that map to good use. (To forestall the letters, the system described in [HOGABOOM03] is not used in operations.)

In the absence of more specific information, the most likely maintenance programmer for your program is, of course, yourself. Strange as it might seem at this point, many—if not most—programmers, in some subconscious fit of masochism, still code in a way that causes needless pain for themselves later on. You know who you are.

If you don't know who's going to take over your code, the question arises: What level of sophistication should you code to? There is much debating on this topic, and more than a few rancorous opinions. I believe you should code to your own level, and not try to satisfy the preferences of a purely hypothetical maintenance programmer. There abounds an absurd notion that there is an objective "best standard" to code to for maintenance, and people fritter away endless hours arguing whether a construction such as:

```
(my $new = $old) =~ s/old/new/;
```

fits this standard,[2] or whether it is clearer to the hypothetical maintainer to rewrite it as:

```
my $new = $old;
$new =~ s/old/new/;
```

If you're going to be the maintenance programmer, the only concern that need affect you is whether *you* will be able to understand the code. That is best determined by how long it took you to write it. If you write something quickly, it is more likely to be readable than something that takes hours of sweating and testing to get right.

If those hours are spent constructing a fiendishly compact brand-new idiom, the odds are you will spend even longer trying to figure it out when you come across it six months later. Leave it out for now and use more obvious code instead; if in some future programming effort the new idiom occurs to you without hours of toil, then you've hit on something useful; but more likely, you will be glad you resisted the temptation to use it.

---

2. Tom Christiansen dubbed this the *en passant* method of setting a variable to a transformation of an expression.

(Writing something quickly doesn't guarantee that it'll make sense in a larger context later on, though, only that you'll understand the syntax. In other words, you may not be able to see the forest for the trees, but at least each tree will be somewhat familiar.)

If, on the other hand, you spend hours developing a small piece of code that doesn't have any apparently clearer representation, you have code that needs commenting. You understand it right now because of all the auxiliary notes that you took, the tests that you ran (which should be rolled into your testing scripts), the articles or texts that you read, and some complex analysis that you performed, none of which appear in the code. If you needed that supporting material to create the code, you'll need it to understand it, so put it in as comments. Later on I'll show how you can insert lengthier information that can be extracted into nicely formatted documents.

4.2.2 The Ten Levels of Perl Programmers

Several years ago, Tom Christiansen created a somewhat tongue-in-cheek list of different levels of Perl programming sophistication ([CHRISTIANSEN98]). With an eye toward classifying maintenance programmers, here's mine. Later on in this book, I'll occasionally refer to one of these levels when I want to indicate the degree of sophistication of some code or technique. It can be helpful to assess at what level the author of a program you are tasked with maintaining was.

Level 1:   Hasn't read any book (or anything else for that matter) on Perl; knows that it's a programming language but knows nothing else about it. Can run a Perl program written by someone else and realizes that they can change parts of the behavior—such as the content of printed strings—by editing parts of the program. Doesn't understand why changes to other parts of the program don't work; has no mental model to fit the language in, so can't differentiate the syntax from languages as diverse as COBOL and C++.

Level 2: Understands the basic block structure syntax, although only to the extent of recognizing that it is similar to a language like JavaScript. Has a notion that blocks create some kind of scoping effect but does not know about lexical variables and has not encountered `use strict` or `use warnings`. Can change the sense of a conditional and use basic arithmetic and logical operators. Thinks that everything they need to do can be achieved by small modifications to programs written by others.

Level 3: Wants to create programs from scratch and realizes that some kind of education is called for; asks people for book recommendations for learning Perl. Someone at this level may acquire the Camel book [WALL00] thinking that it is a tutorial, and attempt to read the whole thing, suffering severe neurological trauma in the process.

Level 4: Learns for the first time about `use strict` and `use warnings`, but thinks they're more trouble than they're worth. Wonders what `my` means. Discovers that there are modules for solving just about any problem but doesn't know how to acquire and use them. Subscribes to a Perl newsgroup and is overwhelmed by the amount of discussion on topics that make no sense to them.

Level 5: Has basic comprehension of regular expressions, operators, I/O, and scoping. Uses `my`, `use strict`, and `use warnings` because everyone says so. A large number of people never advance beyond this level because they can do pretty much anything (aside from creating reusable components), albeit often inefficiently. Learns about references either at this level or the next one.

Level 6: May take a Perl class. Knows how to use objects and realizes that this knowledge and the Comprehensive Perl Archive Network (CPAN) enable them to create powerful programs very rapidly. Wants to advance to the next level to see how far this empowerment trend extends.

Level 7:   Learns how to create their own object-oriented modules and experiences the bliss of code reuse for the first time. Knows about packages and the difference between lexical and dynamic variables. Discovers that Perl's regular expressions aren't regular and are capable of far more than simple text manipulation.

Level 8:   Starts giving back in some fashion: either submitting bug reports or patches, modules to CPAN, documentation suggestions, or help for novices. Discovers advanced features like AUTOLOAD and starts using developer-oriented modules like Class::MethodMaker. Uses complex application modules like DBI or Tk where appropriate; comfortable using CGI.pm to create web-based applications.

Level 9:   Attends a Perl conference, participates in the Perl community in other ways; may frequent `www.perlmonks.org` or #perl (see Chapter 12). Comfortable with creating code on the fly with `eval` and manipulating the symbol table. Thinks often of performance considerations when coding, probably more than necessary. Publishes modules subclassing major modules to add significant functionality.

Level 10:   Takes part in Perl obfuscation and "golf" contests,[3] comfortable writing a single regular expression using embedded code to implement a function that most other people would have needed to write an entire program for; may submit patches to the Perl core, contribute major new modules, or otherwise become a well-known name within the Perl community.

Continuing this progression for a few more levels until reaching one where the only inhabitant is Larry Wall is left as an exercise to the reader.

---

3. Perl golf is a contest of seeing who can solve a problem in the fewest number of characters. The winner is unlikely to be intelligible, but there again, how many other languages allow you to write an entire munitions-grade encryption algorithm (RSA) in three lines that fit on a t-shirt?

4.2.3 What Are the Requirements?

Before rewriting, you must find out how the requirements for the code have changed since the original program was developed. Don't assume that all you have to do is reproduce the functionality unless you've verified that. You may need to optimize the code for different goals; perhaps you're expected to improve its readability, performance, or portability, or extend its functionality.

An important question to ask the original developer is what, if anything, the code was optimized for. For instance, there may be complicated constructions in it that you would simplify if you didn't know that they're required for acceptable performance.

4.3 Style

In [SCOTT01], Ed Wright and I said, "The only believable comment to make about style is that you should have one." I'll go further than that here. Just as in clothing, having a consistent style doesn't necessarily mean other people won't laugh at you. So, to prevent you from accidentally picking a coding style that's equivalent to a 1970s-era pool hustler, here is a suggested style that's rather more conservative.

Of course, some people intentionally dress like pool sharks and may take umbrage at this disparagement of their sartorial tastes. By all means stick with an idiosyncratic style if you've arrived at it through conscious decision and you can live with the consequences. This section is for everyone else. Like many parts of this book, it incorporates a certain amount of personal taste that is one of a number of ways of getting a job done well; I'm not holding it up as the "One True Way."

You can find comments on style in the *perlstyle* documentation page that comes with Perl, parts of which are reflected here.

4.3.1 Layout

The best thing you can do for the layout of your program is to indent it properly. I continue to be amazed by how many people in my classes write programs with no indentation whatsoever, as though there were a price on the head of anyone using white space. My own tendencies are so ingrained in the other direction that I have to fight the urge to indent my one-liners! No matter how brief or short-lived the program, you're doing everyone a favor by indenting it from the beginning. Many editors make this process painless.

perlstyle recommends a four-column indent; I use two columns because it's enough for my eyes to recognize the block structure and I don't want deeply nested blocks crowding the right margin. Some people favor an eight-column indent by virtue of using the tab character for each indentation level, and I personally find this far too large. They sometimes claim that they merely need to set the tab stops in their editors to four columns to get good-looking indentation, but this forces maintenance programmers to fiddle with their editor configuration, something many programmers are so possessive of that you might as well ask them to stop breathing.

When it comes to brace styles for code blocks, programmers break out into confrontations that make Jonathan Swift's big-endian/little-endian battles ([SWIFT47]) look like Amish barn-raisings. I prefer a style called the BSD/Allman style:

```
sub read_dicts
{
  my $dictref = shift;
  my @path = split /:/, $ENV{DICTPATH} || "$ENV{HOME}:.";
  local @ARGV = grep -e, ($DEFDICT, map "$_/.dict" => @path);
  while (<>)
  {
    # Assume the line contains a single word
    chomp;
    $dictref->{$_}++;
  }
}
```

whereas most of the Perl distribution uses the so-called K&R (Kernighan and Ritchie) style:

```
sub read_dicts {
  my $dictref = shift;
  my @path = split /:/, $ENV{DICTPATH} || "$ENV{HOME}:.";
  local @ARGV = grep -e, ($DEFDICT, map "$_/.dict" => @path);
  while (<>) {
    # Assume the line contains a single word
    chomp;
    $dictref->{$_}++;
  }
}
```

which saves a line per block but makes it harder—to this author—to see where the block begins, particularly because a continuation line may be indented. For example:

```
update($controller->connection, $record[$cur_count]->ticket,
       $form_inputs->{params});
```

might force you to check the end of the first line to make sure it wasn't ending with a brace. Another example:

```
if (($best_count == 1 &&   $self->{single_match})
 || ($best_count >  0 && ! $self->{single_match})) {
    $found_match = 1;
}
```

which—even with a four-column indentation—looks more confusing to me than

```
if (($best_count == 1 &&   $self->{single_match})
 || ($best_count >  0 && ! $self->{single_match}))
{
  $found_match = 1;
}
```

with only a two-column indentation. (Although to be fair, some K&R adherents suggest this case is worth an exception.) See also how the continuation line was given a nonstandard indentation so the parallel clauses could line up nicely. Don't underestimate the value of using white space to prettify code in this way.[4]

Although there are at least two ways of conditionally executing a single statement without putting it in an `if` block, if that statement is long enough to overflow the line, using a block for it may be clearer than the other approaches (because it *looks* like multiple statements, even if it isn't):

```
if (@problems)
{
    error("We found the following problems:\n"
        . (join "\n" => @problems)
        );
}
```

The non-block ways of conditional statement execution are:

- *condition* and *statement*

  For example:

  ```
  /(banana|apple|pear)/ and push @fruit, $1;
  ```

- *statement* if *condition*

  For example:

  ```
  warn "Reached line $." if $verbose;
  ```

Code should be as pleasant to look at as you can possibly make it without ornateness that's fragile with respect to modifications—you don't want to shy away from making necessary changes just because they would destroy a beautiful piece of formatting.

---

4. After some conversation with K&R adherents, I am starting to suspect that the difference between them and the BSD/Allman camp is that they tend to look at the ends of lines for semantic clues, whereas we look at the beginnings. Experiment with both styles and see which one you find more appealing.

4.4 Comments

Comments are to your program as the Three Bears' furniture was to Goldilocks; too few aren't good enough, and more are not better. Ideally, code should not need commenting; for example, instead of saying:

```
# If employee was hired more than a week ago:
# get today's week number, convert the employee's
# hire date using the same format, take difference.
use POSIX qw(strftime);
use Date::Parse;
chomp(my $t1 = `date +%U`);
my @t2 = strptime($employee->hired);
if (strftime("%U", @t2) - $t1 > 1)
```

say:

```
if (time - $employee->hired > $ONE_WEEK)
```

by storing times in UNIX seconds-since-epoch format and defining $ONE_WEEK earlier as 60 * 60 * 24 * 7. This is not only easier to read but lacks the bug in the previous code. That tortured tangle of pendulous programming may look absurd, but I have often seen worse. A developer is used to getting a date from the *date* command in shell scripts, does the same in a Perl program, stores the result in the same format, and it goes downhill from there.

Sometimes you can't make the code clear enough. When you add a comment the word to keep in mind is, *Why?* Don't just recapitulate what the code does, but say why you're doing it. This doesn't need to be a verbose justification, but can be as simple as this:

```
if (time - $employee->hired > $ONE_WEEK)  # Past probation?
```

Although then you have to ask why it wasn't written as:

```
if (time - $employee->hired > $PROBATION_PERIOD)
```

So a better example would be something like:

```
if (my ($name) = />(.*?)</s)   # /s: fields can contain newlines
```

which indicates some hard-won piece of knowledge.

4.4.1 Sentinel Comments

Sometimes you need to put a reminder in your code to change something later. Perhaps you're in the middle of fixing one bug when you discover another. By putting a distinctive marker in a comment, you have something you can search for later. I use the string "XXX" because *gvim* highlights it especially for this purpose.[5] (I suppose it also makes the program fail to pass through naive adult content filters.)

4.4.2 Block Comments

People often ask how they can comment out a large piece of code. Wrapping it in an `if (0) {...}` block prevents it from being run, but still requires that it be syntactically correct.

Instead, wrap the code in Plain Old Documentation (POD) directives so it's treated as documentation.[6] There are a number of ways of doing this; here I've used `=begin`:

```
=begin comment

# Here goes the code we want
# to be ignored by perl

=end comment

=cut
```

---

5. Even though I use Emacs most of the time; it helps to hedge your bets in the perennial "Favorite Editor War."
6. See Section 10.3.1.

This will still be interpreted as POD, though. However, in this case, POD formatters should ignore the block because none of them know what a block labeled "comment" is. I needed the =end directive to keep the POD valid (=begin directives should be matched), and I needed the =cut directive to end POD processing so perl could resume compiling the following code. Remember that POD directives need blank lines following them because they are paragraph-based. I'll go into what POD can do for your program in more detail in Chapter 10. For a more creative solution to the multiline comment problem, see http://www.perl.com/pub/a/2002/08/13/comment.html.

4.5 Restyling

What should you do when you're presented with an existing program whose author didn't follow your favorite style guideline and whose layout looks like a Jackson Pollock painting?[7]

Several attempts have been made at writing beautifiers, but the clear winner as of publication time is *perltidy*,[8] by Steve Hancock. You can also download *perltidy* from CPAN. Use Perl::Tidy as the module name to install.

perltidy writes beautified versions of its input files in files of the same name with .tdy appended. It has too many options to document exhaustively here, but they are well covered in its manual page. Its default options format according to the *perlstyle* recommendations. My personal style is approximately equivalent to:

```
perltidy -gnu -bbt=1 -i=2 -nsfs -vt=1 -vtc=1 -nbbc
```

As good as it is, *perltidy* can't make the kinds of optimizations that turn the layout of a program into a work of art. Use it once to get a program written by

---

7. Make than a Pollock imitation. Uri Guttman referred me to an article showing how genuine Pollocks exhibit fractal ordering: [TAYLOR02].

8. http://perltidy.sourceforge.net/

someone else into a "house style," but don't let your style be a straightjacket. For instance, the preceding settings generated this formatting:

```
return 1 if $case_sensitive[length $word]{$word};
return 1 if $case_insensitive[length $word]{lc $word};
```

But I could further beautify that code into:

```
return 1 if $case_sensitive  [length $word]{   $word};
return 1 if $case_insensitive[length $word]{lc $word};
```

Note that you can separate subscripting brackets from their identifiers by white space if you want. In fact, Perl is incredibly permissive about white space, allowing you to write such daring constructs as:

```
$  puppy = ($dog      ->offspring)[0];
$platypup = ($platypus->eggs)      [0];
```

although whether you really want to mix left and right justification without any, er, justification, is questionable.

4.5.1 Just Helping Out?

If you are modifying code that belongs to someone else, but not assuming responsibility for it, follow its existing style. You'll only annoy the author by "helpfully" reformatting their code. That's equivalent to going into the bathrooms at a house you've been invited to and changing the way all the toilet paper rolls are hung.

4.6 Variable Renaming

Easily vying with misindendation for unintentional obfuscation is cryptic variable naming. If you look at a piece of code and can't tell what a variable is for, it has the wrong name. A brief mnemonic is usually sufficient: $func is as good as $function, and unless there are other function references nearby, as good as `$function_for_button_press_callback`. On the other hand, `$f` is not good enough.

Names like `$i` and `$n` are fine if their variables enjoy the commonly accepted usages of an index and a count, respectively, but only over a short scope. Single-letter or otherwise cryptic names can otherwise be acceptable if they are recapitulating a formula that is well-known or included in official documentation for the program, for example:

```
$e = $m * $c ** 2;

# Weighted average contribution, see formula (4):
$v_avg = sum(map $v[$_] * $v_w[$_] => 0..$#v) / sum(@v_w);
```

However, single-character variable names should be confined to small scopes because they are hard to find with an editor's search function if you need to do that.

Don't use `$i`, `$j`, and so on, for indices in hierarchical data structures if the structures are not truly multidimensional; use names representative of what's stored at each level. For instance:

```
$level = $voxels[$x][$y][$z];
```
Okay; these really are x, y, z coordinates.

```
$val = $spreadsheet[$i][$j];
```
Okay; accepted usage.

```
$val = $spreadsheet[$row][$col];
```
Better; more common terms.

```
$total += $matrix[$i][$j][$k];
```
Fine, if we don't know any more about `@matrix` (perhaps this is in a multidimensional array utility method).

```
$e = $o{$i}{$j}{$k};
```
Bad; you have to look up what those variables mean.

```
$employee = $orgchart{$division}{$section}{$position};
```
Much clearer.

```
$emp = $org{$div}{$sec}{$pos};
```
Equally useful; the variables are sufficiently mnemonic to suggest their meaning immediately.

perlstyle has some excellent recommendations for formatting of variable names:

- Use underscores for separating words (e.g., `$email_address`), not capitalization (`$EmailAddress`).
- Use all capital letters for constants; for example, `$PI`.
- Use mixed case for package variables or file-scoped lexicals; for example, `$Log_File`.
- Use lowercase for everything else; for example, `$full_name`. This includes subroutine names (e.g., `raid_fridge`) even though, yes, they live in the current package and are not lexical.

Subroutines that are internal and not intended for use by your users should have names beginning with an underscore. (This won't stop the users from calling the subroutines, but they will at least know by the naming convention that they are doing something naughty.)

4.6.1 Symbolic Constants

I seldom use the `constant` pragma, which allows you to define symbols at compile time; for instance:

```
use constant MAX_CONNECTIONS => 5;
    .
    .
    .
if ($conns++ < MAX_CONNECTIONS) ...
```

It has some advantages:

- You cannot overwrite the value assigned to the symbol. (Well, not easily: The constant is actually a subroutine prototyped to accept no arguments. It could be redefined, but you wouldn't do that by accident.)
- The use of a constant is (usually) optimized by the Perl compiler so that its value is directly inserted without the overhead of a sub-routine call.
- The symbols look constant-ish; identifiers beginning with a sigil ($, @, %) tend to make us think they are mutable.

It also has some disadvantages:

- Constants are visually indistinguishable from filehandles.
- A constant can't be used on the left-hand side of a fat arrow (=>) because that turns it into a string. You have to put empty paren-theses after the constant to ensure that Perl parses it as a subrou-tine call.
- The same is true of using a constant as a hash key.
- Constants do not interpolate into double-quoted strings, unless you use the hair-raising @{ [CONSTANT_GOES_HERE] } con-struction.
- Being subroutines, they are package-based and cannot be con-fined to a lexical scope; but they go out of scope when you have a new package statement (unless you fully qualify their names).

- Being subroutines, they are visible from other packages, and are even inheritable. You may consider this an advantage if you wish but it is not intuitively obvious.

So I tend to define my constants as just ordinary scalars or whatever they might be:

```
my $PI      = 3.1415926535897932384;
my @BEATLES = qw(John Paul George Ringo);
```

Purists argue that constants should be unmodifiable, but Perl's central philosophy is to let you assume the responsibility that goes along with freedom. Anyone who changes the value of π deserves the consequences that go along with altering the fundamental structure of the universe. On the other hand, you might have good reason at various times to add 'Stuart' or 'Pete' to @BEATLES.

4.7 Editing

For those of you who are not *Star Trek* fans, in several series and movies there was a villainous race called the Borg, whose modus operandi was to conquer a people by gradually assimilating them with mechanical body implants. Making someone else's program your own is a similar process of infusing it with your own code and devices until you are certain that you have it under control.

Once you have used a beautifier to make code fit your preferred standard for layout, you can apply *line editing* techniques for reducing code bloat. (If you ever did an exercise in high school English called *précis,* where you took a long-winded screed and condensed it as much as possible, I am talking about the moral equivalent of that process for computer programming.) If you can reduce the amount of code without introducing obfuscation, the result will be clearer and easier to maintain. The more familiar you are with Perl and its efficient idioms, the better you'll be able to do that. As you reduce the bulk of the code through line editing, its purpose will become clearer and you will find it easier to spot inefficient or redundant higher-level constructions.

4.8 Line Editing

Line editing is *not* a process of combining statements to fit as many as possible on each line. It is the conscious conversion of lengthy code into something shorter—or in certain cases, longer—that is at least as clear to you as the original. This can be as simple as replacing an if (! expr) with unless (expr), converting lengthy manual output formatting to use printf(), or something more complicated. Now I'll cover some opportunities to look out for performing line editing.

4.8.1 Needless Repetition

This principle is so fundamental that is is known by an acronym: DRY (Don't repeat yourself; see [HUNT00], p. 27). *Any* repetitive pattern in code should trigger the urge to see if you can elide it. Perl provides a plethora of tools that help in these situations; be especially familiar with:

- foreach loops and their aliasing property: If you modify the loop variable while it points to a writable variable, that variable will be updated. Try this test:

```
my $x = 5;
my @y = 6..8;
for my $z ($x, @y, 17)
{
   $z++ if $z < 10;
}
print "$x @y\n";
```

and then see what happens if you remove the test if $z < 10.

This feature of foreach loops even helps you shorten code when there's no loop to speak of, if you have multiple references to a long variable name. Instead of writing:

```
$music{$artist}{MP3} =~ s#\\#/#g;
$music{$artist}{MP3} = "$MUSICPATH/$music{$artist}{MP3}";
```

you can say:

```
for ($music{$artist}{MP3})
{
  s#\\#/#g;
  $_ = "$MUSICPATH/$_";
}
```

- map() and how it lets you transform one list into another; the output list doesn't even have to have the same number of elements as the input list.

- How to write subroutines and how to implement named parameter passing for clarity, for example:

```
make_sundae(nuts => 'pecan', cherries => 2);
...
sub make_sundae
{
  my %arg = (%DEFAULT_SUNDAE, @_);
  if ($arg{bananas}) ...
}
```

Beginners often don't realize that you can pass hashes around as parts of lists and reconstitute them from arrays.

4.8.2 Too Many Temporary Variables

The less a language intrudes between your understanding of a problem and your expression of it in a program, the better. Temporary variables—also known as *synthetic variables*—are there just because the program required them. They don't actually have any meaning in the language of the problem. Any variable with "temp" in its name is likely a temporary variable (or a temperature). Here's an example of a temporary variable I just inherited:

```
if ($!)
{
  my $msg = "$? $!";
  print ERRFILE "$0: $msg\n";
}
```

Clearly $msg is not used for anything else (because it immediately goes out of scope), so why not save a line:

```
if ($!)
{
  print ERRFILE "$0: $? $!\n";
}
```

Now we can see that it could be shortened still with either a postfixed if:

```
print ERRFILE "$0: $? $!\n" if $!;
```

or a logical and:

```
$! and print ERRFILE "$0: $? $!\n";
```

Sometimes you can avoid temporary variables by crafting a humongous statement involving many function calls and have it still make sense. If you can think of the statement as a pipeline, this is a case where Perl's syntactic generosity in making parentheses on function calls optional can be most helpful. Just put line breaks in the right places. A classic example of this is the Schwartzian Transform (see [HALL98], p. 49):[9]

```
@sorted = map   { $_->[0] }
          sort { $a->[1] <=> $b->[1] }
          map   { [ $_, func($_) ] }
              @unsorted;
```

That would look uglier if parentheses were mandatory:

```
@sorted = map ({ $_->[0] }
            sort({ $a->[1] <=> $b->[1] }
                map ({ [ $_, func($_) ] }
                    @unsorted
            )));
```

---

9. See `http://groups.google.com/groups?selm=4b2eag%24odb%40csnews.cs.colorado.edu` for the original reference.

A pipeline is a natural way to think of the act of using successive functions and operators to transform a list. Here's a really long example for finding particular subdirectories of a directory $dir:

```
1   opendir DIR, $dir;
2   my @kids = map   File::Spec::Link->resolve($_)
3            => grep -d
4            => map  { tr/\n/?/
5                    ? do { warn "Embedded N/L at ? in $_\n"; () }
6                    : $_ }
7            map  "$dir/$_"
8            => grep !/^(?:\.\.?|RCS)$/
9            => readdir DIR;
```

With some creative indentation this is quite easy to read: Some people prefer to read it from top to bottom; most people understand it better when read from bottom to top, that being the order of execution:

9 Return the list of files in $dir.

8 Ignore the current and parent directories, and any file or directory called RCS.

7 Form the full path to the file.

4 Ignore files with embedded newlines, producing a warning instead and substituting an empty list at this point in the pipeline.

3 Select just directories.

2 Use a CPAN module to resolve any symbolic links in the filename.[10]

Yes, newlines are valid characters in UNIX filenames, but they can give some utilities heartburn; this example was designed to protect those utilities while reporting such filenames.

---

10. http://search.cpan.org/dist/File-Copy-Link/

4.8.3 Not Enough Temporary Variables

Conversely, writing obfuscated code to avoid creating a temporary variable is no savings, especially if there is some kind of meaningful name you can assign to that variable. For instance:

```
push @{$person{$ssn}{PHONES}},
   substr($dbh->selectcol_arrayref("SELECT raw_text FROM logs \
                                   WHERE SSN = '$ssn'")->[0],
         $offsets[$WORK_PHONE],
         $offsets[$WORK_PHONE+1] - $offsets[$WORK_PHONE]);
```

Even creative indentation hasn't helped enough. That doesn't mean that every compound expression needs to be replaced by a temporary variable, nor that statements need to be constrained to fit on single lines. Here's one way of making that code clearer:

```
{
  my $sql = "SELECT raw_text FROM logs WHERE SSN = '$ssn'";
  my $record = $dbh->selectcol_arrayref($sql)->[0];
  my $offset = $offsets[$WORK_PHONE];
  my $length = $offsets[$WORK_PHONE+1] - $offset;
  push @{$person{$ssn}{PHONES}},
      substr($record, $offset, $length);
}
```

Notice how the temporary variables are declared in a block that limits their scope.

4.9 Antipatterns

An inexperienced programmer can create code that is far more convoluted than necessary, resulting in decreased maintainability and possibly decreased performance. A team once told me they were about to buy bigger hardware to run a program that was taking more than two hours and 1 GB of RAM each time it ran. When I looked at the program, I saw that it used parallel arrays and linear searches instead of hashes, read large amounts of input into memory, and sorted it there. After editing, a run consumed 20 minutes, 7 MB, and half as much source code. Now I'll cover some inefficient practices to look out for.[11]

4.9.1 Not Using Hashes

The hash has to be the most useful data structure ever invented. This book assumes that you are familiar with their use and therefore know why they are so useful. However, the programmer who wrote your legacy code may not have known this. The complete absence of a hash from that code is a strong clue that the programmer didn't know about hashes, because it's a rare program that can't make good use of a hash somewhere.

Look out for linear searches through arrays. The code may look like this:

```
my $found = 0;
foreach my $element (@array)
{
   $found = 1 and last if $element eq $search;
}
if ($found) ...
```

or:

```
my $found_index = -1;
for (my $i = 0; $i <= $#array; $i++)
{
   $found_index = $i, last if $array[$i] eq $search;
}
if ($found_index >= 0) ...
```

or even:

```
if (grep $_ eq $search, @array) ...
```

---

11. Thanks to Adam Turoff for pointing out that these are best called "antipatterns" [BROWN98].

It's common to create a hash just so you can do lookups in constant time instead of having to perform linear searches over an array. If you only want to do one lookup, then go ahead and use grep(), because creating a hash just for that purpose will be slower and occupy more code. However, consider whether the data should have been stored in a hash in the first place. Needing to perform a lookup or other random access on an array usually indicates that it should have been a hash to begin with.

If you don't care about the ordering of the data, a hash will work. If you do care about the order, sometimes you can use an array in conjunction with a hash. For instance, suppose you are reading information about American states. The data arrives in a particular order, but you want to store it in a two-level hash for random lookup:

```
my @COLS = qw(NAME CAPITAL LARGEST_CITY BIRD FLOWER);
my %state;
while (<DATA>)
{
  my ($abbreviation, @vals) = split;
  @{$state{$abbreviation}}{@cols} = @vals;
}
__END__
AL Alabama Montgomery Birmingham Yellowhammer Camellia
...
```

4.9.2 Magic Numbers

Literal numbers, and some literal strings, in code should be given symbolic names and declared at the head of the program or in some form of configuration input. For example, instead of:

```
open_server('dbms_temp', 442);
```

write:

```
my $DBMS_SERVER = 'dbms_temp';  # Database server name
my $DBMS_PORT   = 442;          # Database server port
```

```
   .
   .
   .
open_server($DBMS_SERVER, $DBMS_PORT);
```

This may occupy more space, but it has three important benefits:

- It attaches a meaning to the value being passed (make the variable or constant name as descriptive as possible).

- It allows you to identify multiple uses of the same thing as opposed to multiple unrelated occurrences of (coincidentally) the same value.

- It puts all the kinds of values that maintenance programmers are likely to want to change in one place where they can change them without having to wade through code you'd rather they didn't change.

These advantages are so key (and applicable to every programming language), you'd wonder why anyone would not follow this rule. Unfortunately, many people don't, and during editing one of the first things you can do is to replace "magic numbers" with symbolic names.

There are cases in which this would be overkill. For instance, subroutine calls with named parameters already tell you what the purpose of a value is:

```
trim_tree(angels => 1, balls => 14, lights => 35);
```

However, it is probably still advantageous to give these values names so they can be adjusted in a global configuration section:

```
my $NUM_ANGELS = 1;
my $NUM_BALLS  = 14;
my $NUM_LIGHTS = 35;
...
trim_tree(angels => $NUM_ANGELS, balls => $NUM_BALLS,
          lights => $NUM_LIGHTS);
```

or, for that matter:

```
my %TREE_TRIM_OPTS = (angels => 1, balls => 14, lights => 35);
...
trim_tree(%TREE_TRIM_OPTS);
```

It may be overkill to use symbolic names for values like 0 and 1, especially if the context is obvious or if you definitely do not want any maintenance programmer changing the assignments, but even here it is possible to make improvements. For instance, subroutines that want a true or false value in a positional parameter won't (or shouldn't) care what kind of true or false value is used, so you can substitute a value that happens to be true but is also symbolic.

So instead of:

```
my $p = HTML::TreeBuilder->new->parse(get($URL));
$p->traverse(\&element_proc, 1);
```

say:

```
my $p = HTML::TreeBuilder->new->parse(get($URL));
$p->traverse(\&element_proc, 'IGNORE_TEXT');
```

to give you a reminder of what the second parameter to traverse() is for.

4.9.3 Ineffective Regular Expressions

Regular expressions are such a huge topic that they deserve their own book . . . and fortunately they already have one [FRIEDL02]. It's a rare Perl program that can't put a regular expression to good use, and if you inherit a program that doesn't have any, take a hard look at it to see whether it should have some. If someone slices up text using substr() and/or split() (which uses a regular expression anyway, although it can be disguised as a string), or searches for multiple substrings using index(), either they are being very smart in solving a problem that requires maximum performance, or they weren't fluent in the language of regular expressions.

Matching text with a regular expression is an art; you want the simplest regex that will match what you want in every possible case. It may not be necessary to make the regex as restrictive as possible. For instance, suppose you are matching uids in lines from /etc/passwd:

```
peter:x:500:500:Peter Scott:/home/peter:/bin/tcsh
```

The colon-separated fields in this sample line are, in order: username, password, **uid**, gid, GECOS, directory, shell. The non-regex solution looks like this:

```
($username, $password, $uid, $gid, $gecos, $dir, $shell) =
split /:/;
```

or, more mercifully:

```
@fields = split /:/;
$uid = $fields[2];
```

Now, a regex-based solution looks hideous if it insists on matching the whole line according to rigid syntax rules:

```
$uid = $1 if /^[a-z][a-z0-9_]*:.*?:(\d+):\d+(?::.*?){3}$/;
```

but really, why bother? In an /etc/passwd line, the uid is the first string composed solely of digits between two colons, because usernames cannot start with digits. So /:(\d+)/ will match a uid. It would be paranoid code indeed that needed to check that a line in /etc/passwd had valid syntax, considering the consequences for the system if a line was corrupted; you'd already know about it.

Is it possible for the encrypted password to be composed only of digits? Most /etc/passwd files have just an "x" in that field these days, leaving the real encrypted password to a more protected /etc/shadow file or an external authentication source, in which case the answer is no. Even if we assume that it *might* be possible for that password field to be all digits, the code for matching the uid need be no more complex than

```
($uid) = /:.*?:(.*?):/;
```

For another example, suppose we're reading an accounting report containing lines like:

```
Total expenditure = $14731.00, fiscal July
```

and we want to extract the dollar amount. What regular expression will do? We don't know, without knowing more about what text could be on those lines. One possibility is to extract text between the $ and ,:

```
/\$(.*?),/ and $amount = $1;
```

but we would need to know that there couldn't be lines like, for instance:

```
surplus of $7443.95 was carried over to August, due to
```

where our regex will match the underlined text. In that event, a regular expression like /\$[\d.]+/ may suffice. Or maybe not, if the report might resort to (admittedly unfiscal) scientific notation:

```
Total expenditure = $7.6324E8, fiscal August
```

in which case we might resort to any of:

```
/\$(\S+),/
/expenditure = $([^,\s]+)/
/\$([\d.e+- ])/i
```

depending entirely on our knowledge of the forms the input can take and how much the lines we want to match can vary.

If the program appears to be using regular expressions for matching any kind of common pattern, then be lazy and use a regex that was generated just for that purpose by someone else's code. Damian Conway's module Regexp::Common (now maintained by Abigail) can generate extremely complex regexes for solving common problems (`http://search.cpan.org/dist/Regexp-Common/`). For matching delimited text—even blocks of Perl code—there's Damian's Text::Balanced (in the Perl core as of version 5.8.1), and for really heavy-duty parsing, there are the full grammar capabilities of his Parse::RecDescent module (`http://search.cpan.org/dist/Parse-RecDescent/`).

4.9.4 Calling Too Many External Programs

A programmer who has migrated to Perl programming from shell scripting is used to calling external programs to do just about everything. Text manipulation in shell programs is accomplished through carefully combining the uses of *sed, awk, head, grep, cut, sort,* and other programs. If a Perl programmer of level 6 or lower calls these programs then they are probably unnecessary, whereas a programmer of higher than level 6 expertise may know what they are doing (see the next section).

Text manipulation is far easier to do in Perl than by calling external programs: You only have one language to learn, the code is portable to systems that don't have those programs, and it is likely to be much faster because of avoiding process creation and interprocess communication overhead. Furthermore, the code is likely to be much briefer and clearer in Perl.

Perl was written to be familiar to shell programmers and users of the common filter programs; often you can take a call to an external program and turn it into Perl without any change to the substantive code. So for instance, instead of:

```
open OUT, ">/tmp/sedin";
print OUT map "$_\n", @entries;
close OUT;
system "sed -e 's/apples/oranges/g' /tmp/sedin > /tmp/sedout";
```

```
open IN, "/tmp/sedout";
while (<IN>)
{
  chomp;
  push @new_entries, $_;
}
@entries = @new_entries;
```

which has many other problems to boot, just say:

```
s/apples/oranges/g for @entries;
```

Even the substantive code will likely be briefer in Perl if regular expressions are involved, due to the expressive power of Perl's regular expressions.

4.9.5 Not Calling Enough External Programs

There's no need to be dogmatic about avoiding external programs, however. Some external programs can do a job faster and clearer than Perl and if there's no need for portability, then you should use them. For instance, suppose you have created an entire tree of temporary files under a root directory named by $temptree. The average programmer would concoct a recursive depth-first unlink scheme using File::Find, because the majority aren't aware of File::Path, which lets you say:

```
use File::Path;
rmtree($temptree);
```

However, it's even more succinct to say:

```
system "/bin/rm -r $temptree";
```

with the added benefit that you can even put the task in the background while you get on with something else:

```
system "/bin/rm -rf $temptree &";
```

I decided to suppress error output at the same time. You can decide whether this meets your requirements better than File::Path on a case-by-case basis; it's not portable, and the -f option may not prevent warnings about unremovable directories, in which case you would have to redirect STDERR.

For another example, imagine you need to know whether a file whose name is in $searchfile contains the string "haddock". You could code this in Perl:

```perl
open my $fh, $searchfile or die "Can't open $searchfile: $!\n";
my $found = 0;
while (<$fh>)
{
  $found = 1, last if /haddock/;
}
close $fh;
```

But you could also just do:

```perl
system "grep -q haddock $searchfile";
```

and test to see if $? is zero (means success; i.e., "haddock" was found). The pitfall is *lack of portability,* and not just to systems that don't have *grep;* not all *grep*s have the -q (for "quiet") option, and some call it -s (for "silent").

Finally, there are legions of programs that for reasons of proprietary code or lack of interest on developers' parts are essentially black boxes and reverse engineering is not cost-effective.

4.9.6 Superfluous Truth

This miniature point is about storing boolean values. When you want to look up a value that is true or false, use Perl's built-in truth values instead of making up something more complex:

Not so good:

```
$found_fruit{apple} = ($rec =~ /apple/) ? 'yes' : 'no';
...
if ($found_fruit{apple} eq 'yes') ...
```

Better:

```
$found_fruit{apple} = $rec =~ /apple/;
...
if ($found_fruit{apple}) ...
```

Not so good:

```
$in_stock{$item} = 1;
...
if (exists $in_stock{pants}) ...
```

Better:

```
$in_stock{$item} = 1;
...
if ($in_stock{pants})...
```

4.10 Evolution

Imagine a very adaptable organism of indeterminate species responding to changes in its environment. Temperature rising? Evolve a thicker skin. Gravity increasing? Add more legs. Water table rising? Grow fins.

Similarly, our code changes as various demands upon it increase: size of input data, number of concurrent users, and so on. You can think of those demands as happening along different dimensions; in other words, they can vary independently of each other and any given program may be subject to one or more type of demand.[12]

---

12. This is the "ontogeny recapitulates phylogeny" argument applied to software. I've always wanted an excuse to use that phrase in a book.

How far along each of those dimensions you are able to evolve your code before it succumbs to the pressures of change depends on your skills; the further along each dimension you go, the more skillful you need to be.

When you're rewriting legacy code, it may help to bump it along these dimensions one step at a time until you get it to where you want. Space doesn't permit me to go into much detail, so I'll just cover some steps of some dimensions broadly.

4.10.1 Modularity

1. Flat scripting: One monolithic block of code.
2. Subroutines: Abstracting common functionality; procedural programming.
3. Using objects, making libraries of reusable subroutines.
4. Subclassing existing modules.
5. Creating application-specific object-oriented modules.
6. Using tieing and overloading (see Section 10.2).

4.10.2 Input Interfaces—Complexity

1. Hand parsing of `@ARGV`.
2. Getopt::Std.
3. Getopt::Long.
4. Configuration files: see Simon Cozens' module Config::Auto (`http://search.cpan.org/dist/Config-Auto/`).

4.10.3 Error Handling—Application Size

1. No error handling at all—"program and pray."
2. Checking return codes from built-in functions.

3. Writing subroutines to return distinct error conditions.

4. Exception handling: using `die()` and `eval()` for throwing and catching exceptions.

5. Throwing objects as exceptions, either with `die()`, or using a module such as Dave Rolsky's Exception::Class (`http://search.cpan.org/dist/Exception-Class/`). Graham Barr's Error.pm, maintained by Arun Kumar U (`http://search.cpan.org/dist/Error/`) provides nice `try` and `catch` keywords, but has a memory leak triggered by nested closures. Such usage is rare, but if you don't want to worry about whether you've unwittingly created a nested closure, don't use it.

4.10.4 Logging—Volume and Granularity

1. What's "logging"? Wait for something to go wrong or evidence needed of past behavior, then panic.

2. Ad-hoc `print()` and `warn()` statements.

3. Ad-hoc `print()` statements directed to specific files, possibly with hand-rolled timestamping, process/host/user identification, and log file rotation.

4. Mike Schilli's Log::Log4perl (CPAN and `http://log4perl.sourceforge.net`) is based on Java's Log4j utility, and provides an object-oriented logging capability with severity levels and completely configurable multiplexing of messages to all kinds of destinations. See Section 10.1.4.

5. Mark Pfeiffer's Log::Dispatch::FileRotate (`http://search.cpan.org/dist/Log-Dispatch-FileRotate/`) automates log file rotation and provides file locking into the bargain. Can be plugged into Log::Log4perl.

4.10.5 External Information Representation—Extensibility

1. External data represented in plain text, likely implicitly assumed to be in the ISO Latin-1 encoding, or (especially in some locales) Unicode UTF-8, but with ad-hoc syntax.

2. Various configuration file formats such as the core modules Data::Dumper and Storable, and CPAN modules for more specific applications such as Config::IniFiles, Config::Auto, DBD::CSV, and so on.

3. When you want a structured markup format that's easy to read, get Brian Ingerson's YAML (originally Yet Another Markup Language; now, hopping on the already overcrowded recursive retronym bandwagon, YAML Ain't Markup Language) from `http://search.cpan.org/dist/YAML/`. A number of Perl modules use it as their data interchange format, such as Ingerson's CGI::Kwiki, which can be used for building Wiki sites [LEUF01].[13]

4. For maximum interoperability, XML (see Section 8.3.7). YAML is extraordinarily capable, but when you need to speak to a third party, they're more likely to understand XML than YAML.

4.10.6 External Data Storage—Complexity, Concurrency, and Volume

1. Plain files—no locking, no structured data.

2. DBM files written by one of the AnyDBM_File modules (*perldoc AnyDBM_File*).

3. DBM files with home-grown locking to avoid concurrent access race conditions.[14]

---

13. As a digression, the need for a human-readable markup format was echoed in the compact format of the RELAX-NG specification for XML schemas (`http://www.oasis-open.org/committees/relax-ng/compact-20020607.html`). Evidently even with so many tools that understand XML, people still want to get their eyes on the raw characters.

14. `http://www.nightflight.com/foldoc-bin/foldoc.cgi?race+condition`

4. Accessing database servers with Tim Bunce's DBI.pm (see Section 8.3.6).

5. Integrating object classes with databases: Tangram (`http://search.cpan.org/dist/Tangram/`), Alzabo (`http://search.cpan.org/dist/Alzabo/`), and so on.

4.10.7 Web Server Processing—Scalability

1. Processing form inputs and generating content for a browser by hand.

2. Using Lincoln Stein's CGI.pm to do either or both.

3. Using Sam Tregar's HTML::Template (`http://search.cpan.org/dist/HTML-Template/`) or Andy Wardley's Template Toolkit (`http://search.cpan.org/dist/Template-Toolkit/`) to separate the output appearance from the code.

4. Using mod_perl on an Apache server for improved performance (see [BEKMAN03]).

5. Using Dave Rolsky's HTML::Mason (`http://search.cpan.org/dist/HTML-Mason/`) for advanced templating under mod_perl.

6. Integrating XML with Matt Sergeant's AxKit (`http://search.cpan.org/dist/AxKit/`) or extending into vertical applications too numerous to mention.

4.10.8 Event Handling—Application Complexity and Interoperability

1. Punt. Event handling is not for the fainthearted.

2. Using Joshua N. Pritikin's Event.pm (`http://search.cpan.org/dist/Event/`).

3. Using Rocco Caputo's Perl Object Environment (POE). See CPAN and `http://poe.perl.org/`. POE can wrap an

event loop around just about any kind and number of asynchronous activity, usually without even needing to start a new thread or process. See also Uri Guttman's Stem (`http://www.stemsystems.com` and CPAN).

4.10.9 Client/Server or Interprocess Communication—Interoperability

1. Again, punt—beginning programmers don't try this.

2. Except at primitive levels like leaving messages in files for other processes to find. Usually has race conditions and other bugs.

3. Using `fork()`. Handcrafted use of signals, pipes, and semaphores.

4. Using higher-level protocols for interprocess communication; see, for example, Graham Barr's Net::Cmd (in the Perl core as of version 5.8.0).

5. Interoperating with other applications using standard remote procedure call (RPC) mechanisms such as XML-RPC [STLAURENT01] and SOAP (both covered in Paul Kulchenko's distribution at `http://search.cpan.org/dist/SOAP-Lite/`).

The dimension of robustness deserves space all to itself, and I'll get to it in Section 10.1.

Chapter 5

The Disciplined Perl Program

"Lack of discipline leads to frustration and self-loathing."
— Marie Chapian

The good news about Perl is that you can start typing programs and they pretty much work right away. The bad news is that you can start typing programs ... Having discovered that this:

```
print "Hello, World!\n";
```

is all that it takes to get going, Perl beginners might never find out that they are venturing down a path fraught with risk; they are on the road to Undisciplined Programs, a land where bugs are hard to locate or fix, and revealing your code in public gets sand kicked in your face by the bigger programmers.

Your two greatest tools in saving yourself from this embarrassment are the strict and warnings pragmas. In this chapter I'll go into them in greater detail than most books do.

5.1 Package Variables vs. Lexical Variables

First I must take a diversion to explain something that will be referred to heavily in the rest of this chapter. Perl enjoys a unique status among languages by having two types of variables: *package variables* and *lexical variables*. You can actually refer to, say, $x, in two places in your program and be referencing two different variables that were both in existence at the same time. Many people are blissfully ignorant of this fact because they either program in the old Perl 4 style (Perl 4 had only package variables, not lexical variables), or they always use my to declare variables (thereby creating only lexical variables). And if you're following good program development practice, which means enabling the strict pragma and declaring all variables with my, you might create Perl programs of your own for years up to level 4, say, without ever being aware of these two variable families. But for maintaining inherited programs, you have to learn about them.

Lexical variables were new in Perl 5, but they are much safer to use because unlike package variables, they are not globally visible; therefore they became the variables of choice for the discerning Perl programmer. You need a good reason to use a package variable these days, although there are some times you have no choice.

Lexical variables are declared with my. If you inherit a program containing a variable that isn't declared with my, that is a package variable and is visible from any part of the program, even other files, and even other packages (as long as they know what package the variable is in). They can just reach right in and do whatever they want with it. Like all strong magic, this can be used for good . . . or evil. For instance, the File::Find module allows you to change its behavior by setting package variables, such as $File::Find::dont_use_nlink if you're using AFS. This is a succinct interface, as is using the variable $File::Find::name to get at the full path to the current file:

```
# Print full paths for symbolic links
use File::Find;
$File::Find::dont_use_nlink = 1;  # For AFS
find(sub { print "$File::Find::name\n" if -l }, '.');
```

But a program that has gone over to the dark side may set and read package variables from all kinds of unexpected places, making it incredibly difficult to tell how it works. Programmers call this kind of gross violation of encapsulation *action at a distance*. Use lexical variables as much as possible and you're less likely to make that mistake.

5.1.1 Your Friendly `local` Perl Function

Some variables can't be declared with my; these are variables that belong to Perl, so you can't go getting possessive over them. An example is the special array @ARGV (which is initialized with the command-line arguments). Sometimes, it's convenient to temporarily reassign to that array. Suppose you want to read information from several configuration files. Perl's "diamond" operator <> makes this easy; it reads lines in succession from all the files named in @ARGV, opening and closing the files behind the scenes for you. So we can appropriate the diamond operator for our use even when the files we want to open aren't listed on the command line, by just setting @ARGV first.

Suppose, however, we want to get at the original command-line arguments after this phase. We can't declare a new @ARGV with my; it doesn't belong to us, because it's special. No problem; we just override @ARGV like this:

```
{
  local @ARGV = @CONFIG_FILES;
  while (<>)
  {
    # Do something with $_
  }
}
```

The local function hides the previous version of @ARGV in a location that will be restored on exit from the current scope. The new version it creates is initialized with a copy of the array @CONFIG_FILES, which our program earlier set to the list of configuration file names. We can then use the diamond operator to read those files, safe in the knowledge that when we exit the outer block, the original copy of @ARGV is restored to its rightful place. "Naked blocks" like the outer block in this example are frequently useful for creating a temporary scope.

You can find other variables that don't belong to you listed in the *perlvar* documentation page. However, there are some other variables—package variables—that Perl also puts to special use. For instance, if you call a subroutine that doesn't exist, but have defined a subroutine in that package called AUTO-LOAD, Perl calls that subroutine instead. This feature is handy when you don't want to define subroutines at compilation time, but you would like to know what subroutine the user was attempting to call; so Perl sets the $AUTOLOAD package variable to the name of that subroutine:

```
# Let's say we're in package 'MyPack'
sub AUTOLOAD
{
  my $method = $MyPack::AUTOLOAD;  # Copy to private variable
  $method =~ s/.*:://;             # Strip off package
  # Now the name of the subroutine being called is in $method
}
```

Other package variables that are also useful to Perl include: $VERSION (version number of current package), @ISA (classes we inherit from), and @EXPORT and similar variables used by the Exporter module.

5.1.2 With a Little Help from our Friends

Perl 5.6.0 introduced the our function, which makes life easier when you want to work with package variables. It is equivalent to use vars in that it allows you to refer to variables in the current package without fully qualifying them, but unlike use vars, it is lexically scoped, so its variable names aren't valid in your program long after you were done with them. (Yes, it is a little weird to speak of a declaration of package variables being lexically scoped. Just remember that the "lexical" part refers to the scope over which you can refer to the variable by its unqualified name, even though the value of that variable is globally visible.) use vars, on the other hand, is file scoped.

Take for example our earlier AUTOLOAD function. It was a nuisance to have to hard-code our package name in there (not that we couldn't have gotten around it with __PACKAGE__ and a symbolic reference, mind). With our, we don't need to:

```perl
sub AUTOLOAD
{
  our $AUTOLOAD;            # Now I can just say $AUTOLOAD
  my $method = $AUTOLOAD;   # Copy to private variable
  $method =~ s/.*://;       # Strip off package
  # Now the name of the subroutine being called is in $method
}
```

5.1.3 Lexical vs. Dynamic Scoping

Why are variables declared with my called lexical variables? Because that describes their scope. If you open a Perl program in an editor, start selecting text from the statement following a my declaration, and highlight code until the end of the enclosing block (or the end of file, if that comes first), everything you've highlighted is the scope of the variable in the declaration. Subroutines called from within that highlighted text won't see the variable unless they are also highlighted.

```
while (<SOMEFILEHANDLE>)
{
  my @words = split;
  # @words can be seen until the end of this block
}
# Now @words can no longer be used as a variable name
# (except by declaring a new variable with that name)
```

Package variables (and most of Perl's special variables listed in *perlvar*) can be saved temporarily with `local`. On the other hand, lexical variables can't be localized, but don't need to be; if you want to temporarily override a lexical variable just declare it again with my in an inner scope. Declaring a lexical variable twice at the same scope level triggers a warning.

Dynamic scoping derives its name from the fact that it is determined at run time. A package variable can always be referred to, even if nothing has ever set it, just like you can refer to a member of a hash even if it hasn't been set, and get undef back.[1] So in terms of where you can use its name, a package variable has global scope.

As to the lifetime of the value of that package variable, if you assign a temporary value with `local`, that value is seen by all code that runs until Perl exits the block containing the `local`, at which point it returns to its previous value. By way of example:

```
1   $main::global = "outer";
2   {
3       my $lexical = "private";
4       check_vars();
5       local $main::global = "inner";
6       check_vars();
7   }
8   check_vars();
```

---

1. It's even more like that than it seems; package variables are accessed via special hashes.

```
9
10  sub check_vars
11  {
12    print $main::global;
13  }
```

At line 1 I assign a value to the package variable $main::global. (Because I use strict, it forces me to refer to the variable with its full name like that. More on use strict later.) The block that follows defines a lexical variable $lexical. If any code referred to that variable, it would have to be on lines 4, 5, or 6. Even though check_vars() is called from the same block, the code for check_vars() isn't *in* that block, and so that subroutine can't refer to $lexical. If I want that subroutine to see $lexical, I'll have to pass it in the argument list.

But $main::global is a different story. The check_vars() on line 4 will see a value of "outer" for that package variable. The check_vars() on line 6 will see a value of "inner." The check_vars() on line 8 will see a value of "outer" because the block in which the variable was localized has ended. See [DOMINUS98] for more about scoping.

5.2 *Warnings and Strictness*

Because use strict and use warnings—two examples of pragmas (directives that affect the compilation of a program)—are so important in program maintenance, I'm going to give them a more thorough treatment than is common.

It's not hard to see why warnings and strict are vital. Without them—well, watch:

```
% perl
do you, each reader, accept risks, close calls
and wait until failure
and then; alarm rings and people, listen shocked, horrified
or do you, "use strict" and "use warnings" and sleep soundly;
```

```
my main $message; study earnestly while you-can;
do this, cos I, tell you
and you, can be free;
^D
%
```

This doggerel not only *compiles*, it actually *runs* without error. (Fortunately, it doesn't actually do anything.)

In fact, if you just consider legal compile-time syntax, virtually anything goes:

```
% perl -c
There was a young man from Maastricht
Whose programs just never had clicked
One day he discovered
The bugs he had smothered
Not using warnings or strict
^D
- syntax OK
```

Unless you want to program in an environment where poetry—bad poetry—can just as easily be legal syntax as your best coding efforts, use warnings and strict in every program.

Of course, using these pragmas is not a substitute for critical and analytical thinking. It is worth understanding exactly what they mean so you can tell what their diagnostics denote and when it is appropriate to suppress them. Until you arrive at that understanding, however, your life will be easier if you enable the pragmas than it will if you don't, even if you don't know what they're doing.

In fact, both warnings and strict are abbreviations for a host of different types of protection, like broad-spectrum antibiotics. Let's look under the hood.

You may be unfamiliar with some of the command-line flags used in this chapter, but they're very useful. Here's a brief overview:

- -c Compile only. Useful for syntax checking; if you have been making extensive modifications to a program and you know it's bound to have syntax errors, you can find out what they are without risking the program being run. Code in BEGIN or CHECK blocks will be run, because their purpose is to facilitate the compilation of later code during this phase. In particular, this means that code in modules that are used will be run.

- -e *CODE* Execute *CODE* as Perl instead of reading the program from a file. This switch allows you to make "one-liners" of Perl code without having to create a file to put that code in. Very handy for testing constructions you're unsure of and aliasing shell shortcuts so you don't have to create a new file in ~/bin.

- -M*MODULE* Equivalent to putting "use *MODULE*" at the beginning of the code to be executed. To pass arguments to the import() routine, add them after an =. Thus "-Mstrict=subs" is equivalent to "use strict qw(subs)", and "-Mstrict=subs,vars" is equivalent to "use strict qw(subs vars)".

- -I *DIRECTORY* Equivalent to "use lib '*DIRECTORY*'".

- -l Automatically append a newline to the arguments of all print (but not printf) statements. This also removes trailing newlines when the -n or -p switches are used to wrap an input loop around code.

For more details on these switches, see the *perlrun* manual page.

A handy way of executing a few lines of Perl without having to put them in a file is to feed them to the standard input of perl from the command line. I've shown this here by terminating the input with the usual end of input character for UNIX shells, control D (^D). What follows after that point is the output of the program. You can't edit lines you've already entered, so this is of limited use, but I use it often here as a convenient way of demonstrating code.

5.3 `use strict` *in Detail*

`use strict` is actually the same as saying

```
use strict 'vars';
use strict 'subs';
use strict 'refs';
```

Each of these statements confers a different benediction. Let's consider each one in detail.

5.3.1 `use strict 'vars'`

`use strict 'vars'` forces you to use `my`. Well, more or less. This is a cunning way of catching typos. `use strict 'vars'` requires that all variables either be declared with `my` or that they be fully qualified with their package names (since they must be package variables if they are not declared with `my`). The two exceptions to this rule are package variables declared with `our` or named by `use vars`; they need not be fully qualified.

No, it is not good enough to say, "Okay, I'll use `my`, just don't make me `use strict 'vars'`." It's too easy to make a mistake no matter how careful your typing. Suppose you decide that a good way to announce a successful return from a function is:

```
my $x = func() and print "\$x is true: set to $x\n";
```

Unfortunately, the `$x` in the `print()` is not the same `$x` declared by `my`. The scope of the new `$x` has not yet started (it starts with the *following* statement). Therefore the `$x` in the `print()` is in fact the *package variable* `$x`, which may be set to a completely different value or none at all. Only with `use strict` will you get the error:

```
Global symbol "$x" requires explicit package name
```

The scoping becomes clearer when we discover that internally, Perl converted the and to an if. You can see this with the B::Deparse module:

```
% perl -MO=Deparse -e 'my $x = func() and print $x'
print $x if my $x = func();
```

That shows us that even within the same statement, the print comes before the my. "But wait," you cry, "isn't the postfixed if exactly equivalent to a real if?" Not in this case. Observe:

```
% perl -Mstrict -wle 'print $x if my $x = $]'
Global symbol "$x" requires explicit package name at -e line 1.
Execution of -e aborted due to compilation errors.
% perl -Mstrict -wle 'if (my $x = $]) { print $x }'
5.008003
```

I printed a variable instead of a literal because with a literal, Perl warns about finding an assignment inside a condition. The $] variable contains the version number of the perl program. In order to turn a version number like "5.8.3" into a value that can be compared as a true number, Perl formats it as you see here.

So you should make sure that the use of any lexical variable does not start until at least the statement following its declaration. Perl provides some helpful shortcuts that you might consider to violate this distinction. You can declare a lexical variable in a condition or as a for/foreach loop variable:

```
if (my ($word) = /(\w+)/) { ... }
for my $person ($db->person_search) { ... }
```

and Perl will restrict the scope of the lexical to the attached block, as though you had written:

```
{
  my $word;
  if ($word = /(\w+)/) { ... }
}
{
```

```
  my $person;
  for $person ($db->person_search) { ... }
}
```

In fact, Perl allows you to put my just about anywhere. It's really just a modifier on a variable. For example, if you need to pass a reference to a variable to some function, so that function can write into the variable, you can write:

```
func(\my $foo);
print "func() set \$foo to $foo\n");
```

which, bizarre as it might look, works. A realistic use of this feature is in the getopts() function exported by Getopt::Std, which can populate a hash with command-line options if a reference to the hash is passed as the second argument:

```
use Getopt::Std;
getopts("dif:v", \my %Opt) or die $Usage;
$Opt{f} or die "The -f option is mandatory\n";
```

Note that subroutines are still package variables. There are no lexical subroutines this side of Perl 6. If you're paranoid about people calling your internal subroutines and want to keep them private, then make them anonymous subroutine references and assign them to lexical variables, like so:

```
# Before:
sub dumpit
{
  require Data::Dumper;
  print Data::Dumper::Dumper(\@_);
}
# [...]
dumpit(@args);

# After:
my $dumpit = sub { require Data::Dumper;
                   print Data::Dumper::Dumper(\@_)
                 };
# [...]
$dumpit->(@args);
```

Now nothing outside the lexical scope of `$dumpit` can get at that subroutine.

5.3.2 `use strict 'subs'`

This stricture disables the use of barewords as strings. Let's take a deep breath and find out just what Perl thinks our poem-cum-admonishment means:

```
% perl -MO=Deparse
do you, each reader, accept risks, close calls
and wait until failure
and then; alarm rings and people, listen shocked, horrified
or do you, "use strict" and "use warnings" and sleep soundly;

my main $message; study earnestly while you-can;
do this, cos I, tell you
and you, can be free;
^D
'???';;
do 'you', 'use strict' and 'use warnings' and sleep 'soundly'
unless alarm 'rings' and '???', listen(shocked, 'horrified');
my $message;
study 'earnestly' while 'you' - 'can';
'???', 'be'->can('free') if do 'this', cos 'I', tell you;
- syntax OK
```

Explaining why Perl interprets this piece of creative writing this way would be somewhat off topic.[2] Notice instead that many of the words in the input were interpreted as strings, as we see from the quotes that Deparse put around them.

Now let's see what happens with `use strict 'subs'`:

```
% perl -Mstrict=subs -c
[...]
```

---

2. But incidentally, the `'???'` is Deparse notation for "a string that had a constant value that Perl put somewhere I can't get at."

```
^D
Bareword "people" not allowed while "strict subs" in use at -
line 4.
Bareword "then" not allowed while "strict subs" in use at - line
1.
Bareword "rings" not allowed while "strict subs" in use at -
line 3.
[...]
- had compilation errors.
```

Just as use strict 'vars' expects variables either to be declared lexical or used fully qualified, use strict 'subs' expects subroutines either to be declared prior to being referenced as barewords, or called using explicit subroutine invocation syntax.

It is *not* a compilation error to call a subroutine that hasn't been defined. Perl is permissive enough to let you define subroutines at run time, so it's impossible to say at compilation time that a subroutine is missing.

Here are examples of the effect of use strict 'subs' on calling a subroutine with no arguments:

```
outgrabe;     # ok only if sub outgrabe has already appeared
outgrabe();   # ok
&outgrabe;    # ok
&outgrabe();  # ok
```

There is no such restriction on method calls; when Perl sees - > followed by an identifier or simple scalar it knows that it must be a method call regardless of whether it has seen its declaration yet or not.

If for some reason you want to call a subroutine without parentheses before Perl has seen its declaration, you can put a forward declaration of that subroutine earlier than the call, like so:

```
sub outgrabe;   # No code body
# [...]
outgrabe;
```

Now the Perl compiler knows that `outgrabe` is a subroutine call. It doesn't need to have seen the code for that subroutine because while it's compiling it just needs to know how to interpret each token it finds in the source. As long as the code for `outgrabe` exists by the time the Perl run time system reaches the last line everything will be fine.[3]

Alternatively, just as variables can be snuck past `use strict 'vars'` with `use vars`, Perl can be persuaded to refrain from complaining about barewords if you claim that they're subroutines-to-be with `use subs`:

```
use subs qw(outgrabe);
# [...]
outgrabe;
```

`no strict 'subs'`—the opposite of `use strict 'subs'`—is referred to in Perl as "poetry mode," for reasons that should now be plain. It interprets any bareword that doesn't look like a subroutine call as a string, as though it had quotes around it.

5.3.3 use strict 'refs'

If you're expecting consistency, you've come to the wrong language. `strict` is billed as a pragma, a module that affects the compilation of a program. But `use strict 'refs'` takes effect at *run time,* so we can't say that it *prohibits* code containing symbolic references; what Perl does instead is to issue a fatal exception when it tries to execute such a reference. However, here's the puzzle: Until Perl 5, symbolic references were the only ways of referring to things indirectly. So why the hard line? Let's look closer.

This question appears on Perl newsgroups so often that it should have its own song: How can I access a variable whose name I have in another variable? The questioner is developing something along the lines of:

---

3. Provided that, if either the forward declaration or the real declaration of the subroutine uses a subroutine prototype, both use the same prototype.

```
my %names_of_badges;  # Keys: badge numbers. Values: names.
my %names_of_users;   # Keys: usernames. Values: names.
print "Lookup by (b)adge or (u)sername? ";
chomp(my $answer = <STDIN>);
my $choice = ($answer =~ /^b/ ? "badges" : "users");
# How do I get at %"names_of_$choice"???
```

The answer to the question is, "Don't try." The way to do what this code is really attempting to accomplish is either with a hash, a "hard" reference, or both.

The questioner is thinking that having formed a string equal to the name of the hash they want to access, they must have nearly solved the problem. And with a symbolic reference, they would be right. But symbolic references have several problems. One is that they only work on package variables, so there's no way to access the lexical hashes in the example above using symbolic references.

Another, and more important problem is that they're the wrong approach. If you want to get at one of two possible hashes you shouldn't do it using an accessor—in this case, the string containing the hash name—whose possible values span the entire universe of strings. One typo and your program is toast. The proper solution is to make a hard reference to each original hash, so that now you just have to choose between the two references. I'll show examples of this in Section 6.2.13.

So symbolic references are bad, but they were all we had in Perl 4. Now that we no longer need to use them—save for mostly esoteric purposes I'll touch on later—we use strict 'refs' to ensure that we don't put in any by accident. Symbolic references are also used for manipulating the symbol table, and there are better ways to do that if that's what you have in mind.

5.3.4 use strict 'DWIM'

No, there really isn't a pragma to "Do What I Mean" with strictness. But if you put that statement in, Perl will not complain, because it just silently ignores any

type of strictness you request that it doesn't know about.[4] It's better to say use
strict and get every kind of strictness than to try selectively enabling only
the ones you think you need; one day, you, like, I, will type use strict
'sbus' by accident. I'll talk about how to turn off ones that get in your way
in Section 5.5.

5.4 use warnings *in Detail*

use warnings is equivalent to saying:

```
use warnings 'all';
```

which is in turn short for:

```
use warnings 'chmod';
use warnings 'closure';
use warnings 'exiting';
# ...Lots more of the same...
```

that is, it enables a whole host of warnings. It is a fairly recent pragma (introduced in Perl 5.6) and you might not have seen it; you are more likely to be
familiar with its venerable command-line cousin, -w:

```
#!/usr/bin/perl -w
# Now warnings are enabled
```

So why so much extra typing for something that does the same job?
Because use warnings is much more powerful. You can disable parts of it
instead of the all-or-nothing proposition presented by -w (more on that in the
next section), and you can also restrict its scope lexically. You can also use it to
turn off some warnings that are otherwise enabled even if you *don't* use -w (the
so-called default warnings). As if that isn't enough, you can selectively turn

---

4. Unless you're using Perl 5.8.1 or later, wherein this has been fixed.

warnings into fatal exceptions, and you can even make up your own warning classes.

5.4.1 `use warnings` vs. Modules

Because of the lexical scoping, `use warnings` will not propagate its effect to modules you use (whereas `-w` does). In your own modules, add `use warnings` near the top. Other people's modules may or may not be so enlightened. Now, it's really the module author's business and responsibility to make their code warnings-safe, but sometimes the author of a module you are using may not have put a `use warnings` statement in it.

Why should you care? Because quite often you can get a clue that there's something wrong with your code from a warning generated inside a module. You may have created an undefined value somewhere and passed it into a module where it finally triggered a "use of uninitialized value" warning. That's helpful. And you'd get that warning with `-w`. But with `use warnings`, you won't get it unless the module author also had a `use warnings` statement.

Therefore, *for maximum safety when using third-party modules, add the* `-w` *flag to your shebang line.* As regressive as that may sound, it will ensure that you see every warning that you can. Wherever a `warnings` pragma appears, whether in your code or a module you use, the `-w` flag for the code under the control of that pragma will be ignored by Perl, so you still benefit from the additional pragma power where it applies.

You can make all warnings fatal with the `FATAL` argument:

```
use warnings FATAL => 'all';
```

That turns all warnings (or whatever warning classes you specify) into fatal exceptions. Now your code will simply die when it would generate a warning.

I'll talk about how best to deal with warnings when writing your own modules in Section 10.4.

5.4.2 Pragmas, Meet AutoLoader

If you use the AutoLoader module to load subroutines on demand, be aware that any `strict` or `warnings` pragmas in the main module will not be visible to the autoloaded subroutines. You need to add `use strict` and `use warnings` to the beginning of each autoloaded subroutine for them to take effect.

5.5 Selective Disabling

As you might have guessed by now, I am in favor of cranking up warnings and strictness to their maximum levels. Sometimes, however, it makes sense to silence them because you're violating the rules intentionally and you know what you're doing.

5.5.1 Learn How to Say `no`

There's no need to turn off strictness or warnings altogether just because they get in your way. If you can't make a reasonable adjustment to your code to avoid triggering them, disable just the part that's in the way, and only for long enough to get the job done. You can do this with the `no strict` pragma; for example:

```
no strict 'refs';
```

`no` is the opposite of `use`; it disables the specified part of the pragma for its lexical scope. All other parts of the pragma remain in force.

5.5.2 Turning Off Strictness

no strict 'vars' I cannot think of a single case where this would be necessary. Any time you feel the urge to turn off `strict 'vars'`, use `our` or, in perls that precede the introduction of `our`, use `vars`. It's certainly legitimate to want to avoid fully qualifying package variables in situations where you don't

want to hard-code the package name, or might not even know what it is, but
our/use `vars` will still do the job without turning off strictness.

I have looked at many programs that used `no strict 'vars'`, and in
every case, they could have easily been written without it.

no strict 'subs' There is even less reason to resort to this. The last remotely
good reason to do so was to pass filehandles to subroutines:

```perl
open(REPORT, "evil-empire.takeovers");
my @totals = extract_totals(REPORT);
# [...]
sub extract_totals
{
  local *FH = shift;
  # [...]
```

But (imagine a Californian teenager accent here) that is *so* Perl 4. In fact,
even in Perl 4 you could satisfy strictness by passing the typeglob instead:

```perl
@totals = extract_totals(*REPORT);
```

(Well, aside from the fact that Perl 4 didn't have the `strict` pragma, but
you get the idea.) See Section 7.9.1 for more information on how to improve
this code with more modern Perl features.

no strict 'refs' Finally we have a candidate for Most Useful Negation of a
Strict Pragma. There are indeed times when a symbolic reference really is the
right thing to do, and you have to ask `strict 'refs'` to step aside. For
instance, creating a bunch of look-alike accessor methods:

```perl
sub _attr
{
  my ($self, $name) = splice @_, 0, 2;
  $self->{$name} = shift if @_;
  return $self->{$name};
}
```

```
for my $method (qw(email name telephone address))
{
  no strict 'refs';
  *$method = sub { _attr($_[0], $method, @_[1..$#_] };
}
# Now with a $person object we can call
# $person->email, or $person->name, etc
```

This approach has the advantage that all the methods share the same piece of code rather than having separate implementations each taking up their own space. Without disabling `strict 'refs'` Perl will object to the assignment to `*$method`:

```
Can't use string ("email") as a symbol ref while "strict refs"
in use...
```

In case you're unfamiliar with the `*` notation, this is called a *typeglob,* a frighteningly arcane term meaning all the types of package variable with the name that follows the `*`. In this code, what follows the `*` is not a word but a variable, which is therefore used as a symbolic reference. Because we are assigning a reference to the typeglob, Perl can tell the type of variable we want to assign, and therefore populates only that type of package variable and not every entry in the typeglob. In our code, the reference is a code reference, and so we are creating a new subroutine (subroutines are package variables) whose name is whatever is stored in `$method`.

We have, however, created all of the methods regardless of which ones we end up actually using, so you might prefer to create methods only when they're needed:

```
1   # Same _attr() method as before, and then:
2   sub AUTOLOAD
3   {
4     (my $method = our $AUTOLOAD) =~ s/.*:://;
5     no strict 'refs';
6     *$method = sub { _attr($_[0], $method, @_[1..$#_]) };
7     goto &$method;
8   }
```

Incidentally, it's line 6 that needs `no strict 'refs'`, not line 7; for what it's worth, calling subroutines indirectly with `goto` does not violate `strict 'refs'`.

This just-in-time method creation is fine, but somewhat permissive; we really need to limit the user to just the methods we want. No problem:

```
1    sub AUTOLOAD
2    {
3       (my $method = our $AUTOLOAD) =~ s/.*://;
4       { map { $_ => 1 } qw(email name telephone address)
5       }->{$method}
6          or croak "Invalid method $method"
7       no strict 'refs';
8       *$method = sub { _attr($_[0], $method, @_[1..$#_]) };
9       goto &$method;
10   }
```

I've added a highly concise construction in lines 4 through 6 for checking whether the given method is in the allowed list; a level 6 idiom at least. Set membership is best done with a hash, so I made a reference to an anonymous hash whose keys are the allowed methods, then dereferenced the element with key `$method`. If it's in the hash, it'll have the (true) value 1. If it isn't, the hash lookup will return the (false) value `undef`, and the code will call `croak()`. A more maintainable module would enumerate its object attributes at the top of the code in a global hash, which we could then reference instead of the literal list in line 4.

Both the all-at-once and the on-the-fly approaches to creating methods suffer from the disadvantage that the methods are created at run time and therefore static analysis tools won't see them. Using the all-at-once approach and wrapping that code in a BEGIN block may help.

There are other legitimate uses of `no strict 'refs'` besides creating methods, such as exporting a variable to your caller's package (although arguably that's just generalizing method creation to other types of package variable).

5.5.3 Turning Off Warnings

Temporarily disabling lexical warnings is a snap: Find out the name for the class of warning you want to ignore, and wrap a block containing a `no warnings` pragma for that class around the code that violates it.

Here's an example: Suppose you want to override an existing subroutine and make it do something else. Two good reasons for wanting to do this are temporarily overriding one of your own subroutines for debugging purposes, and overriding a method in a module you didn't write so that you can change its behavior. For instance, I've done this with a graphing module from CPAN when I needed to get it to produce some graphs whose margins were beyond its usual repertoire. The easiest way of overriding a subroutine is just to define it again:

```
# Adjusting from Celsius for USA-centric users
sub temperature
{
  my $self = shift;
  return ($self->{temperature} + 40) * 9 / 5 - 40;
}
```

But Perl will warn us that this might be a mistake:

```
Subroutine temperature redefined at...
```

We can handily take care of that with:

```
{
  no warnings 'redefine';
  # Adjusting from Celsius for USA-centric users
  sub temperature
  {
    my $self = shift;
    $self->{temperature} * 9 / 5;
  }
}
```

Yes, it's possible to redefine a subroutine in such a way as to not need to disable warnings, but the preceding code is perfectly clear. Well, . . . here's how you would do it:

```
BEGIN
{
  undef &temperature;
  *temperature = sub
  {
    my $self = shift;
    return ($self->{temperature} + 40) * 9 / 5 - 40;
  };
}
```

First we undefine the old subroutine, then install a new one by assigning to the typeglob. We have to put it in a BEGIN block to get the same effect as we had with our earlier warning-disabling code, because saying "sub temperature" creates a subroutine definition at *compile time;* but assigning to a typeglob is a *run time* action and therefore any calls to temperature() before we get to that code will call the old subroutine unless we preemptively hoist the redefinition into the compilation phase.[5]

There; wasn't it easier just to disable the warning?

5.5.4 Disabling Warnings with $^W

If you're using a Perl that precedes the introduction of lexical warnings, their moral equivalent is the special variable $^W. When that flag is set to 1, warnings—all warnings—are enabled, as if you'd typed -w on the shebang line, and when it is set to 0, warnings are off. You can thus enable and disable warnings to your heart's content throughout your code. To have warnings revert to their previous state when you're done modifying them, make the assignment to $^W temporary via local() and put it in a block to limit its scope:

---

5. If we just wanted to replace all calls to temperature() *after* the run time point of redefinition, then we could say local *temperature = sub { ... }.

```
{
  local $^W = 0;   # Disable warnings
  $x = $y + $z;    # Use possibly undef variable
}
```

Remember, however, that assigning to any variable is a *run time* action and many warnings happen at *compile time;* to affect them you must put your assignment in a BEGIN block. Disabling warnings for the subroutine redefinition example is particularly difficult because you cannot just redefine the subroutine the obvious way in the same BEGIN block as the assignment to $^W:

```
BEGIN
{
  local $^W = 0;              # WON'T WORK
  sub temperature { ... }
}
```

The subroutine will be compiled before the assignment is executed because that's how things are done, whether they're in BEGIN blocks or not. You either have to use the typeglob assignment from earlier:

```
BEGIN
{
  local $^W = 0;
  *temperature = sub { ... };
}
```

or you have to do something even more despicable:

```
{
  my $warn_save;
  BEGIN
  {
    $warn_save = $^W;
    $^W = 0;
  }
  sub temperature { ... }
  BEGIN
  {
```

```
      $^W = $warn_save;
  }
}
```

This shows you how useful lexical warnings are, now that you see how unpleasant the alternatives can be!

5.5.5 Redirecting Errors and Warnings

There are some warnings you don't want the user to see in detail, though; they might reveal too much about your code. This is even more true of fatal exceptions, which often incorporate (via the `croak()` or `confess()` functions of the Carp module) details of function calls and their arguments. And the worst environment for that to happen in is a public web site whose users are not normally entitled to read program source code and among whose number could lurk unsavory characters to whom you'd rather not allow your database password to be exposed.

Randal Schwartz addressed this in a *Linux Magazine* column[6] with a module called FatalsToEmail, designed to send the text of fatal exceptions in e-mail to the developer while leaving the user with a nondescript apology.

Here's my version, a module called EmailErrors designed to fulfill a similar purpose, but with a few key differences. It allows exceptions to propagate normally if the code is running in an eval block, or if it's being run at the command line instead of via the web. It handles warnings as though they were exceptions. However, you'll have to insert some code to handle your specific use of the module where indicated by "##":

Example 5.1 EmailErrors Module

```
package EmailErrors;
use strict;
use warnings;
```

6. `http://www.stonehenge.com/merlyn/LinuxMag/col14.html`

```perl
BEGIN
{
  # If we're in an eval, or not being used from the web,
  # allow the exception to be handled normally.
  # Otherwise, if we die, send it to an error handler.
  $SIG{__DIE__} = sub
  {
    return unless $ENV{REMOTE_ADDR};
    my $in_eval = 0;
    for (my $stack = 1;
         my $sub = (CORE::caller($stack))[3];
         $stack++)
    {
      $in_eval = 1 if $sub =~ /^\(eval\)/;
    }
    unless ($in_eval)
    {
      goto &throw;
    }
  };


  # For warnings, do the same thing.
  $SIG{__WARN__} = sub
  {
    CORE::warn(@_) and return unless $ENV{REMOTE_ADDR};
    local $SIG{__WARN__};  # Avoid possible recursion
    goto &throw;
  };


  sub throw
  {
    my $text = shift;
    $text = do { require Carp::Heavy; Carp::longmess($text) };
    ## Handle denial of service issues
    ## Print desired text to user
    ## Log error text
    ## Email error text
  }
}

1;
```

Here's what you'd do with those comments: If you're using the code in a web application and you're worried about bad guys slowing your server down by triggering many e-mails in succession, then keep a first-in, first-out cache of warnings and timestamps; if a warning is repeated too soon, ignore it. Decide what you want the user to see; in a web application, you might use a special error template. If you're keeping logs of what your application does, log the error. Finally, send the e-mail message containing the actual error text to whoever in your organization is unlucky enough to be detailed to handle such things.

5.5.6 Don't Rush to Disable

Don't disable a warning when you don't know why it happens. I have lost count of how many times I have heard someone ask what was wrong with their program, and on inspection, I discovered that they did not have warnings enabled. If they had, they would have received a giant clue as to what the problem was—but they said they had disabled the warnings because of all the messages that were produced. This is plugging your ears when your mentor is yelling, "I THINK THERE'S SOMETHING WRONG HERE!"

5.6 Caveat Programmer

use strict and use warnings may be very helpful, but don't assume that they're going to catch all your mistakes. Perl leaves a lot of checking to run time. Look what happens when we take the limerick and make an innocuous change:

```
% perl -Mstrict -Mwarnings -c
There was a young man from Maastricht
Whose programs just never had clicked
Until he discovered
The bugs he had smothered
Leaving out warnings & strict
^D
- syntax OK
```

Perl's compiler thinks this is just dandy. Fortunately it doesn't *do* anything, but the run time error is the same without `warnings` and `strict` as with.

So much for panaceas.

Another word of warning: You'll find many examples of code in documentation and books that isn't warnings- or strict-safe, usually by omitting to declare variables with `my`. Don't take them to be endorsements of programming without the `strict` and `warnings` pragmas; their authors are simply being economical with their example code and don't view the pragmas or `my` keywords as being important to understanding the examples.

5.7 *Perl Poetry*

As you saw earlier, it can be quite easy to write Perl that compiles and executes cleanly while also harboring some artistic value . . . however subjective. There is a recognized pastime of composing Perl prose like this, the definitive paper on which was written by Sharon Hopkins (`http://www.wall.org/~sharon/plpaper.ps`). Perl haiku contests pop up on the net and at Perl conferences, allowing more right-brain exercise for the creative programmer.

See Damian Conway's Coy.pm (`http://search.cpan.org/dist/Coy/`) for a mind-boggling example of just what someone with a lot of talent and a little free time can do.

Chapter 6

Restructuring (The Operating Table)

"The end of art is to figure the hidden meaning of things and not their appearance; for in this profound truth lies their true reality, which does not appear in their external outlines."

— Aristotle

Beyond simple rewriting lies the deeper analysis and restructuring of your program. In this chapter I'll cover several important aspects of restructuring inherited code.

6.1 Keep It Brief

A big problem with the maintainability of many programs is that their code units are just too long. (By "code unit" I mean a subroutine or the main program.) Once a code unit exceeds the length of what you can view all at once, it becomes harder to maintain. Therefore, consider the number of lines displayed per screen by your editor to be a strong suggestion for the maximum size of a code unit.

Sometimes you can make the case for extending the definition of "code unit." For instance, an exception-handling block may be sufficiently decoupled from the code preceding it that it can be considered a separate code unit for maintainability purposes.

When you're faced with a massive lump of code, break it down into smaller code units. Isolate a section of code that operates on only a few variables, and put it into a subroutine that takes those variables as input and/or output. Find a section of code that is repeated and put it in a subroutine.

You have to be able to invent a plausible name for the subroutine that describes what it is doing. There is little benefit to having a subroutine with a long name that is still so obscure that you can't remember what it does without looking at its source. As you create each subroutine, write documentation for it that describes how to use it. If the documentation takes a long time to write, that's a clue that you haven't picked a good section of code to isolate.

6.2 Cargo Cult Perl

Perl provides so many ways of solving a problem that it's not surprising that sometimes people pick ways that do work, but are suboptimal for reasons of performance, readability, or maintainability. It might sound harsh to characterize something that gets the job done as a mistake, but we're working on being better than just "good enough" here.

During World War II, air crews visited islands in the South Pacific such as Melanesia that had seen few, if any, white people before. The appearance and vehicles of these crews resembled some local legends and they were revered as deities. Following their departure, islanders emulated the behavior and clothing of these airmen in the hope that they would return, even building landing strips to encourage their arrival. These ad hoc religions were termed *cargo cults* because they venerated the cargo left behind by the airmen.

Cargo cult code is a pejorative but colorful term given to code that is used without the author knowing what it does, but because he or she saw someone else doing it and assumed it was right for their purpose. Remember, the more you think about your programming, the more valuable you will be as a programmer. Be conscious of when you make blind use of code idioms, because the next person to read your code may also have seen the advice I am about to give: When you see cargo cult code in programs you are given to maintain, it will help you gauge the experience level of the author. This helps you decide how seriously to take code that you cannot understand at all.

As in any art, the most advanced practitioners of Perl make their own rules. If you know that the code you're inheriting came from someone who knew what they were doing, the presence of apparent cargo cult code in their program probably does not mean they were suffering from premature dementia. They likely had a good reason for putting it in.

Here are some examples of cargo cult code. They range from the harmlessly redundant to the just plain wrong, but all of them are worth looking out for, to make sure that you don't use them unwittingly.

6.2.1 Useless Stringification

When I see a scalar variable enclosed in double quotes with nothing to keep it company—like so:

```
print "$x";    # Useless stringification
```

I think, "Ah, a shell programmer was here." This code is identical to:

```
print $x;      # No stringification
```

(with a caveat I'll get to in a moment). In the Bourne shell, there are times you *must* put a variable in double quotes to avoid a possible error; there are no such times in Perl.

Harmless, you say? Mostly. But the reason we refer to quoting an expression as "stringification" is more than a desire to coin a horrible neologism. In fact it describes an actual operation. Not everything in Perl is unaffected by stringification. References—including objects—are not the same after being stringified:

```
% perl -Mstrict -Mwarnings
my $ref = { dog => 'bark', cat => 'purr', llama => 'hum' };
my $notref = "$ref";
print "Reference: $ref->{dog}\n";
print "String:    $notref->{dog}\n";
^D
Reference: bark
Can't use string ("HASH(0x80fbb0c)") as a HASH ref while
"strict refs" in use...
```

Stringification is also a process that can be affected by the programmer. If an object in a class overloads stringification, putting quotes around it will invoke its stringify method. This may sound too esoteric for you to be concerned about, but there are a number of common modules that do in fact overload stringification, such as URI.pm:

```
% perl -Mstrict -Mwarnings -MURI
my $url = URI->new("http://www.perlmedic.com");
my $nonurl = "$url";
print "Object: ", $url->host, "\n";
print "String: ", $nonurl->host;
^D
Object: www.perlmedic.com
Can't locate object method "host" via package
"http://www.perlmedic.com" (perhaps you forgot to load "http://
www.perlmedic.com"?)...
```

Useless stringification is also inefficient. If you're stringifying a scalar that started life as a number only to use it as a number again anyway, Perl ends up performing a redundant string conversion; overhead that could be detrimental if you're in a loop that gets executed often.

6.2.2 Pointless Concatenation

This is not using variables between double quotes *enough*. (A number of these sections will seem to contradict others. There isn't really a contradiction, but I don't mind you speculating that there is one if that encourages you to think about everything.) This isn't an error per se, but more of a cumbersome style. Many languages don't have variable interpolation, so people who are used to those languages write Perl code like this:

```
$title = "Report at " . $time . " on " . $date . "\n";
```

I've even seen—don't laugh:

```
$title = join (" ", "Report at", $time, "on", $date, "\n");
```

the result of which happens to differ from the first by a trailing space, but regardless of that is needlessly obfuscated. Instead, use interpolation:

```
$title = "Report at $time on $date\n";
```

6.2.3 Superfluous Use of `scalar()`

There is no point in using the `scalar()` function if the context is already scalar. Understanding list and scalar contexts is crucial to being a good Perl programmer, and the canonical reference work [WALL00] does not mince words: "You will be miserable until you learn the difference between scalar and list context" (p. 69).

Therefore you have to wonder how well someone who wrote this:

```
if (scalar @items) { ... }
```

understood context. Clearly the code is intended to execute the following block if there is anything in the `@items` array. But the condition of an `if` statement is *already* in scalar context.[1] It couldn't be otherwise; the condition has to be evaluated to see whether it's true or false; both of those alternatives are single values (i.e., scalars).

Even more blatant is code like this:

```
my $n_values = scalar(values %hash);
```

Assigning anything to a scalar will put the expression in scalar context anyway, so the `scalar()` is superfluous.

Understanding context will make a world of difference in, for example, how you use regular expressions in conditions. Can you tell the difference between the following two constructs?

```
1. while   (/(\w+)\s+(\d+)/g) { ... }
2. foreach (/(\w+)\s+(\d+)/g) { ... }
```

---

1. Strictly speaking, it's in *boolean* context. But that's a special case of scalar context (as are string and numeric contexts), and you'd be hard pressed to tell the difference.

The `while` statement puts its condition in scalar context, and a `/g` regular expression match in a scalar context acts as an iterator, repeatedly returning true while the pattern matcher advances along the input string (`$_` in this case) until there are no more matches. We're saving the portions of interest in `$1` and `$2` via the capturing parentheses, and therefore the code in the block had better use them.

The `foreach` statement imposes a list context between the parentheses, and a `/g` regular expression match in a list context returns a list of all the capturing parentheses matches. Inside the block `$_` will be set in turn to each of the successive `$1` and `$2` from each match. If you actually wanted to differentiate between the `$1` and `$2`, this would not be good code, because you'd have no idea inside the block whether your `$_` represented the word (`$1`) or the number (`$2`), unless you counted how many times you'd been through the block and looked to see if that count was even or odd.

Let's look at an example to make that clearer:

```
$_ = <<EOT;
  apples  42
  oranges 57
  lemons  21
  pears   91
EOT

my %stock;
while (/(\w+)\s+(\d+)/g)
{
  my ($fruit, $count) = ($1, $2);
  $stock{$fruit} = $count;
}
```

This is using the right tool for the job; because we need to differentiate between the fruit and the count in the loop, we want to get two elements at a time. Had I tried this with a `foreach` loop, not only would the loop not have started executing until I'd accumulated all the matches in a list, but the block would have executed first for `apples`, then for `42`, then for `oranges`, and so on.

If you understood that, try this example. Suppose we decide to combine the regular expression match with the assignment to $fruit and $count:

```
while (my ($fruit, $count) = /(\w+)\s+(\d+)/g) #Wrong!
{
  $stock{$fruit} = $count;
}
```

This is a big mistake! The code will loop forever on just the first values of $fruit and $count. We've confused the behavior of m// in a list context with the behavior of /g in a scalar context. In a list context, a match will return the list of what matched in capturing parentheses, and a global (/g) match will return the list of all lists of capturing parentheses matches. There is no iterative behavior; once the /g match is complete, another attempt to execute it will start from the beginning again.

Even though the while statement puts its condition in a scalar context, the list assignment is inside that condition and therefore takes precedence for setting the context of the m//g. The list assignment itself is evaluated in scalar context, and *perlop* tells us that a list assignment in scalar context evaluates to the number of elements that were assigned. So as long as there was a match, there will be an assignment, and the condition will be true.

When I need to force a scalar context, I seldom use scalar(); it's just too much typing. Instead I take advantage of an operator that imposes a scalar context. Here's what I mean: Say I want to print a report of the number of elements in an array. These don't work:

```
print "There are ", @items, " items in the array\n"; # Wrong
print "There are @items in the array\n";       # Also wrong
```

The first puts @items in a list context and therefore prints out all the items; the second puts @items in a string context and therefore prints all the items with a space between consecutive elements. But wait! Don't reach for that scalar() button! With much less effort, . will do the job:

```
print "There are " . @items . " items in the array\n";
```

(Either dot could have been replaced with a comma; one is enough to force `@items` into scalar context.)

Now suppose I have an array `@recs` of data records and I need to set a `count` parameter in a hash to the number of elements in `@recs`, say for some web page template. I can't do this:

```
my %param = (count => @recs, ... );
```

It's tempting to think, "Why not? `@recs` is right where I'd put a scalar in a hash initialization list, so isn't it in scalar context?" No it isn't; elements in a list are in list context, and there's no special hash context (until Perl 6); a hash on the left-hand side of an assignment puts the right-hand side in list context, and there's only one kind of list context.

Here I *can* make a case for `scalar()`; to see why, let's look at the alternative. I want a count, so I can use an arithmetical operator to force scalar context:

```
my %param = (count => 0+@recs, ... );
```

Yes, I could use other variants like `1*@recs`, but `0+@recs` is the least surprising to the eyes. But here I am using the + for its side effect of imposing scalar context, and I have no interest in the addition per se, whereas in the previous example I certainly did want to perform string concatenation and the dot operator was therefore not surprising. So the next person to look at this might wonder why I am performing a superfluous addition. They may realize the reason within a fraction of a second, but good coding requires paying attention to even that level of detail, because any program will contain many potential places where the reader might waste that fraction of a second. So by all means write that as:

```
my %param = (count => scalar @recs, ... );
```

It's handy to know the alternatives, though, in case one day you're writing a throwaway script in a hurry and want to minimize typing.

6.2.4 Useless Slices

Beginners often get confused over the syntax for an array element, and write @array[4] where they should have written $array[4]. Today we can ascribe a more charitable interpretation to their actions and say that they are merely anticipating Perl 6, where that *is* the syntax; however, in Perl 5 it means something else. The programmer has inadvertently stumbled across the array slice, a useful way of getting several elements from an array:

```
my @pilots = qw(Scott Virgil Alan Gordon John);
my @ships = (0, 3, 4);
for (@pilots[@ships]) { ... }  # Scott Gordon John
```

What appears between the brackets is the list of indices to use. You *can* slice only one element from an array; however, with warnings enabled, Perl will tell you about it:

```
% perl -Mstrict -Mwarnings -le 'print @INC[2]'
Scalar value @INC[2] better written as $INC[2] at -e line 1.
/usr/lib/perl5/site_perl/5.6.1/i386-linux
```

Why should it bother? Since the definition of an array slice is that @array[*a*,*b*,*c*,...] is equivalent to the list ($array[*a*], $array[*b*], $array[*c*],...), then @array[2] is the same as $array[2], isn't it?

Not quite, and the difference again is that magic word *context*. @array[2] is a list containing one element; but $array[2] is a scalar. Therefore each will impose a different context if given the chance:

```
% perl
$element[0] = localtime;
@slice[0]   = localtime;
print "Element: ", $element[0], "\n";
print "Slice:   ", @slice[0], "\n";
^D
Element: Fri Apr 18 20:10:09 2003
Slice:   9
```

The warning is only generated for a literal list of one element. If you use an expression for the index list—say, @slice[@items]—you don't get a warning even if @items happens to contain one element. Otherwise you'd be forced to check the size of @items first, and that kind of constraint is quite anti-Perlish.

Here's an even better reason not to use a slice accidentally:

```
% perl -Mstrict -Mwarnings
my @cats = ( {name => 'Jake', fur => 'orange'} );  # etc
print @cats[0]{name};
^D
Scalar value @cats[0] better written as $cats[0] at - line 2.
syntax error at - line 2, near "]{name"
Execution of - aborted due to compilation errors.
```

I tried to access the name element of the first hashref in the array @cats; Perl warned me that I probably didn't want a slice, but left the code the way it was, which turned out to be a syntax error. (Out of curiosity, there is no syntax error if the implied arrow is put back: @cats[0]->{name}. But I'd sooner you stay off the road with the landmines than keep going just because I point out where the first one is.)

Lists and hashes can also be sliced:

```
my ($uid, $gid) = (stat $file)[4,5];
my @fields = @data{@field_names};
```

That second line shows a handy way of extracting hash values in a particular order, useful in code for database applications. See [GUTTMAN98] for more information.

6.2.5 Not Testing a Regular Expression Before Using $1

This is when you do a regular expression match that captures text, and then use $1 and friends without checking that the regex matched:

```
$line =~ /height = (\d+) in, weight = (\d+) lbs/;
print "Go metric! Height = ", $1 * 2.54, "cm, weight = ",
      $2 * 0.45, "kg\n";
```

and it is flat out wrong. Assume that a regular expression matched when using $1 and you may end up with a $1 that was set by a *previous* regular expression match. Always check to see if the regex match succeeded, or you could end up with quite bogus results like this:

```
% perl -Mstrict -Mwarnings
for (qw(1 2 3 banana 4))
{
  /(\d+)/;
  print "\$1 = $1\n";
}
^D
$1 = 1
$1 = 2
$1 = 3
$1 = 3
$1 = 4
```

and no warning that anything is amiss. The same goes for s/// (although it's less common to want to capture text in a substitution). Proper code looks like:

```
for (qw(1 2 3 banana 4))
{
  /(\d+)/ and print "\$1 = $1\n";
}
```

or some other variant of only performing the action if the match succeeded.

6.2.6 Not Checking Return Codes from System Functions

This is also wrong. The only time it is appropriate not to check the return code from a function that might fail is when your program should do the same thing whether or not the function succeeds. Usually that requires more thinking than putting in a check every time. Most system functions return false and set $! on failure, so checking is as simple as this:

```
open my $fh, $filename or die "Can't open $filename: $!\n";
```

Look in *perlfunc* at the lists under the headings "Input and output functions" and "Functions for filehandles, files, and directories" for system functions. Note that people rarely check the return code of print(), even though it can return false if, for instance, it is printing to a file on a filesystem that has run out of space. Although you see that error when you call close(),[2] if you've spent a lot of time or written (so you think) a lot of data before getting to the close(), this may be small comfort. So check the return code from print() if you want to be really safe. Remember, if the return code signals an error, your program should get the reason for that error from $! and put it somewhere that it can be seen.

6.2.7 `map()` in Void Context

The reason I bring this one up is that a large number of people think of it as cargo cult programming, even though it's a small nit to pick. And one of those people may be evaluating your competence based on your use of this idiom. What they are all worked up about is using map() for its side effects and ignoring its return value. Because map() is designed to transform a list and therefore its raison d'être is to return another list, to ignore that output list is to obscure your point; and here the detractors are right. They also argue that Perl wastes memory constructing this list, and they're right again there, although Perl as of version 5.8.1 has been modified not to bother constructing the list in a void context. The final nail in the coffin is that there's no savings in readability or typing, because:

```
map EXPR, LIST
```

is identical to

---

2. Don't count on it; I found a situation with AFS where this wasn't the case.

```
EXPR for LIST
```

except the second doesn't create the unnecessary list, and it's even one character shorter. The same goes for the block form:

```
map BLOCK LIST
```

is identical to

```
for (LIST) BLOCK
```

although granted, the second is a whopping two characters longer.

6.2.8 Reading an Entire Stream into Memory Only to Process It Line by Line

For reasons I have never been able to discover, a surprising number of people write code like this:

```
# Don't really do this
my @lines;
while (<>)
{
  push @lines, $_;
}
for (@lines)
{
  # Process $_
}
```

There are two things wrong with this approach. First, processing doesn't start until the whole stream has been read. Second, memory is wasted on a temporary array. Both of these problems make this program a poor implementation for a filter in a pipeline processing an arbitrarily long stream. Just write this instead:

```
while (<>)
{
  # Process $_
}
```

If the stream has to be processed in a different order from its input—via some kind of sorting, say—then you will need the temporary array after all. Don't confuse that requirement with the need to sort some product of the lines; if, for example, you're reading lines that contain stock inventory such as:

```
apples 10
oranges 16
lemons 12
```

and you need to work with this data sorted in descending order of stock count, then populate a hash on the fly:

```
my %stock;
while (<>)
{
  my ($fruit, $count) = /(\w+)\s+(\d+)/ or next;
  $stock{$fruit} = $count;
}
my @sorted_fruit = sort { $stock{$b} <=> $stock{$a} }
                        keys %stock;
```

Or, if speed is of the essence, use an external sorting program:

```
open my $fh, "sort -nr -k2 @ARGV|" or die $!;
my (%stock, @sorted_fruit);
while (<$fh>)
{
  my ($fruit, $count) = /(\w+)\s+(\d+)/ or next;
  $stock{$fruit} = $count;
  push @sorted_fruit, $fruit;
}
```

6.2.9 Reinventing File::Find

This one sounds like it should be a public service announcement. Imagine Charlton Heston—or Alan Alda, if you prefer—solemnly intoning, "Every year, hundreds of beginner Perl programmers get caught in an insidious trap. Seduced by the temptation to try out recursion and the apparent simplicity of filesystem traversal, they write programs and even modules to descend through directory trees. But along the way, something goes horribly wrong . . . "

It looks so easy and fun to write directory traversal code. In five minutes one can dash off a `find()` function that takes a callback routine to call on each file found under a set of starting points. In fact, just to prove the point, I'll take five minutes to write one:

```perl
sub find                 # Don't really use this!
{
  my ($callback, @tops) = @_;
  for my $top (@tops)
  {
    _dofile($top, $callback);
  }
}

sub _dofile
{
  my ($file, $callback) = @_;
  -d $file and _dirfind($file, $callback);
  $callback->($file);
}

sub _dirfind
{
  my ($dir, $callback) = @_;
  opendir my $dh, $dir or warn "Can't open $dir: $!" and return;
  while (defined(my $file = readdir $dh))
  {
    next if $file =~ /^\.\.?$/;
    _dofile("$dir/$file", $callback);
  }
}
```

So quick, so simple, so wrong. The insidious nature of this beast is that it appears to work at first, and might in fact work for every test case *you* happen to use it for. Unfortunately, in addition to interface flaws (no order of traversal is guaranteed, and some programmers may want to traverse all the children of a directory before the directory itself, or vice versa), there are potentially fatal problems. One of those is the handling of cyclic symbolic links; the preceding code will loop until the filesystem gets tired of generating ever longer paths. Another is portability across filesystems.

Other optimizations performed, and problems solved, by File::Find, I deliberately omit here; the point is that you don't need to know what they are, because the authors of File::Find have done the work for you. Instead of typing all the preceding code, all you need to type instead is this:

```
use File::Find;
```

which is a massive win for efficiency, maintainability, readability, and portability. If you don't mind going to CPAN, Richard Clamp has written File::Find::Rule (`http://search.cpan.org/dist/File-Find-Rule/`), a module that makes it even easier to construct filesystem traversal code.

6.2.10 Useless Parentheses

This is being very nitpicky, but in statements like this:

```
my ($cheese) = shift;
my ($wine);
```

the parentheses are unnecessary. You only need them when you are declaring more than one variable or when you need to put the right-hand side in list context. Their use like that suggests that the programmer thought that my is a function rather than a variable modifier and would therefore be unaware of the more subtle aspects of my, such as its separate compile time and run time effects.[3]

---

3. Yes, I know my is listed in *perlfunc*. Whether that's the right place for it is debatable.

If you do have more than one variable to declare, make sure you *do* have the parentheses; I once spent a long time debugging a problem caused by:

```
my $words, $lines = (0, 0);
```

But that was in the Dark Ages before I was using strict everywhere. Had I used strict, Perl would have told me that $lines was undeclared.

6.2.11 Superfluous Initialization

As long as I'm picking nits, hashes and arrays automatically start life empty; there is no equivalent of undef for an aggregate. Therefore this:

```
my @foo = ();
my %bar = ();
```

is just the same as this:

```
my (@foo, %bar);
```

It might be a small point, but when I'm compressing legacy code so I can see enough of it to understand it better, every line saved helps.

6.2.12 Thinking tr and the Right Side of s/// Use Regular Expressions

This is another one for the Just Plain Wrong camp. For some reason, tr (*transliterate*) is an operator that is bound to a variable via =~, just as the operators m// and s/// are. When Perl was invented, transliteration constituted a more important part of the language and its applications than it does now, and so it made sense to minimize its syntax; if you're transliterating $_, you don't even need to use =~ at all, for example:

```
tr/a-zA-Z/n-za-mN-ZA-M/;          # rot-13
```

Unfortunately, seeing `tr` in the company of `=~` so often leads some people to believe that it is an operator that takes regular expressions, so they write code like this:

```
tr/[a-z]/[A-Z]/;                    # Don't use this
```

thinking that they are employing character classes that will uppercase text. By coincidence, they get the result they wanted, without realizing that this code means, "Turn left square brackets into left square brackets, turn lowercase letters to uppercase letters, and turn right square brackets into right square brackets." They have made an incorrect assumption that will lead them into trouble when they try something different with `tr`.

To find out how `tr` is really used, see *perlop*.

Likewise, because the second argument of the substitution operator, `s///`, is so close to the first one, people sometimes put regular expression syntax there. This can be benign:

```
s/\.txt\b/\.doc/g       # Superfluous backslash
```

or malignant:

```
s/\.txt\b/\.doc\b/g     # Superfluous backslash and backspace
```

The second argument—or right side, if you like—of `s///` is treated as a double-quoted string, which obeys different syntax rules from a regular expression.

6.2.13 Using Symbolic References

I promised back in Section 5.3.3 that I would expand on how to avoid symbolic references. The first symbolic reference avoidance tool is the hash. When you see code like this:

```
$bob = 42;  # Bob's age
```

```
$jim = 71;  # Jim's age
$art = 57;  # You get the idea...

$name = 'bob';  # Or set $name some other way
$age = $$name;  # Get their age with a symbolic reference
```

it means that the programmer didn't know about hashes. This is a pity, because it's a rare Perl program that can't make good use of them. In this case, the code should be turned into:

```
my %age = (bob => 42, jim => 71, art => 57);
my $name = 'bob';          # Or set $name some other way
my $age = $age{$name};     # Get their age from the hash
```

The second symbolic reference avoidance tool is the "hard" reference. Too few programmers know how to use hard references. (I'll mostly call them "references" from now on, and say "symbolic references" when I mean the other kind, because that's how Perl people talk.) Unfortunately the most common tutorial for learning Perl [SCHWARTZ01] doesn't cover them. Fortunately, Randal Schwartz and Tom Phoenix rectified that omission with a book specifically covering references and objects [SCHWARTZ03a].

A reference is preferable to a symbolic reference because the only way to create a reference is to have something to refer to. So if you receive a reference, you know you can dereference it. A symbolic reference, on the other hand, is just a string. There may or may not be an entity in your program with the same name; who knows how the symbolic reference was constructed. So, as your mother might tell you, put that symbolic reference down, you don't know where it's been.

Here's some code that doesn't know about references:

Example 6.1 Symbolic References

```
1  my (%title, %author, %pubyear, %artist);
2  my $isbn        = '0-201-79526-4';
3  $title{$isbn}   = "Perl Medic";
```

```
4   $author{$isbn}  = "Peter Scott";
5   $pubyear{$isbn} = 2004;
6   $artist{$isbn}  = "Ann Palmer";
7
8   # Later that same program...
9
10  foreach my $isbn (sort keys %title)
11  {
12    print "$isbn: ";
13    foreach $attribute (qw(title author pubyear artist))
14    {
15      print "$attribute: ", $$attribute{$isbn}, " ";
16    }
17    print "\n";
18  }
```

Aside from the use of a symbolic reference in line 15, this code commits at least two other offenses: First, it separates attributes (title, author, etc.) that all belong to the same entity (a book) into different data structures. Secondly, because of that separation, it is forced to assume that all those data structures have the same keys and arbitrarily pick one of them to get a list of keys from. This also wastes space.

But with references, we can make a multidimensional data structure:

Example 6.2 Multidimensional Hash

```
1   my %book;
2   my $isbn            = '0-201-79526-4';
3   $book{$isbn}{title}   = "Perl Medic";
4   $book{$isbn}{author}  = "Peter Scott";
5   $book{$isbn}{pubyear} = 2004;
6   $book{$isbn}{artist}  = "Ann Palmer";
7
8   # Later that same program...
9
10  foreach my $isbn (sort keys %book)
11  {
12    print "$isbn: ";
13    foreach my $attribute (sort keys %{$book{$isbn}})
```

```
14   {
15     print "$attribute: $book{$isbn}{$attribute}, ";
16   }
17   print "\n";
18 }
```

This is good, but our itch to remove superfluous code needs scratching. Our knowledge of references enables us to remove duplicate code in lines 3–6:

Example 6.3 Loading Multidimensional Hash

```
1   $book{$isbn} = { title   => "Perl Medic",
2                    author  => "Peter Scott",
3                    pubyear => 2004,
4                    artist  => "Ann Palmer")
5                  };
```

By just assigning an anonymous hash reference to the primary key we now have code that looks exactly like what it does with no extra verbiage.

6.2.14 Reinventing CGI.pm

Chapter 8 covers this mistake in detail, but it is so endemic among novice and intermediate users that I must mention it here. If reinventing File::Find deserves a public service announcement, then reinventing CGI.pm merits a hazmat team from the Centers for Disease Control. Countless people waste untold hours writing code to parse form submissions to CGI scripts. The lines of code for decoding hexadecimal encoding multiply around the Internet like the Black Death devastating Europe. Aside from being occasionally egged on by misguided bystanders pretending to know what they're talking about, there is no rhyme or reason to people's spreading this plague.

It is *not* easy to do CGI decoding properly; Lincoln Stein has done a fantastic job of staying on top of all the issues in his CGI.pm. In Section 8.3.1, I'll show you how to use it.

6.2.15 Returning `undef`

All subroutines return something, whether you use it or not. You don't even need to use a `return` statement in a subroutine to make it happen; the value of a subroutine is the value of the last expression evaluated in the subroutine if Perl didn't encounter a `return` statement before the end of the subroutine.

Often we write a subroutine whose job is to extract some feature from an item of data, and we have to decide what the subroutine should do in the event that feature doesn't exist. For example, suppose we're returning a person's work phone number, but they're unemployed. This is a natural use of Perl's `undef` value, so you sometimes see people write that like this:

```
sub work_phone
{
  # ...
  # No work phone!  Not even self-employed...
  return undef;
}
```

But this is a mistake. Granted, it works when used like this:

```
$bus_fone = work_phone(...);
```

or:

```
if (defined(work_phone(...)))
```

But what if it is called in a list context? For instance:

```
push @biz_fonez, work_phone(...);
```

Then the array will have an undefined element in it. What makes more sense is for nothing to get pushed on the array in the first place; that is, `work_phone()` should return an empty list when called in a list context. "A-ha!" you say, "I know that `wantarray()` will tell me what context I am called in." And so you write:

```
sub work_phone
{
  # ...
  # No work phone!  Not even self-employed...
  return wantarray ? () : undef;
}
```

Well, guess what? That's exactly what the default argument to `return` is. So you could have just said:

```
return;
```

to begin with.

6.2.16 Using `for` Instead of `foreach`

Iterating through an array using the C-style `for` loop:

```
for (my $i = 0; $i <= $#array; $i++)
{
  # Do something with $array[$i]
}
```

reveals that the programmer is unaware of the much clearer option of `foreach`:

```
foreach my $item (@array)
{
  # Do something with $item
}
```

Perhaps they knew about `foreach`, but wanted to change each element of the array, and thought that the `foreach` loop variable was just a copy of each element. Not so; it is in fact an *alias* for any writable member of the `foreach` list:

```
foreach my $item (@numbers)
{
  $item **= 2;      # Square it
}
```

Not only that, but `foreach` uses `$_` as a default loop variable, and can also be used in a suffix form. Perl even allows you to use `for` as a synonym for `foreach` (because it can tell the difference based on whether it sees a list or statements separated by semicolons). Combining all these features gives us a highly concise construction:

```
$_ ** = 2 for @numbers;    # Square each element of the array
```

In general, `$#array` is abused far more often than it is used appropriately, so question every use of it that you see.

6.2.17 Useless Regular Expressions

Using Perl's regular expression engine is like summoning a genie: You don't want to invoke that kind of power just to ask for a diet soda. So using a regular expression to test for straightforward string equality:

```
if ($tree = ~ /^larch$/)
```

is unnecessarily confusing. If you want to test for equality, say so:

```
if ($tree eq "larch")
```

Conversely, don't be afraid to use a regular expression even where there are alternatives if it's clearer:

```
if ($tree =~ /larch/)           # Regex check for substring...
if (index($tree, "larch") >= 0)  # ... is clearer than this
```

Use `index()` if you need to know the position the substring matched at, if you need to start searching from a particular offset, or if performance is crucial.[4]

---

4. Okay, so you might have spotted that there's a tiny difference between the effect of the match and the effect of eq: the regular expression can match not only the string "larch" but the same string with a newline appended. That's one of those convenience features of Perl (in this case, the meaning of the `$` in the regular expression) that many people aren't aware of, but just does what they want anyway. But most people who write /^larch$/ aren't doing it because they know the string might end with a newline.

6.3 Escaping the Global Variable Trap

Far too many programs that I read start with dozens of variable declarations:

```
my @e1badges;
my @e2badges;
my $optemp;
my $found_match = 0;
my $total1;
my $total2;
my %linecount;
my $lines_per_page;
# etc ad nauseam for at least a dozen more lines
```

And that's just the ones that are savvy enough to use my. This type of code is hard to maintain because of how much there is to keep track of. Where is $optemp used? What parts of the code are allowed to use it? Who can modify it? You must go on a fishing expedition to find these things out, wearing out the "find" function of your editor. Sometimes a variable is no longer used elsewhere at all.

Some students of formal life-cycle methodologies decide that comments are the cure for this problem, and the more the better. Their version of the preceding starts with:

```
##########################################################
# Global variable: @e1badges                             #
# Type: Array                                            #
# Purpose: First set of badge numbers read from file     #
# Index range: 0 through last badge number               #
# Sentinel values: none                                  #
# Exception indications: none                            #
##########################################################
my @e1badges;
```

This is as much of a pain to read as it is to type. Only someone getting paid by the line could love this code. In the process of adding only minimal information, its obesity squeezes more valuable code out of view. Remember, the real estate on the maintenance programmer's screen is precious; every part of it should count as much as possible, and that means comments have to carry their weight.

The first way we can improve this situation is to note that Perl is unlike many procedural languages that require all the variables that are going to be used within a block to be declared before any executable code in that block. You can put declarations anywhere you want in Perl, as long as they precede all other references to their variables. So declare a variable as close as you can get to its first use; if you ever remove the use of the variable you're more likely to see the superfluous declaration and remove it, too. An exception to this guideline is a constant assignment intended to be configurable. For the sake of convenience, these are usually clustered near the top of the code so a casual maintenance programmer isn't tempted to go further into code you'd rather they didn't try to modify.

Next, see if you can reduce the scope of the variables by putting them inside blocks. Look for all the uses of each variable in turn; if they're bunched in a relatively small area, that suggests that you may be able to turn that area into a subroutine. Then, identify purely temporary variables. If a variable is used only over a few lines of code and isn't an input or output then it is probably a synthetic variable. Either eliminate it using the guidelines in Section 4.8.2, or isolate it with a naked block around the area of its use.

6.4 Debugging Strategies

Imagine you've inherited a program, and when you go to run it, it doesn't work. (I know—what are the odds, eh? But let's pretend.) You need strategies for finding and fixing the problems.

6.4.1 Divide and Conquer

One of the simplest, yet most effective, techniques is to selectively remove as much of the code as possible until you've isolated the cause of an error message. If you can get the code down to a screenful, then even if *you* can't find the problem, other people to whom you show the code have a chance of being able to help you.

If you want to hide code temporarily (perhaps because you're not sure whether it's being used), then you can insert a line consisting precisely of:

```
__END__
```

(that's two underscores on each side and no leading or trailing white space) in your program, and everything that comes after it will be ignored (actually, it's available for reading via the DATA filehandle—make sure there isn't already an __END__ or __DATA__ line in the file). You can shuttle pieces of code in and out of that section.

Usually a syntax error is easy to locate because Perl tells you the line it occurred on, or the following line. Sometimes, however, the real culprit can be many lines earlier. If you're trying to locate the source of a really strange error that appears caused by bad syntax, you can move an __END__ line up and down the file in a binary chop and use perl's -c run-time flag to do syntax checking only (see *perlrun*).

To comment out a block of code in the middle of a file, use POD directives as described in Section 4.4.2.

When you're making modifications to how the program works, the golden rule to remember is this:

Change only one thing at a time!

You will go batty trying to figure out what caused strange new behavior if you make a whole slew of changes before trying the program out again. Once again the importance of having automated tests comes into the limelight.

For details on how to use Perl's run-time debugger, see Section 9.4.

Chapter 7

Upgrading (Plastic Surgery)

"When we inherit property, it does not occur to us to throw it away, even when
we do not want it."

— Mark Twain, *A Connecticut Yankee in King Arthur's Court*

Perl has remained extraordinarily backward compatible. The vast majority of programs written for Perl 4.018 will work identically on Perl 5.8.3. Thanks to the zealous efforts of a group affectionately—or otherwise—called the "backward compatibility police," only a handful of changes were made during that decade that could change the behavior of existing code.[1]

This cozy state of affairs (how many applications today will accept a file written by a 15-year-old version of themselves?) means that a program you inherit could have been written for a truly ancient version of Perl. Or it could have been written by a programmer who was only familiar with a truly ancient version of Perl, which amounts to the same thing. As long as you're porting the program—and especially if you're rewriting it—you should take the opportunity to use the labor-saving devices available in modern Perl. So much has been added to the language that you may be able to radically simplify the code.

In this chapter I'll show you how you can tell what version of Perl a program's creator was programming to, and how you can improve it by using features in more modern versions of Perl.

7.1 Strategies

What version of Perl was the application written for? Earlier I told you how to tell what version of Perl a particular program in a particular environment is running under, but that program could have been written by someone who was using only features provided by an earlier version of Perl. (There are still many people writing Perl 4 code, even though their programs are running on more modern Perls.)

You can find out what modules (and what versions of those modules) were installed with any release of Perl using the *corelist* program that comes with

---

1. This will not be the case with Perl 6, however. The developers concluded that backward compatibility had been taken as far as it could go, and if they wanted to realize significant gains in syntactical power, consistency, and learnability, it was time to bite the bullet.

Richard Clamp's Module::CoreList (`http://search.cpan.org/dist/Module-CoreList/`).

Once you've cast an eye over your inherited program source and you have an idea of what version of Perl the programmer was coding for, your next step is to upgrade the code that can be replaced with more succinct idioms that work in the newer version of Perl that you are using. In each section that follows, I'll tell you how you might recognize a program written for that version of Perl, and then how you can upgrade a program written for an earlier version of Perl to that one. Those recommendations are cumulative; that is, you can apply the recommendations of each section until you reach the one for the version of Perl you're running.

7.2 Perl 4

Most easily recognized by the absence of:

- `use`
- `my`
- `=>`
- References
- Objects
- `::` as a package component separator (instead of `'`)
- POD

There were many, many other things added in Perl 5—such as BEGIN and END blocks, the `/x` modifier on regular expressions—but the preceding are going to be your major markers.

This code is likely to contain more uses of `eval()`, `do()`, `local()`, and typeglobs (`*`) than you would see in Perl 5 programs.

7.2.1 Upgrading to Perl 4

There being no prior versions of Perl I wish to consider for this purpose, this section is intentionally left blank.

7.3 Perl 5.000

At this point it's no longer useful to point out what each version of Perl lacked, so from now on I'll say what they added. Yes, there were several subversions of each of these major versions, but I'll just consider the last one in each case. Although many changes went into each release of Perl, I will just mention the major features noticeable at the level of writing code. Much more was visible to programmers of embedded applications, for instance. There were many other changes made behind the scenes; for instance, Perl 5.8.1 randomizes the order of hash elements from one run to the next to defeat potential denial-of-service attacks.

Perl 5.000 of course added the object-oriented system, modules, pragmas, lexical variables, and references, to name only a few features.

7.3.1 Upgrading to Perl 5.000

Add `use strict` and ensure that all barewords that are implicit strings are quoted. Make all user variables lexical (declare them with `my`). Do list transformation with `map()` instead of temporary arrays. Turn symbolic references into hard references. Look for lengthy subroutine parameter lists and analyze the information flow to see where you can construct object classes. Look for lengthy operations that can be replaced by calls to core or CPAN modules.

If the program requires a customized perl built from Perl source and additional code, look for a CPAN module that does the same job or convert the additional code to XS and write a dynamically loadable module. Alternatively, small amounts of foreign code can be included directly and transparently in a

Perl program using the Inline:: series of modules (Inline::C, Inline::Java, Inline::Python, etc.).

7.4 Perl 5.001

Added the `$SIG{__DIE__}` and `$SIG{__WARN__}` handlers, closures, and Exporter tags.

7.4.1 Upgrading to Perl 5.001

If the application goes to unusual lengths to find out whether it has emitted a warning or an exception, it might benefit from using the `$SIG{__WARN__}` or `$SIG{__DIE__}` handlers. See *perlvar*. If it uses global variables to pass data to anonymous subroutines, consider rewriting to use closures.

7.5 Perl 5.002

Added subroutine prototypes and the `$^E` and `$^O` predefined variables.

7.5.1 Upgrading to Perl 5.002

If the application is running on VMS, OS/2, Win32, or MacPerl and would benefit from more verbose reporting of system errors, output `$^E` in addition to `$!`. If the program contains code purely to check the number and type of arguments to a subroutine, this would probably have been better written with a subroutine prototype (see *perlsub*). However, because dynamic checking is done at run time and prototypes are checked at compile time, a prototype may not work as a drop-in replacement for the dynamic checking code without other modifications. Consider instead Params::Validate (see Section 10.1.1).

7.6 Perl 5.003

Added the `IO::` modules and the FindBin module. This is also the first version of Perl where you could say `use <version>` to require that the running perl be at least at level `<version>`. Otherwise, the main purpose of this version was to plug a security hole in the *suidperl* program. This is the version of Perl that the second edition of *Programming Perl* [WALL96] was written for.

7.6.1 Upgrading to Perl 5.003

If the program is resorting to extraordinary shenanigans to find out where it is located, use FindBin.pm instead.

7.7 Perl 5.004

Allowed `my` to appear inside control structures, so that `while (my $x = pop)`, for instance, would create a new lexical variable scoped just to the `while` loop. Added the use of the arrow operator for dereferencing subroutine references, tied filehandles, and the UNIVERSAL methods `can()` and `isa()`. The regular expression anchor `\G` was added along with the concomitant `/c` modifier. The `constant` pragma and CGI.pm were added to the core modules.

7.7.1 Upgrading to Perl 5.004

Where a `for`, `foreach`, `while`, or `until` loop uses a lexical loop variable that is not used or should not be used elsewhere in the program, you can ensure it is isolated by embedding it in the loop statement:

```
for (my $i = 0; $i < 10; $i++) { ... }
foreach my $rocker (@Beatles, @Stones) { ... }
while (my $soda = pop) { ... }
```

If the program defines de facto constants using argumentless subroutine prototypes, for example:

```
sub avogadro () { 6.023E23 }
```

then they can be replaced by calls to the `constant` pragma:

```
use constant avogadro => 6.023E23;
```

if you find that more appealing.

It is unlikely that you would rapidly recognize a regular expression that would benefit from the \G anchor. See *perlfaq6* for an explanation of the purpose of \G.

7.8 Perl 5.005

Threads were added, but perl had to be compiled with a special option to use them; nevertheless `lock` became a reserved word. Regular expressions added look-behind, code evaluation, and non-backtracking matches. Pseudo-hashes were added (later to be regretted), and `<>` could read fixed-length records (look for $/ being set to a reference to an integer). It became possible to create compiled regular expression objects with `qr//`, and `foreach` was allowed as a suffix on a statement (e.g., `$_++ for @stocks`). The `$^S` variable (true inside `eval()` blocks) was added.

New modules in the core included the `attrs` pragma, base classes for tieing arrays and hashes, and Data::Dumper. The new `fields` pragma plus some internal magic makes it possible to catch references to invalid object attributes if objects were "typed"; for example, `my Kangaroo $skippy`.

7.8.1 Upgrading to Perl 5.005

Again, it is unlikely that you can quickly spot code that would be improved by the use of look-behind or the other new features in regular expressions. If the code contains a subroutine called `lock`, it should be renamed.

Where a `foreach` loop contains a single statement and the loop variable is either `$_` or a variable scoped just to that loop, it can be turned into the post-fixed form:

```
foreach ($text =~ /((?:\d+\.){3}\d+)/g)
{
  $ip{$1}++;
}
```

becomes:

```
$ip{$1}++ for $text =~ /((?:\d+\.){3}\d+)/g;
```

You can even extend this to multiple loop statements under the right circumstances:

```
foreach my $rock (@rocks)
{
  return "Paydirt" if is_gem($rock);
}
```

becomes:

```
is_gem($_) and return "Paydirt" for @rocks;
```

Note that you cannot chain postfixed control modifiers:

```
return "Paydirt" if is_gem($_) for @rocks;  # WRONG
```

The new object-oriented features in the next version of Perl are more useful for new applications than for retrofitting onto existing code.

7.9 Perl 5.6.0

This version of Perl was longer in the making than most of the others, but that was because so much was added. Therefore the version number format was altered to denote the importance of this update. A number of people did not recommend this version due to certain bugs. Others were unaffected and wondered what the fuss was about.

Lexical warnings (use warnings) were added, as was the initial support for Unicode (use bytes/use utf8). The our declaration made its first appearance. User-defined attributes showed up, and replaced the limited attrs pragma. Version strings were added, amid some controversy: Numbers beginning with v, or with more than one period in them, were automatically converted to a packed binary form.

open() came in for some enhancements: If the filehandle was an undefined variable, open() would store the filehandle there, so you could say open my $fh, ..., and have a lexically scoped filehandle that would automatically be closed on being garbage collected. The three-argument form of open() appeared, as did binary literals and lvalue subroutines. You could now call exists() on subroutines and array elements, and delete() on array elements.

7.9.1 Upgrading to Perl 5.6.0

Remove the -w command-line flag and add the use warnings pragma in every file; look for where the $^W special variable is set to 0 and change that to a no warnings pragma for the appropriate warning class.

Replace use vars with our and look to see whether it can be placed in a small lexical scope. Use scalar variable filehandles (e.g., open($fh, ...)) and declare them in the smallest scope necessary; you can then remove a close() statement at the end of that scope if you do not need to check its return status. Convert open() statements to the three-argument form, especially if they are preceded by code that attempts to tell whether the filename argument might contain shell metacharacters.[2]

Lvalue subroutines are still experimental. It would be unwise to go looking for opportunities to insert them into legacy code.

7.10 Perl 5.6.1

Many improvements were made in Unicode integration, many bug fixes and things were made easier behind the scenes, but there were no additions to the core language aside from the `open` pragma for setting I/O disciplines. An important security hole discovered in the *suidperl* and *sperl* programs was fixed; see `http://www.cpan.org/src/5.0/sperl-2000-08-05/sperl-2000-08-05.txt`.

7.10.1 Upgrading to Perl 5.6.1

In the event that you have `binmode()` being called on many filehandles, you might want to take advantage of the `open` pragma for making this a default within a lexical scope. The more interesting line disciplines came in Perl 5.8.0.

7.11 Perl 5.8.0

Along with more Unicode integration, Hash::Util added restricted hashes, which allowed you to prohibit inserting new keys or even changing the values of existing ones. The `-t` command-line flag allowed taint problems to be downgraded from exceptions to warnings.

---

2. Some rather clever code might rely on the magical behavior of `open()`, assuming that it is used by experts who are familiar with its special abilities. If the code was written by an expert, there is a small chance this might be happening.

The Filter::Util::Call and Filter::Simple modules from CPAN were added to the core so you could perform source filtering, that is, modify the source of a program before the Perl parser saw it. (You might think that this module would be used by those novelty modules that turn your program into white space or punctuation characters, but apparently that would be too easy.)

A panoply of other modules were rolled into the core, including Attribute::Handlers, Digest::MD5, the libnet bundle, List::Util, Memoize.pm, MIME::Base64, Scalar::Util, Storable.pm, Switch.pm, Test::More, Test::Simple, Text::Balanced, Tie::File, and Time::HiRes.

The `sort` pragma was introduced, allowing you more control over the internal behavior of the `sort()` function. The *suidperl* program was finally deprecated after consensus was reached that its security could never be fully guaranteed.

7.11.1 Upgrading to Perl 5.8.0

If you have a CGI program that was never taught about taintedness with the `-T` command-line flag, you can start out with the `-t` flag and get warnings on all the uses of tainted data so you can fix them all at once.

7.12 Perl 5.8.1

Use of pseudo-hashes triggered a warning that they were deprecated (and will be gone entirely in Perl 5.10.0). The `$*` variable (an ancient way of turning on multiline regular expression matching) was also deprecated.

7.12.1 Upgrading to Perl 5.8.1

If you're using pseudo-hashes, use something else, or wrap their use with this:

```
no warnings 'deprecated';
```

Pseudo-hashes had little use aside from being used internally by the `fields` pragma, which will continue to work as advertised, by using something other than pseudo-hashes behind the scenes. Their main use was to restrict the keys of a hash so that new ones couldn't accidentally be created. You can avail yourself of this functionality with the `lock_keys()` function in the core module Hash::Util (and that is just what the `fields` pragma now does).

Use the `/m` modifier on regular expressions instead of setting `$*`.

7.13 Perl 5.8.2

At this point the Perl developers' strategy shifted to one of releasing new versions every three months so that bug fixes appeared in stable versions faster. Consequently, although many bugs were fixed, internal operation improved, and documentation updated, there were no significant changes to the language.

7.14 Perl 5.8.3

Now we come to the current version of Perl. The SCALAR() method was introduced for tied hashes used in a scalar context, and a program called *prove* was added, allowing the running of specific tests at several levels of granularity.

7.14.1 Upgrading to Perl 5.8.3

If you've actually got a use for putting a tied hash in a scalar context, you can now do so in a meaningful way.

The extent of what is possible by using all the modules that were integrated from CPAN in versions 5.8.0 and 5.8.1 in particular is too great to go over here. For that, I need the next chapter.

Chapter 8

Using Modules (Genetic Enhancement)

"A working model may be requested in the case of applications for patent for alleged perpetual motion devices."

— U.S. Patent and Trade Office Web Site

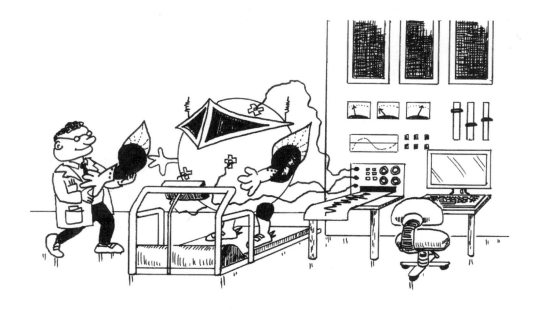

Western society values independence and self-reliance. One of my favorite activities is to hike in the back country until I'm lost, and then find my way out with maps and a compass.[1] Using a global positioning satellite (GPS) unit, cellular telephone, or helicopter are not on my list of options, efficient though they may be.

When it comes to programming however, it's a different story. If I had nothing better to do, I might enjoy reinventing code that other people had already written. Because it's been more than 20 years since I had nothing better to do, though, I need to be more prudent with my time and my clients' money.

8.1 The Case for CPAN

It surprises and disappoints me how often people waste time reinventing code for which a module already exists. Here are some reasons why they might be doing that:

- They don't know that there are non-core modules for Perl, or they don't know where to find them.
- They don't trust non-core modules.
- It takes them too long to find a module to do what they want.
- Their management has a policy against using non-core modules.
- They think it will be faster to write the code themselves than to figure out how to use a module.

Let me address each of these issues in turn.

---

1. My wife inserted a note in a draft version of this manuscript to the effect that I "no longer do such silly things since getting married." We'll see . . .

8.1.1 Yes, Virginia, There Is a Code Repository

The first concern is easily handled. There is a repository of contributed code; it is called the Comprehensive Perl Archive Network, or CPAN; and it is as easy to reach as you can imagine. It is replicated on hundreds of computers around the world for your convenience, far more than even really necessary these days (the mirroring structure was set up when networks were less reliable, bandwidth much smaller, and machines less powerful). The upshot of this is that under any circumstances short of World War III, at least part of CPAN will be accessible to you at all times if you can reach any reasonable chunk of the Internet. Elaine Ashton's all-encompassing FAQ also makes entertaining reading (`http://www.cpan.org/misc/cpan-faq.html`). See Section 8.1.3 for more information on how to use CPAN.

8.1.2 Trusting CPAN

How much can you trust code from CPAN? The bad news is that it is true that there is little quality control on CPAN: Anyone can upload any code they want; the only central controls are on the apportionment of the module namespace. There is a testing group (see `http://testers.cpan.org/`), but they just test that a module passes its own tests on as many different platforms and configurations as they can.[2] Technically, someone could place malicious code on CPAN.

The good news is that this has not yet happened. Every CPAN distribution has a corresponding checksum (generated automatically by the server when the distribution is uploaded) stored on CPAN so that when you download code you can compare the checksum with what it is supposed to be. (CPAN.pm does this automatically. See Section 8.2.1.)

The reliability of code on CPAN is a separate issue, but still not a pressing concern. I have found the modules I have tested to be of very high quality, but

---

2. You can also reach the test results for any module via `search.cpan.org`, if you navigate to the root of a module's distribution, then click on the "CPAN Testers" link. See Figure 8.4.

that doesn't mean that there are no poor CPAN modules. I would suggest you apply these heuristics to estimate the pedigree of a module:

- See if there are reviews of the module at the new site `http://cpanratings.perl.org/`.

- Is the module written by a prominent name in the Perl community? If you don't recognize the name, have they written any modules you recognize? (Using `search.cpan.org`, click on the author's ID near the top of the page to get a listing of their modules.) Do a Google search for their name and "Perl" in Web pages and Usenet articles, and see if you like what you read. At the time of writing there are more than 2,800 authors listed on CPAN and there are so many specialties I have not investigated that it would be grossly unfair to give any kind of list of reputable authors at this point in the context of assessing module reliability.

- Does the module pass its tests? If it doesn't *have* tests, or isn't delivered to work properly with CPAN.pm (or Module::Build), those would be red flags.

- Check the date the module was last updated; if it has been altered in the last three months then the author is giving it regular care and you are more likely to be able to get their attention if you have a problem than you would if the module is very old.

- If the module has not been touched in two years, it is likely moribund; investigate to see if it has been superseded by another module. However, it is quite possible that if it is a simple module, it doesn't need frequent changing. The module Geography::States, for instance, contains mappings between state names and abbreviations for several countries, and these just don't change often.[3]

- Complex modules often have SourceForge projects[4] so that multiple people can cleanly work on them concurrently. This site will

---

3. As luck would have it, I looked at Geography::States and found that it hadn't been updated with the (recent!) assignment of the abbreviation for Nunavut in Canada. (The definition of "state" is a bit broad in this module.) I notified the author.
4. `http://sourceforge.net/`

be a valuable source of information about the current state of the module.

- Do a Google search of Usenet articles for the module and sort by date to see if there have been any recent postings indicating approval or otherwise.

8.1.3 How to Find a CPAN Module

Like many things, finding a CPAN module is very easy when you know how. The easiest way to access CPAN is through `http://search.cpan.org/` (see Figure 8.1).

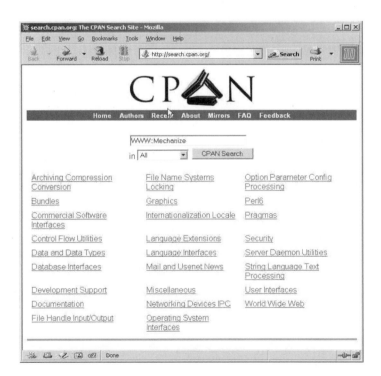

FIGURE 8.1 Front page of search.cpan.org.

If you want to find out more about CPAN and get some different views of its data, you can go to `http://www.cpan.org` and browse. One type of data you can find through `www.cpan.org` but not `search.cpan.org` is scripts (pre-written programs). `search.cpan.org` just has modules (reusable libraries of functions and methods).

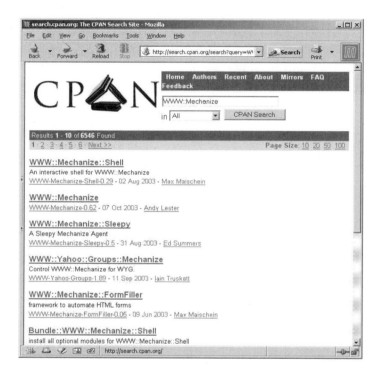

FIGURE 8.2 Hits from a search on search.cpan.org.

After entering a query on `search.cpan.org`, clicking on the desired hit (Figure 8.2) will give you the documentation for the module: its POD automatically rendered into HTML (Figure 8.3). Clicking on the distribution link in the header will take you to a listing of the files that make up the distribution (Figure 8.4); this is a handy way to find the README file that comes with the module, and also displays the `cpanratings.perl.org` rating. If the module is delivered with any examples, this is a way to inspect them without having to download the whole distribution. The Download link on this page gives you a direct link to the tarball containing that version of the module; but use this only if CPAN.pm won't work for you, because that'll be a much easier way to install a module (see Section 8.2.1).

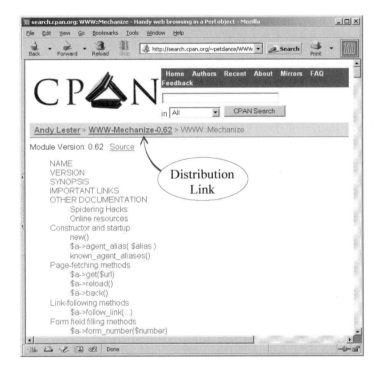

FIGURE 8.3 Module documentation seen via search.cpan.org.

Clicking on the Source link under the header will take you to the module source code, which allows you to answer any remaining questions you might have about how the module works.

FIGURE 8.4 Module distribution seen via search.cpan.org.

8.1.4 Dealing with an Anti-CPAN Policy

A policy that says "No CPAN code" is born out of fear or ignorance. Every day, companies and governments trust millions, even billions of dollars to CPAN modules. Refer your management to "Perl Success Stories" [OREILLY99] for examples. If they are concerned about quality control, point out that modules such as PerkTk and DBI are nearly as complex as the entire Perl core (and presumably they already trust the Perl core or you wouldn't be reading this) and receive attention from dozens of maintainers and thousands of users. Sadly, though, many organizations suffer from the "Not Invented Here" syndrome, which causes them to be blind to important new technologies.

8.1.5 Make or Buy?

Our final concern arrives in the form of a venerable question that takes on a special aura when applied to modules. We programmers have a well-known tendency to underestimate the time it takes to create code. If we were right the first time about interface and design decisions, never hit any problems, didn't have to write tests because the code worked to begin with, and could leave out documentation, then our schedule estimates might only be too optimistic by a factor of two.

Otherwise, with the exception of a few people in CMM-SW (Software Engineering Institute Capability Maturity Model for Software) level 5 environments [CMU03] or devout adherents of the Personal Software Productivity process [HUMPHREY94], we're likely to be way off the mark. "Create a module for parsing CGI form inputs—no problem! Three, four hours at the most," we think. This is not just abusing the virtue of hubris, this is mugging it in a dark alley.

Before you decide to hack out your own module without looking for an equivalent on CPAN, consider what you will have to do, one way or another, sooner or later, in your module:

- Document it (in POD of course).
- Comment it for maintenance programmers.
- Port it to any platforms or versions of Perl that might be required by users.
- Write regression tests for users.
- Respond to user feedback and requests.

The only time it makes sense not to use a CPAN module that already does what you want is if it is such a bad fit in other respects that you will spend longer learning its documentation or working around unnecessary interfaces than it would take to create a module that does only what you want. Of course, false hubris makes us think that this is true 90 percent of the time. But if you truly believe that a particular CPAN module is not worth the effort after reading this chapter, then as a last resort before you proceed to do it yourself, consider whether you can eliminate the interface problems by subclassing the module.

8.2 Using CPAN

You can of course download *tarballs* (compressed archives of file trees created with the *tar* program) of modules from CPAN and build them manually. I'll show you how to do that shortly. But first, I'll show you the easy way.

8.2.1 Using CPAN.pm

Perl makes it phenomenally easy to install most modules by providing a handy layer of automation for talking to CPAN right in the core. That layer is implemented by—you guessed it—a module, amazingly enough called CPAN.pm.[5]

Installing a new module with CPAN.pm is extremely easy, especially if you are the system administrator or otherwise have write access to the directories in perl's @INC where it wants to install new modules. To install a module called, say, Mac::iTunes, just type:

```
% perl -MCPAN -e 'install Mac::iTunes'
```

What launches CPAN.pm into the realm of superstardom is that it can detect and install *dependencies;* when the module you are installing requires other modules to work (and Mac::iTunes requires a bunch), but you don't already have them. Provided the module author properly listed those prerequisite modules (and the Mac::iTunes author did), then CPAN.pm will install those modules; and if any of *them* have unrequited prerequisites, CPAN will install them, and so forth. If a module in this dependency chain did not specify its prerequi-

---

5. In Perl 5.10 CPAN.pm will be superseded by a module called CPANPLUS.pm, which you can currently find on CPAN. CPANPLUS.pm will provide a cleaner interface for using CPAN. As of this writing it is still somewhat leading edge, so I am not covering it further here, but feel free to experiment with it.

sites properly, you can usually get around it by reissuing the original install command after the first attempt fails.

If you want to use CPAN.pm to install modules to a private directory (perhaps because you don't have administrator privileges to install to the site_perl targets in the @INC compiled into perl), you have to work a little harder. CPAN.pm uses a configuration file that contains settings for, among other things, where to build downloads and where to install completed modules. You need to make a version just for you that has special settings. This file needs to be called MyConfig.pm and live in a directory .cpan/CPAN under your home directory. You can let CPAN.pm build this file for you by typing this command:

```
% perl -MCPAN -e shell
```

and answering the questions. However, if the superuser has already done so, you may get a message about permission being denied to access their .cpan directory. In that case, first copy the CPAN::Config module that is part of the installed perl so you can edit it:

```
% mkdir ~/.cpan
% mkdir ~/.cpan/CPAN
% cp `perl -MCPAN::Config -e 'print $INC{"CPAN/Config.pm"}'` \
    ~/.cpan/CPAN/MyConfig.pm
```

Then edit ~/.cpan/CPAN/MyConfig.pm to change the paths of the build_dir, cpan_home, and keep_source_where parameters to point to directories you have write permission for.

Now you can now run CPAN.pm in interactive mode:

```
% perl -MCPAN -e shell
cpan shell -- CPAN exploration and modules installation (v1.76)
ReadLine support available
```

Now, give a configuration command to the CPAN shell:

```
cpan> o conf makepl_arg PREFIX=/home/peter/myperl
```

In this case, /home/peter/myperl is the private directory where you want to install new modules. (Don't try using ~ in this path.) Finally, commit the configuration change (cause the change to `makepl_arg` to become permanent) and exit the CPAN shell:

```
cpan> o conf commit
commit: wrote /home/peter/.cpan/CPAN/MyConfig.pm
cpan> q
Lockfile removed.
```

You can now build a module using CPAN.pm and the `install` command will put the installed module under /home/peter/myperl. You will need to add the directory /home/peter/myperl/lib/perl5/site_perl to perl's `@INC` to find the modules that are installed there.[6] Therefore a Perl program that wants to use these modules should start out:

```
use lib qw(/home/peter/myperl/lib/perl5/site_perl);
```

because that directory is not in the default `@INC`.

8.2.2 Manual Module Installation

On rare occasions CPAN.pm won't work for some reason. You may have an idiosyncratic environment, or the module may require some configuration. Modules that require your input to configure are supposed to engage you in an interactive dialog when you issue the CPAN.pm `install` command. The module author programs this dialog in a file called Makefile.PL (see Section 3.3). If the CPAN.pm `install` command doesn't work for a particular mod-

---

6. The full story is a bit more gory. Modules can be installed not just under /home/peter/myperl/lib/perl5/site_perl, but under version- and architecture-specific subdirectories therein. So why don't I have to add those directories to `@INC` as well? Because Perl's use lib pragma and -I command-line option will do it for me: If version- or architecture-specific subdirectories exist for any directory I add to `@INC` using those operations, they will be added to `@INC` automatically. That's another good reason to avoid modifying `@INC` directly.

ule, then you can build it by hand and invoke Makefile.PL yourself. First download the module; the `look` command in the CPAN.pm shell is ideal for that:

```
% perl -MCPAN -e shell
cpan> look Foo::Bar
[output deleted]
Working directory is /home/peter/.cpan/build/Foo-Bar-0.44
%
```

It might look from that last prompt as though the perl command has returned, but in fact it's still running, and has downloaded and unwrapped the latest version of the Foo::Bar module and launched a shell in the build directory for you to play with the module. The manual equivalent of the `look` command is to download the module's tarball from CPAN (that Download link on search.cpan.org), then:

```
% gunzip Foo-Bar-0.44.tar.gz
% tar xf Foo-Bar-0.44.tar
% rm Foo-Bar-0.44.tar
% cd Foo-Bar-0.44
```

The first two steps can be combined if your *tar* program accepts the `-z` option.

Now look for a README file and peruse it. Normally, the steps to build the module are:

```
% perl Makefile.PL
% make install
```

`make install` will expand in this case to `make; make test; make install`, with each step being executed only if the previous one succeeds.

Since you're presumably building this module by hand because the CPAN.pm `install` command isn't good enough, rather than some masochistic desire to make life difficult, you'll need to intervene at this stage. Most likely you'll be editing Makefile.PL before the first command. It's hard to imagine legitimate circumstances for editing the Makefile before running *make* given that you can set just about every parameter in that Makefile that matters through arguments to the first command. To find out more about those arguments, read the documentation for the ExtUtils::MakeMaker module. (That's what Makefile.PL uses to create a Makefile.)

If you began this build process with the CPAN.pm `look` command, remember that you're in a subshell and you need to exit it:

```
% exit
cpan> q
%
```

I sometimes forget this and only find out that I'm still in the CPAN.pm shell when I log out at the end of the day.

8.2.3 PPM

On a Windows platform CPAN.pm will not be useful due to the absence of the *make* program. You can either get a version for Windows such as *nmake*[7] or *dmake,* get one in a UNIX emulation environment such as Cygwin,[8] or you can take the easier step of using the *ppm* (Perl Package Manager) program included in ActiveState's Windows Perl distribution.[9] PPM only knows about modules that have been ported to the PPM repository, so it will always lag behind CPAN; but on the other hand, all the compilation has already been done for you, so installation of modules with binary components can be much easier than on a UNIX machine. An extreme example of this is PerlTk, which on UNIX requires that you first acquire and build the underlying Tk and Tcl libraries, whereas on Windows everything will be installed for you with the single PPM `install` command.

---

7. `ftp://ftp.microsoft.com/Softlib/MSLFILES/nmake15.exe`
8. `http://www.cygwin.com/`
9. *PPM3* in recent versions of Active Perl.

8.2.4 Module Distribution

When you want to package your own module for distribution, the obvious choice today is called ExtUtils::MakeMaker. That's a core module that's invoked by *h2xs* to create the Makefile.PL when you first create a new module.

If, however, you want to do more than what the default Makefile.PL does, you need to edit it and insert directives drawn from the ExtUtils::MakeMaker documentation. Some people have pointed out lately that this interface is not as easy to use as they would like, and they have started developing alternatives:

- Ken Williams' Module::Build generates a Build.PL file that can be used to build a distribution without a *make* utility. As time goes by, more CPAN modules will incorporate Module::Build and CPAN.pm and CPANPLUS.pm will be upgraded to recognize Build.PL files (`http://search.cpan.org/dist/Module-Build/`).

- However, Module::Build addresses how a user installs a module, not how a developer creates one. Geoffrey Avery created an alternative to *h2xs* in Extutils::ModuleMaker (`http://search.cpan.org/dist/ExtUtils-ModuleMaker/`). It even knows how to generate Build.PL files.

- Autrijus Tang's PAR (Perl ARchive) can create self-contained executables that encapsulate all their dependencies. It employs highly sophisticated code to find those dependencies and works on a wide variety of platforms (`http://search.cpan.org/dist/PAR/`).

Expect that in the next few years these modules will get greater attention and more widespread use.

8.3 Improving Code with Modules

Vast amounts of legacy code have been expended duplicating functionality that now resides in modules. You can slim down programs drastically when you find code that you can excise in favor of a module that does the same job. Here are some common opportunities to look out for.

8.3.1 CGI.pm

For some reason, legions of programmers never got the word that there is a module for doing the common functions they need to perform in a CGI program. If you encounter a CGI program that's not using CGI.pm, unless it has some unusual performance requirements, do yourself a favor and convert it.

The most basic and important functionality of CGI.pm is to return the values supplied by a user to form inputs. When you see code like this:

```
foreach (split /&/, $ENV{QUERY_STRING}
{
  ($key, $val) = split /=/, $_, 2;
  s/%([A-Fa-f0-9]{2})/pack("c", hex($1))/ge for ($key, $val);
  $data{$key} = $val;
}
```

you're looking at (flawed) code for decoding (some) form inputs. (It might not be exactly the same as that.)

CGI.pm makes reading form inputs ridiculously easy. No matter what type the input field is, if its name is, say, `myforminput`, then your program can retrieve its value with:

```
use CGI qw(param);
my $myforminput = param('myforminput');
```

Even when handling a file upload for an input named, say, `myfileupload`, CGI.pm makes this as easy as could be:

```
use CGI qw(param);
my $upload = param('myfileupload');

# Use $upload as a string, get the file name:
use File::Basename;
my $saveto = basename($upload);

# Use $upload as a filehandle, get the upload contents:
open(OUT, '>', $saveto) or die $!;
print OUT while <$upload>;
close OUT;
```

You can get at all of the parameters at once using the Vars() method:

```
use CGI qw(Vars);
my %param = Vars();
```

CGI.pm also contains methods that can generate HTML, but don't feel you have to use them; I prefer a templating system such as HTML::Template so I can get an HTML expert to take care of the appearance of a site without any assistance from me.

The other CGI.pm methods that I use routinely with templates are header() to generate the HTTP header, and various reflective functions such as url() for finding out the URL my program was invoked with.

Some programs don't do the input decoding themselves but use an older library called cgi-lib.pl. This exports a function called ReadParse() that places form inputs in a package hash called %in. CGI.pm has a compatibility mode that allows you to migrate such scripts painlessly. Where the program currently says:

```
require 'cgi-lib.pl';
&ReadParse;
```

replace those lines with:

```
use CGI;
CGI::ReadParse;
```

That's it. Of course, a lot of useful CGI.pm functionality will be missing because it wasn't in cgi-lib.pl. For instance, multiple form inputs with the same name will show up in `%in` as a single value with null characters separating the different inputs. CGI.pm does it that way because that is what cgi-lib.pl does, whereas the CGI.pm `param()` method returns those inputs as a true list.

8.3.2 Date Parsing and Manipulation

So many people seem wedded to the idea of calling an external program to find out the date. Granted, this is the way it's done in shell scripts, but we can do better in Perl. You can:

- Get the values for seconds, month, and so on, from `localtime()`.

- Format a date string any way you want, using the `strftime()` function exported from the (core) POSIX module.

- Parse a date string in virtually any format into a UNIX time (seconds since epoch), using the (CPAN) Date::Parse module. For example:

```
% perl -MDate::Parse -le \
  'print str2time("Thursday")'
1057215600
```

- Parse a date string in even more formats (at the expense of noticeable compilation time) using the (CPAN) Date::Manip module. For example:

```
% perl -MDate::Manip -le \
  'print ParseDateString("Next Wednesday")'
2003070900:00:00
% perl -MDate::Manip -le \
  'print ParseDateString("Last Wednesday")'
2003070200:00:00
```

Also, you can perform numerous operations with Date::Manip, such as working with recurring events and finding out the dates of holidays.

• Perform calculations on dates and times with the (CPAN) module Date::Calc. Life is too short to write yet more code for handling base-60 calculations. For example, to find the number of days between April Fool's Day and Canada Day in 2003:

```
% perl -MDate::Calc=:all -le \
  'print Delta_Days(2003, 4, 1, 2003, 7, 1)'
91
```

8.3.3 Socket.pm and IO::Socket

Socket programming in Perl has been simple since 1995, when Graham Barr's Socket.pm module hit the archives, and even simpler since 1996, when his IO::Socket module came out. Instead of using constants from a .ph file and using `pack()` and `unpack()`, with Socket.pm you can easily get, say, the IP address of a machine from its name:

```
% perl -Mstrict -Mwarnings -MSocket -l
my $addr = gethostbyname("www.perlmedic.com")
  or die "Lookup failed";
print inet_ntoa($addr);
^D
204.95.83.7
```

IO::Socket—and in particular, IO::Socket::INET—provide object-oriented packaging for sockets that make client/server programming a snap.

For a comprehensive treatment of just what you can do with IO::Socket, see [STEIN00].

8.3.4 HTML Parsing

Thousands of people want to parse HTML because they believe that's the only way to get at the result of some kind of operation they want to perform. Unfortunately, they're usually right. Face it, if what you want to know is, say, your bank balance, then just about the most annoying way you could think of for finding it out would be to submit several sets of inputs gleaned from successive HTML forms, finally parsing the quantity out of a morass of tags whose layout changes every other week. It would be much nicer if the bank provided you with an application program interface (API) like this:

```
$balance = get_balance($account, $PIN);
```

although, yes, it would be more likely to work like this:

```
$acct = BankAccount->new($username, $PIN) or die ...;
$balance = $acct->balance($account);
```

but we're still dreaming; banks don't do that. One day banks might become enlightened enough to provide SOAP interfaces, or at least some kind of XML API, but until then people like me who want to automate this task face some kind of HTML parsing.

You may not be accessing an online banking service, but that doesn't make any difference to the ease or difficulty of the task of parsing HTML. So find out first of all whether the creator of the pages you think you need to parse can provide them in a more palatable format. RSS, for instance, may be available for content resembling news stories.[10] If you are the creator of the HTML pages, don't force yourself to parse the HTML to extract content when you could provide an interface to that content some other way.

If you're stuck with no alternative but to parse HTML, you're in good company. So don't reinvent the wheel when so many people have constructed entire fleets of articulated trucks before you.

---

10. RSS stands for RDF Site Summary; RDF stands for Resource Description Framework.

The temptation to parse HTML with regular expressions appears irresistible, judging by how many people do it. Not, to quote *Seinfeld,* that there's anything wrong with that. If you can accept the risks and limitations of that style of parsing, it can certainly be more succinct and readable than the alternatives. However, you need to know what the risks and limitations are in order to accept them.

The risks are that you will mislabel some part of the content; you might be looking for anchor tags, for instance, and accidentally find some that were embedded in comments or JavaScript that have nothing to do with what you were looking for. If you know the provenance of the content well enough to know that this has no chance of happening, then go ahead:

```
@links = $content =~ /<A\s+HREF\s*=\s*"(.*?)"/ig;
```

Or suppose you're scanning for form input tags, and you know the source well enough to know that the TYPE attribute will always precede the NAME attribute. Then you can use:

```
@inputs = $content =~ /<INPUT\s+TYPE="text"\s+NAME="(.*?)"/ig;
```

But the list of caveats for these examples builds up rapidly—are we sure that there will always be enclosing quotation marks, for instance? Browsers can work without them. When you get too nervous, it's time to invoke the no-nonsense power of a true HTML parser, such as HTML::Parser, HTML::TreeBuilder, or—if all you want is just hyperlinks—HTML::LinkExtor. For further reading, see [BURKE02]. Randal Schwartz also pointed out advantages to using XML::Parser to parse HTML in [SCHWARTZ03b].

8.3.5 URI Parsing

Uniform Resource Identifier (URI) is the proper technical term now for what 99 percent of the world still calls a Uniform Resource Locator (URL). Common operations you may need to perform on a URI include:

• Extracting one of the components (scheme, path, server, etc.).

- Changing one of those components.
- Turning a relative URI into an absolute one.

Rather than trying to figure these things out via regular expressions, use the URI.pm module, which has methods for all of them.

8.3.6 Database Interaction

Too few modules that should be using proper databases really are using them. Whenever concurrent access is a possibility, in particular, a database may be appropriate, since a proper relational database will handle locking for you automatically and provide transaction semantics. Use DBI.pm and whichever of the myriad DBD:: family of modules speaks to the database of your choice. MySQL and PostgreSQL are two excellent free relational databases, so procurement cost need not be an obstacle. You will have to learn SQL (unless you use any of a number of CPAN modules that attempt to insulate you from that task), but it's not that difficult and the gains are well worth it if you're going to make much use of the database.

If concurrency is not an issue and you don't want to go through the trouble of putting up a database server, a DBM file offers significant advantages over a plain text file. You can use core modules such as DB_File to manage random access to the data, and store complex hierarchical structures with MLDBM (`http://search.cpan.org/dist/MLDBM/`). Best of all, you can do this using `tie()` as the interface, so if, say, you've got a program that is running out of memory to store a particular hash in, with a couple of lines you can tie it to a DBM file and instantly perform the trade-off of execution time for memory. (Just make sure that the code doesn't call `keys()` or `values()` in a list context, or use the hash in a list context, or it'll pull the whole database into memory to do so.)

If you want to do your own locking to handle concurrency, you can, but this is *not* easy to get right (see the section "Locking: The Trouble with `fd`" in the documentation for the DB_File module).

There are many modules on CPAN that provide abstraction layers on top of DBI. One such worth checking is Michael Schwern's Class::DBI, now maintained by Tony Bowden (`http://search.cpan.org/dist/Class-DBI/`).

For further reading, see [DESCARTES00].

8.3.7 Mail Processing

A plethora of modules exist to make mail sending and reading easy. For sending mail, Mark Overmeer's Mail::Send is very easy to use (`http://search.cpan.org/dist/MailTools/`). The same distribution includes Mail::Internet, a module for parsing mail messages into objects. Mark's Mail::Box (`http://search.cpan.org/dist/Mail-Box/`) is a new module that takes this concept and extends it to mail folders. For creating and parsing messages with attachments, use Eryq's MIME::Lite (`http://search.cpan.org/dist/MIME-Lite/`), maintained by Yves Orton.

To read mail from a server, use the core Net::POP3 module, or David Kernen's Mail::IMAPClient (`http://search.cpan.org/dist/Mail-IMAPClient/`).

I use Simon Cozens' Mail::Audit (`http://search.cpan.org/dist/Mail-Audit/`) in conjunction with Justin Mason's wildly popular Mail::SpamAssassin (`http://www.spamassassin.org/` and CPAN) to manage the flood of garbage that pollutes the mailbox of anyone with an address published in the Perl change log.

For further reading, see [STEIN00].

8.3.8 XML Manipulation

XML and Perl have a rich history of association. It is impossible to do justice to that in the space I have. XML is a complex technology spawning many even more complex technologies such as XSL, SOAP, WSDL, and so on. There are many modules for making XML easier; in particular see XML::Simple, XML::Parser, XML::TreeBuilder, XML::Writer, XML::SAX, XML::DOM, and XML::Grove. HTML::Parser has an XML parsing mode that doesn't depend on your having the *expat* program that XML::Parser requires. See Matt Sergeant's AxKit (`http://axkit.org/`) for a spectacular example of how much can be done with XML and Perl on a web server.

To really explore what you can do with Perl and XML takes a whole book; see [RAY02].

8.4 Custom Perls

Back in the wild and woolly days of Perl 4, integrating custom C code into Perl took sweat, ingenuity, and guts. Whereas in Perl 5 custom binary code can be dynamically loaded faster than you can say "perldoc *perlxs*," in Perl 4 you had to build a special version of perl that contained the new code you wanted. You would edit some template files to load the new source files that you placed in the right subdirectory, and make perl from source all over again.

To keep this and other custom perls separate from the unaltered, common or garden-variety perl, it was customary to give them different names depending on what functionality had been added. Thus, a perl that had Oracle database intelligence embedded would be called *oraperl.* A perl that knew how to speak the Lightweight Directory Access Protocol (LDAP) to an X.500 directory user agent would be called *duaperl.* (Theoretically, a perl that had both capabilities ought to have been called *oraduaperl* or *duaoraperl,* but I never heard of this happening.)

Once Perl 5 appeared on the scene with dynamic loading of shared libraries (or DLLs), these custom perls were consigned to the scrap heap of history. Unfortunately, legacy code might still be using these relics of a bygone era; that's why they call it "legacy." Here is a guide to common types of custom perl and what to do with them.

8.4.1 Btreeperl

Btreeperl, by John Conover, was for interfacing with BSD NDBM database files. No compatibility mode module was written, but the NDBM_File module, bundled in the core as of Perl 5.8.0, supplies a cleaner tied interface to NDBM files.

8.4.2 Cisamperl / rocisperl

Cisamperl, by Mathias Koerber, was for accessing Informix C-ISAM files. No DBD module exists because the interface does not use SQL. The closest compatibility mode is Philippe Chane You Kaye's Isam module (`http://search.cpan.org/dist/Isam/`).

8.4.3 Ctreeperl

Ctreeperl, by John Conover, was for accessing Faircom c-tree databases. Robert Eden's Db::Ctree module (`http://search.cpan.org/dist/Db-Ctree/`) is a close object-oriented translation. However, there is no DBD module.

8.4.4 Duaperl

Duaperl, by Eric Douglas, was for accessing X.500 directory servers via LDAP (DUA is a directory user agent in X.500 terminology). Stephen Pillinger made a Perl 5 module (`http://search.cpan.org/dist/Dua/`) that, while not providing an exact emulation mode (it is object-oriented), does have a one-to-one correspondence between its methods and the duaperl functions. It is, however, quite old, unsupported, and does not build without expert attention. You can migrate programs to more maintainable code by changing them to use Graham Barr's Net::LDAP (`http://search.cpan.org/dist/perl-ldap/`) instead.

8.4.5 Ingperl / sqlperl

Ingperl (also called sqlperl), by Ted Lemon, was for accessing Ingres databases. Henrik Tougaard maintains an emulation module, Ingperl, in the DBD-Ingres distribution (`http://search.cpan.org/dist/DBD-Ingres/`). You can migrate programs to more maintainable code by changing them to use his DBD::Ingres module in the same distribution.

8.4.6 Interperl

Interperl, by Buzz Moschetti, was for accessing Interbase databases. Edwin Pratomo's DBD::Interbase (`http://search.cpan.org/dist/DBD-InterBase/`) fulfills the same purpose. There is no compatibility module.

8.4.7 Isqlperl

Sometimes inaccurately referred to as infoperl, this module by Bill Hails was for accessing Informix databases. No compatibility module was ever written. DBD::Informix, by Jonathan Leffler, handles the functionality for Perl 5.

8.4.8 Oraperl

Oraperl, by Kevin Stock, was for accessing Oracle databases. You can use the Oraperl module in Tim Bunce's DBD-Oracle distribution (`http://search.cpan.org/dist/DBD-Oracle/Oraperl.pm`), which provides an emulation mode allowing you to port old oraperl programs to run under new perls. You can migrate programs to more maintainable code by changing them to use DBD::Oracle (`http://search.cpan.org/dist/DBD-Oracle`) instead.

8.4.9 Pgperl

Pgperl, by Igor Metz, was for accessing Postgres databases. There appears to be no emulation module; the closest equivalent is the Pg module in Edmund

Mergl's pgsql distribution (`http://search.cpan.org/dist/`
`pgsql_perl5/Pg.pm`). The migration path to more maintainable code is via
his DBD::Pg (`http://search.cpan.org/dist/DBD-Pg/`).

8.4.10 Sybperl

Sybperl was for accessing Sybase databases. Michael Peppler maintains an
FAQ [PEPPLER02]. You can use his CPAN module Sybase::Sybperl (`http://`
`search.cpan.org/search?dist=sybperl`), which provides an emulation mode that allows old sybperl programs to run under new perls. The migration path to more maintainable code is via DBD::Sybase (`http://`
`search.cpan.org/dist/DBD-Sybase/`), by the same author.

8.4.11 Tkperl

In a break from the relentless stream of database-specific perls, tkperl, by Malcolm Beattie, was for creating Tk graphical user interfaces. It has been superseded by Nick Ing-Simmons' Perl/Tk (`http://search.cpan.org/`
`dist/Tk/`). See [LIDIE02].

8.4.12 Uniperl

Uniperl, by Rick Wargo, was for accessing Unify databases. H. Merijn Brand's
DBD::Unify (`http://search.cpan.org/dist/DBD-Unify/`) brings
that capability to Perl 5, and also contains a Uniperl.pm module providing
backward compatibility with uniperl.

Chapter 9

Analysis (Forensic Pathology)

"Facts which at first seem improbable will, even on scant explanation, drop the cloak which has hidden them and stand forth in naked and simple beauty."

— Galileo Galilei, *Discourses Concerning Two New Sciences*

9.1 Static Analysis

You'd like to know more about the program you're working on. But it's so long and boring that reading it all is likely to cause premature senility. Fortunately there are some tools that can help you get a handle on your morass of Perl source code.

If you're looking for an interactive development environment (IDE) for Perl, the bad news is that there aren't many; not nearly as many as for languages like Java and C++. One very good reason for this is that static analysis of Perl is rather unsatisfying if you're an IDE developer because so much of the environment of a Perl program is not determined until run time (late binding). Considering that Perl programs can not only create subroutines at run time, but import new classes and even modify the inheritance hierarchy while they are running, it's not surprising that IDE developers don't find Perl attractive. A class browser would have to be capable of updating itself at run time in order to be reliably accurate, and that implies a positively incestuous relationship between the IDE and the Perl run-time system. Most Perl IDEs consist of bundling a syntax highlighting editor, an interface to the Perl debugger, and perhaps a browser for Perl documentation. Getting really good at an editor like *vi* or *emacs* that can let you switch between multiple buffers and shell command modes quickly is what you'll find most of the top developers doing.

The good news is that large projects can be developed in Perl without the need for an IDE, as long as the programmers agree to use the same layout style and code to a particular level of sophistication (see Section 4.2.2). If you want an IDE, there are a number of free ones and a very capable commercial tool called *Visual Perl* from ActiveState Corporation (see Figure 9.1).

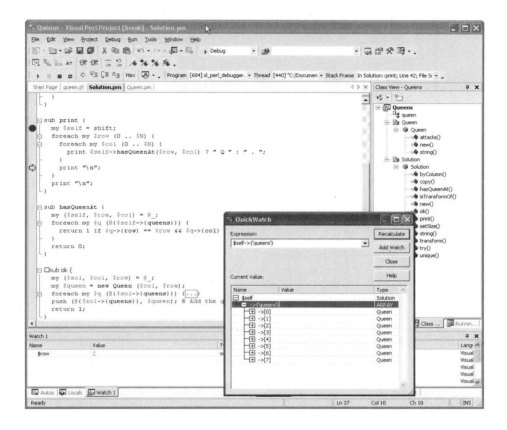

FIGURE 9.1 ActiveState's Visual Perl IDE.

Now I'll list some of the modules that can help tell you things about a program you're trying to analyze.

9.1.1 YAPE::Regex::Explain

Jeff Pinyan wrote this module, which provides plain English explanations of regular expressions. If you've got some legacy code that employs regexes beyond your current comprehension, YAPE::Regex::Explain can give you a useful head start on understanding them, by feeding them to its `explain()` method. Here's an example:

```
% perl -Mstrict -Mwarnings
use YAPE::Regex::Explain;
my $regex = qr/\G([\w-]+).+?\b/;
my $xplnr = YAPE::Regex::Explain->new($regex);
print $xplnr->explain;
^D
The regular expression:

(?-imsx:\G([\w-]+).+?\b)

matches as follows:

NODE                    EXPLANATION
----------------------------------------------------------------
(?-imsx:                group, but do not capture (case-sensitive)
                        (with ^ and $ matching normally) (with . not
                        matching \n) (matching whitespace and #
                        normally):
----------------------------------------------------------------
  \G                    where the last m//g left off
----------------------------------------------------------------
  (                     group and capture to \1:
----------------------------------------------------------------
    [\w-]+              any character of: word characters (a-z,
                       A-Z, 0-9, _), '-' (1 or more times
                       (matching the most amount possible))
----------------------------------------------------------------
  )                     end of \1
----------------------------------------------------------------
  .+?                   any character except \n (1 or more times
                       (matching the least amount possible))
----------------------------------------------------------------
  \b                    the boundary between a word char (\w) and
                       something that is not a word char
----------------------------------------------------------------
)                       end of grouping
----------------------------------------------------------------
```

Note that we need to feed a regex object or a string to the `new()` method, but either way, if we need to specify regex modifiers, they have to be embedded in the regex using the `(?:xxx-xxx)` notation. This leads to a somewhat esoteric discussion (level 7) that you only need heed if you're really interested in how to explain modifiers. Suppose the regex in the original code appears as follows:

```
while ($line =~ /\G([\w-]+).+?\b/csig)
```

then to get YAPE::Regex::Explain to explain the modifiers, they have to be embedded like this:

```
my $regex = qr/(?si:\G([\w-]+).+?\b)/;
```

Why did I leave the `c` and `g` modifiers out? Because they only affect the operation of the `m///` operator and are not part of the regular expression itself. See *perlre* for more information on `(?:xxx-xxx)`, *perlop* for more information on `m///`, and especially [FRIEDL02] for the definitive treatment of regular expressions.

9.1.2 Benchmark::Timer

This module by Andrew Ho is like a stopwatch for your program. You can time the duration of specific sections of code and get a report on how much time your program spent in them and how many times it executed them. You label each section with a unique tag in a call to the `start()` method, and then call the `stop()` method when the code you're measuring is done. Multiple sections of code (or the same section of code executed multiple times) can receive the same label and therefore be lumped together. Here's an example program that performs some relatively time-consuming operations (sending GET and HEAD requests for a web page):

Example 9.1   Demonstration of Benchmark::Timer

```
#!/usr/bin/perl
use strict;
use warnings;
```

```
use Benchmark::Timer;
use LWP::Simple;

my $timer = Benchmark::Timer->new;

my $url = "http://www.perlmedic.com/";

$timer->start('head');
head($url);
$timer->stop();

$timer->start('get');
get($url);
$timer->stop();

$timer->start('head');
head($url);
$timer->stop();

$timer->report;
```

When we run this program, we see:

```
% ./timertest
2 trials of head (1.192s total), 596.092ms/trial
1 trial of get (177.013ms total)
```

demonstrating that for some counterintuitive reason, LWP::Simple's head() function takes longer than its get() function.

9.1.3 Benchmark::TimeTick

Here's a simple little module along similar lines that I wrote for this book. Its purpose is to output a list showing exactly how long your program took to reach each of a series of points you mark with a call to its timetick() method. Its source code is in the Appendix; here is its documentation:

NAME

Benchmark::TimeTick—Keep a tally of times at different places in your program

SYNOPSIS

```
use Benchmark::TimeTick qw(timetick);
# Your code...
timetick("Starting phase three");
# More of your code...
```

DESCRIPTION

`Benchmark::TimeTick` provides a quick and convenient way of instrumenting a program to find out how long it took to reach various points. Just use the module and call the `timetick()` method whenever you want to mark the time at a point in your program. When the program ends, a report will be output giving the times at which each point was reached.

The times will be recorded using `Time::HiRes::time()` if `Time::HiRes` is available, otherwise `time()` will be used. (Because `time()` has one-second granularity this is unlikely to be useful.)

CONFIGURATION

You can customize the action of `Benchmark::TimeTick` via the package hash `%Benchmark::TimeTick::Opt`. Recognized keys are:

suppress_initial If true, do not put an initial entry in the report when the module is loaded.

suppress_final If true, do not put a final entry in the report when the program terminates.

reset_start If true, report all times relative to the time that `Benchmark::TimeTick` was loaded rather than the actual start of the program.

format_tick_tag If set, should be a reference to a subroutine that will take as input a $tag passed to `timetick()` and return the actual tag to be used. Can be helpful for applying a lengthy transformation to every tag while keeping the calling code short.

format_report If set, should be a reference to a subroutine that will take as input a list of time ticks for reporting. Each list element will be a reference to an array containing the time and the tag, respectively. The default **format_report** callback is:

```
sub { printf("%7.4f %s\n", @$_) for @_ }
```

suppress_report If true, do not output a report when `report()` is called; just reset the time tick list instead.

For either **suppress_initial** or **reset_start** to be effective, they must be set in `BEGIN` blocks before this module is used.

METHODS

Benchmark::TimeTick::timetick($tag) Record the time at this point of the program and label it with the string $tag.

Benchmark::TimeTick::report() Output a report (unless **suppress_report** is set) and reset the time tick list.

Benchmark::TimeTick::end() Add a final time tick (unless **suppress_final** is set), and output a report. Called by default when the program finishes.

OPTIONAL EXPORTS

`Benchmark::TimeTick::timetick()` will be exported on demand. This is recommended for the sake of brevity.

EXAMPLE

```
BEGIN { $Benchmark::TimeTick::Opt{suppress_initial} = 1 }
use Benchmark::TimeTick qw(timetick);
# ... time passes
timetick("Phase 2");
# ... more time passes, program ends
```

Output from `Benchmark::Timetick`:

```
0.7524 Phase 2
0.8328 Timeticker for testprog finishing
```

9.1.4 Debug::FaultAutoBT

Stas Bekman wrote this module, which intercepts signals that would otherwise cause a core dump, and attempts to extract and dump a *gdb* backtrace instead. Use this if you are trying to debug some XS code.

9.1.5 Devel::LeakTrace

This module by Richard Clamp requires Perl 5.6.0 or later, and will report on any storage allocated after the program started but not freed by the time the program went through its END blocks. If it finds any they are probably due to cyclic references, in which case the cure is Tuomas J. Lukka's WeakRef module (`http://search.cpan.org/dist/WeakRef/`).

9.1.6 Module::Info

Mattia Barbon maintains this module created by Michael Schwern; it scans the source of a module to provide information about it. Some of that information may not be completely reliable, just because of how infernally difficult it is to parse Perl. It can tell you things like the list of `package` declarations in the module, the subroutines defined in it, and the subroutines called by it.

9.1.7 Class::Inspector

Adam Kennedy wrote this module that provides convenience methods for reflective functions about loaded modules: source filename, subroutines, and methods.

9.1.8 B::Xref

This module by Malcolm Beattie was added to the Perl core in version 5.005. It will generate a report that can help you track where variables and subroutines are defined and referenced. Because it's a compiler back end like B::Deparse, it doesn't actually run your code. Invoke it via the O front end:

```
% perl -MO=Xref program arguments...
```

and what will appear is the report, showing variables and subroutines and the lines they appeared on, broken down by file.

9.2 Eliminating Superfluous Code

When you're faced with a mountain of code dripping all over your editor, you might want all the help you can get telling whether it's all used. It's not uncommon for people to write code that might have been used to begin with, but eventually became superfluous. So here are some ways of spotting unused code en masse.

9.2.1 Devel::Coverage

Randy J. Ray's Devel::Coverage is a module for code coverage analysis; reporting the lines of code that are visited during execution of a program. The module hasn't been changed in a while, but it still works with the current development version of Perl 5.9.0 as of the time of writing.

Devel::Coverage is a debugger plug-in, which means that it is invoked by enabling Perl's run time debugger hooks, which fire on each statement about to be executed, among other things. The interactive command-line debugger that comes with perl is itself a debugger plug-in. Devel::Coverage, however, generates a data file in response to those hook calls. That data file is not intended to be human-readable; you should run it through the program *coverperl* that comes with Devel::Coverage.

You use Devel::Coverage by invoking it on the command line as an argument to the -d flag:

```
% perl -d:Coverage program arguments...
```

The program will run, and the coverage file *program*.cvp will be created. The following is a fragment of output from *coverperl* for a module called Solution.pm:

```
12   Solution::print
         12    line 37
         12    line 38
         96    line 39
        768    line 40
         96    line 42
         12    line 44
0    Solution::setSize
          0    line 107
          0    line 108
          0    line 109
          0    line 112
7522 Solution::string
       7522 line 94
      75220 line 95
3761 Solution::transform
       3761 line 99
       3761 line 100
      37610 line 101
       3761 line 102
       3761 line 103
```

There is a line printed for every subroutine and every executable line; the first token on each line is the number of times that subroutine or line was executed. We can see here that the `setSize()` function has not been exercised at all in this test.

9.2.2 Devel::Cover

Paul Johnson's Devel::Cover module (`http://search.cpan.org/dist/Devel-Cover/`) is a more modern module with many more options than Devel::Coverage, but is still, according to its documentation, in its infancy.

Devel::Cover comes with a program, *cover,* that generates a database. The range of options is too great to go into here, but you can generate a coverage report at the granularity of lines by running

```
% perl -d:Cover=-coverage,statement program arguments...
```

and then generating a readable report from the database created in the default directory `cover_db` by running the program *cover* that comes with Devel::Coverage:

```
% cover -report text
```

9.3 Finding Inefficient Code

When an application is taking too long to run, one cure starts with finding out how long each part takes to run. Knowing where to expend your optimization efforts is key; if you happen to pick a piece of code that only consumes 1 percent of the total run time, then no matter how efficient you make it you cannot achieve more than a 1 percent increase in speed (roughly 1.01 percent, for the pedants). Optimizing a piece that consumes 90 percent of the run time can lead to a speed-up of up to a factor of 10. However, you should not rely on being able to determine by inspection alone which piece of code is which. People are notorious for being wrong in such assessments and the only thing that separates the experts from the neophytes is that the experts know that they shouldn't trust their guesses. What they use instead is a profiling tool, and there are two available for Perl: Devel::DProf and Devel::SmallProf. Be aware that both of these modules unavoidably introduce inaccuracies into the times they report. Because they involve running additional code for every subroutine or statement that Perl executes (and because both invoke Perl's internal debugging hooks), profiled programs will take longer to execute than their unaltered forms.

9.3.1 Devel::DProf

Devel::DProf is included in the Perl core; its purpose is to show you the execution profile at the level of subroutines. This means that it will show you the number of times those subroutines are called and the time spent executing them. Like Devel::Coverage and Devel::Cover, it is invoked as a debugger plug-in:

```
% perl -d:DProf program arguments...
```

It will log timing information to a file tmon.out that can rapidly get extremely large for even a moderately complicated run; monitor the size of the file from another window and terminate the run when you don't like how large it's become. The filename can be changed by setting the environment variable PERL_DPROF_OUT_FILE_NAME.

The tmon.out file is not for human consumption and you need to run the program *dprofpp* to generate a report. As with any Perl program that's installed with perl, you can use *perldoc* to view its documentation.

dprofpp will give good output without any arguments; you can give it several options to change its default behavior. By default it shows only the time spent inside the lexical scope of each subroutine, not the cumulative time spent in that subroutine and all subroutines called from it; but that's what you want anyway.

Regrettably there is no way to pipe the DProf output into *dprofpp* and avoid creating tmon.out, because DProf `seek()`s to near the beginning of the file periodically.

9.3.2 Devel::SmallProf

Ted Ashton's Devel::SmallProf is being maintained by Salvador Fandiño and is available from CPAN (`http://search.cpan.org/dist/Devel-SmallProf`). Its purpose is similar to Devel::DProf, but it can show results at the finer granularity of execution lines (hence, "small"). Ensuring that you have at most one statement per line will maximize the benefit of using this module, so make sure you have deobfuscated and beautified the code first.

Devel::SmallProf generates a file called smallprof.out. It is not possible to cause the output to go elsewhere, but unlike Devel::DProf, the size of that file is not dependent on the length of run time but instead on the amount of source code, because what it contains is all the source code, annotated with the number of times each line was called and how much wall clock time and CPU time was spent executing it.

The smallprof.out file is ordered by source code line number, which isn't terribly helpful; the point of profiling is to find out what code is taking the longest to run. The commands for sorting the file given in the Devel::Small-Prof documentation aren't as helpful as one would like, because smallprof.out contains page headers that clutter the output, and the filenames get separated from the source code lines when sorted.

I therefore wrote a program that will sort either by CPU or wall clock time, and output the filename of the source as well. (The truncated line of original source code that was at the end of each smallprof.out line had to be removed to make room for the filename.) It's called *smallprofpp* and you'll find it in the Appendix.

Here is an example of the first few lines of output from that program, sorted by wall clock time:

```
% ./smallprofpp | head -5
   count wall tm  cpu time line
    1140 0.999952 0.150000 /usr/lib/perl5/5.6.1/Exporter.pm:57
     545 0.999952 0.050000 substr2:36
       1 0.999952 0.000000 /usr/lib/perl5/site_perl/5.6.1/LWP/Simple.pm:319
       1 0.238549 0.000000 substr2:9
```

and here by CPU time:

```
% ./smallprofpp -c | head -5
   count wall tm  cpu time line
     727 0.000000 0.360000 substr2:33
    1140 0.999952 0.150000 /usr/lib/perl5/5.6.1/Exporter.pm:57
     247 0.000000 0.110000 substr2:43
     397 0.000000 0.090000 /usr/lib/perl5/5.6.1/Exporter.pm:55
```

Note that there is a significant difference between the lines that took the most wall clock time and the ones that took the most cpu time. Generally, you should investigate the highest CPU time consumers first when seeking to improve performance; the excess of wall clock time over CPU time may be due to I/O or other processes getting attention. Improving time spent doing I/O is a very tricky activity, and even determining whether I/O is the reason for the delay is problematic.

9.3.3 Optimization Tips

If your efforts to improve the speed of a Perl program aren't approaching the target, there are a number of strategies that may get you unstuck:

- Rewrite parts of it in another language. Having identified a section of code that's taking a large proportion of execution time, if it is small enough, consider rewriting it in, say, C. Note that if the code is just performing text manipulation this might not improve the running speed because Perl works like a Complex Instruction Set Computer (CISC); its operators are implemented by highly optimized compiled C code. You can most easily include your C code by using Brian Ingerson's Inline::C (http://search.cpan .org/dist/Inline/).

- Rewrite all of it in another language. Some applications are just better off that way. I would not write a windowing system in Perl, for instance, nor a guidance system for a cruise missile. If it has to run as fast as possible, C is a better bet. Beware that many people will say "it has to run as fast as possible" when that isn't really the case, however. They usually have a standard in mind and if you can meet it with Perl, they'll be happy even if you could have shaved some time off using another language.

- Improve the algorithms. Algorithms are an often-neglected but critical component of the education of any programmer. The right algorithm can make the difference between a program finishing in less than a second or exceeding the lifetime of the universe. See [AHO74], [AHO83], [BENTLEY82], and [ORWANT99] for a start.

9.4 Debugging

Debugging is just an extreme case of dynamic analysis. Third-party code can be extremely convoluted (so can your own code, of course, but you don't usually think of it that way because you're familiar with it; you knew it when it was just a subroutine); sometimes you just can't tell how part of the code fits in, or whether it's called at all. The code is laid out in some arrangement that makes no sense; if only you could see where the program would actually go when it was run.

Well, you can, using Perl's built-in debugger. Even though you're not actually trying to find a bug, the code-tracing ability of the debugger is perfect for the job.

This isn't the place for a full treatment of the debugger (you can see more detail in [SCOTT01]), but fortunately you don't need a full treatment; a subset of the commands is enough for what you need to do. (Using the debugger is like getting in a fight; it's usually over very quickly without using many of the fancy moves you trained for.)

You invoke the debugger with the -d command-line flag; either edit the program to add -d to the shebang line, or run the program by invoking Perl explicitly:

```
% perl -d program argument argument...
```

Make sure that the perl in your path is the same one in the shebang line of *program* or you'll go crazy if there are differences between the two perls.

The commands in Table 9-1 will account for nearly all of your use of the debugger:

TABLE 9-1 **Basic Debugger Commands**

Command	Description
h / h h	Brief / verbose help (verbose / brief help prior to 5.8.0)
b *subroutine*	Set breakpoint at first executable statement of *subroutine*
b *line*	Set breakpoint for line *line*
b *place condition*	Set breakpoint for *place* (either *line* or *subroutine*) but trigger it only when the Perl expression *condition* is true
c	Continue until end of program or breakpoint
c *line*	Continue until line *line*, end of program, or earlier breakpoint
x *expression*	Examine the value of a variable or expression
n	Execute current statement, skipping over any subroutines called from it
s	Execute next Perl statement, going into a subroutine called from the current statement if necessary
l	List source code from current line
r	Execute statements until return from current subroutine, end of program, or earlier breakpoint
T	Display stack trace
q	Quit

Armed with these commands, we can go code spelunking. Suppose you are debugging a program containing the following code fragment:

```
77 for my $url (@url_queue)
78 {
79   my $res = $ua->request($url);
80   summarize($res->content);
81 }
```

and you know that whenever the program gets to the URL `http://www.perlmedic.com/fnord.html` something strange happens in the `summarize()` subroutine. You'd like to check the HTTP::Response object to see if there were any redirects you didn't know about. You start the program under the debugger and type:

```
DB<1> b 80 $url =~ /fnord/
DB<2> c
```

The program will run until it has fetched the URL you're interested in, at which point you can examine the response object—here's an example of what it might look like:

```
DB<3> x $res
0   HTTP::Response=HASH(0x70f340)
    '_content' => '\cF\cN\cO\cR\cD'
    '_headers' => HTTP::Headers=HASH(0x70f790)
      'cache-control' => 'private,max-age=60'
      'client-date' => 'Tue, 01 Jul 2003 01:21:55 GMT'
      'client-peer' => '204.95.83.7:80'
      'client-response-num' => 1
      'connection' => 'close'
      'content-type' => ARRAY(0x23f470)
         0   'text/html'
         1   'text/html; charset=iso-8859-1'
      'date' => 'Tue, 01 Jul 2003 01:21:54 GMT'
      'expires' => 'Tue, 01 Jul 2003 01:22:54 GMT'
      'last-modified' => 'Tue, 01 Jul 2003 01:21:54 GMT'
      'refresh' => 1800
      'server' => 'Apache/1.3.27 (UNIX)'
      'title' => 'This page intentionally left blank'
    '_msg' => 'OK... sort of...'
    '_previous' => HTTP::Response=HASH(0x6af660)
      '_content' => ''
      '_headers' => HTTP::Headers=HASH(0x6af66c)
```

```
        'client-date' => 'Tue, 01 Jul 2003 01:21:49 GMT'
        'client-peer' => '204.95.83.7:80'
        'client-response-num' => 1
        'connection' => 'close'
        'content-length' => 0
        'content-type' => 'text/html'
        'date' => 'Tue, 01 Jul 2003 01:21:48 GMT'
        'location' => 'http://www.perlmedic.com/fnord/'
        'server' => 'Apache/1.3.27 (UNIX)'
      '_msg' => 'Moved Temporarily'
      '_protocol' => 'HTTP/1.1'
      '_rc' => 302
      '_request' => HTTP::Request=HASH(0x4a60d0)
          '_content' => ''
          '_headers' => HTTP::Headers=HASH(0x4a60a0)
            'user-agent' => 'libwww-perl/5.69'
          '_method' => 'GET'
          '_uri' => URI::http=SCALAR(0x27e668)
            -> 'http://www.perlmedic.com/fnord.html'
  '_protocol' => 'HTTP/1.1'
  '_rc' => 299
  '_request' => HTTP::Request=HASH(0x623e40)
      '_content' => ''
      '_headers' => HTTP::Headers=HASH(0x68e6f4)
        'user-agent' => 'libwww-perl/5.69'
      '_method' => 'GET'
      '_uri' => URI::http=SCALAR(0x6e55e8)
        -> 'http://www.perlmedic.com/fnord/'
```

You can see from this that there was indeed a redirect, and find out exactly what was returned. (You can gain a fine control over this procedure for web page fetching with the LWP::Debug module, but the approach I have illustrated will work for any type of object.) Then you can see what happens to the content in summarize() by stepping into the routine:

```
DB<4> s
main::summarize(/home/peter/bin/url_summarizer):177:
    my $content = shift;
```

Find out more about how to use the debugger in *perldebtut, perldebug,* or [SCOTT01].

There are a few special tricks you can use to enhance your use of the debugger. For instance, suppose you're getting a warning, but it's emerging from deep in code that you didn't write and you can't tell where; you'd like the debugger to breakpoint at that place so you can display a stack trace and find out how you got there.

Perl 5.8.0 and later will give you a stack trace anyway if you run a program under the debugger and some code triggers a warning. But suppose you are either running under an earlier perl, or you'd really like to have a debugger prompt at the point the warning was about to happen.

You can combine two advanced features of Perl to do this: *pseudo-signal handlers,* and *programmatic debugger control.*

A signal handler is a subroutine you can tell Perl to execute whenever your program receives a signal. For instance, when the user interrupts your program by pressing Control-C, that works by sending an INT signal to your program, which interprets it by default as an instruction to stop executing.

There are two pseudo-signals, called __WARN__ and __DIE__. They aren't real signals, but Perl "generates" them whenever it's told to issue a warning or to die, respectively. You can supply code to be run in those events by inserting a subroutine reference in the %SIG hash (see *perlvar*) as follows:

```
$SIG{__WARN__} = sub { print "Ouch, I'm bad" };
```

(Try it on some code that generates a warning.)

The next piece of the solution is that the debugger can be controlled from within your program; the variable $single in the special package DB determines what Perl does at each statement: 0 means keep going, and 1 or 2 mean give a user prompt.[1] So setting $DB::single to 1 in a pseudo-signal handler will give us a debugger prompt at just the point we wanted.

---

1. The difference between the two values is that a 1 causes the debugger to act as though the last n or s command the user typed was s, whereas a 2 is equivalent to an n. When you type an empty command in the debugger (just hit Return), it repeats whatever the last n or s command was.

Putting the pieces together, you can start running the program under the debugger and give the commands:

```
DB<1> $SIG{__WARN__} = sub { warn @_; $DB::single = 1 }
DB<2> c
```

Now the program will breakpoint where it was about to issue a warning, and you can issue a T command to see a stack trace, examine data, or do anything else you want.[2] The warning is still printed first.

Unfortunately, no __DIE__ pseudo-signal handler will return control to the debugger (evidently death is considered too pressing an engagement to be interrupted). However, you can get a stack trace by calling the confess() function in the Carp module:

```
DB<1> use Carp
DB<2> $SIG{__DIE__} = sub { confess (@_) }
```

The output will look something like this:

```
DB<3> c
Insufficient privilege to launch preemptive strike at wargames line
109.
        main::__ANON__[(eval 17)[/usr/lib/perl5/5.6.1/
perl5db.pl:1521]:2]('Insufficient privilege to launch preemptive
strike at wargames line 109.^J') called at wargames line 121
        main::preemptive('Strike=HASH(0x82069d4)') called at wargames
line 109
        main::make_strike('ICBM=HASH(0x820692c)') called at wargames
line 74
        main::icbm('Silo_ND') called at wargames line 32
        main::wmd('ICBM') called at wargames line 22
        main::strike() called at wargames line 11
        main::menu() called at wargames line 5
Debugged program terminated.  Use q to quit or R to restart,
  use O inhibit_exit to avoid stopping after program termination,
  h q, h R or h O to get additional info.
```

---

2. Under some circumstances, the breakpoint might not occur at the actual place of warning: The current routine might return if the statement triggering the warning is the last one being executed in that routine.

I've often found it amusing that the debugger refers to the program at this point as "debugged."

9.4.1 Debugging Regular Expressions

Not for the fainthearted, if you want to see how a regular expression runs when used in a match or substitution, use the core re pragma with its debug option:

```
% perl -Mstrict -Mwarnings
use re qw(debug);
$_ = "cats=purr, dog=bark";
my %sound = /(\w+)=(\w+)/g;
^D
Compiling REx `(\w+)=(\w+)'
size 15 first at 4
   1: OPEN1(3)
   3:    PLUS(5)
   4:       ALNUM(0)
   5: CLOSE1(7)
   7: EXACT <=>(9)
   9: OPEN2(11)
  11:    PLUS(13)
  12:       ALNUM(0)
  13: CLOSE2(15)
  15: END(0)
floating `=' at 1..2147483647 (checking floating) stclass `ALNUM' plus
minlen 3
Guessing start of match, REx `(\w+)=(\w+)' against `cats=purr,
dog=bark'...
Found floating substr `=' at offset 4...
Does not contradict STCLASS...
Guessed: match at offset 0
Matching REx `(\w+)=(\w+)' against `cats=purr, dog=bark'
  Setting an EVAL scope, savestack=3
   0 <> <cats=purr, d>    |   1:  OPEN1
   0 <> <cats=purr, d>    |   3:  PLUS
                             ALNUM can match 4 times out of 32767...
  Setting an EVAL scope, savestack=3
   4 <cats> <=purr, d>    |   5:    CLOSE1
   4 <cats> <=purr, d>    |   7:    EXACT <=>
   5 <cats=> <purr, d>    |   9:    OPEN2
   5 <cats=> <purr, d>    |  11:    PLUS
```

```
                          ALNUM can match 4 times out of 32767...
  Setting an EVAL scope, savestack=3
   9 <=purr> <, dog=b>     | 13:       CLOSE2
   9 <=purr> <, dog=b>     | 15:       END
Match successful!
Guessing start of match, REx `(\w+)=(\w+)' against `, dog=bark'...
Found floating substr `=' at offset 5...
By STCLASS: moving 0 --> 2
Guessed: match at offset 2
Matching REx `(\w+)=(\w+)' against `dog=bark'
  Setting an EVAL scope, savestack=3
  11 <urr, > <dog=bar>     | 1:        OPEN1
  11 <urr, > <dog=bar>     | 3:        PLUS
                          ALNUM can match 3 times out of 32767...
  Setting an EVAL scope, savestack=3
  14 <rr, dog> <=bark>     | 5:        CLOSE1
  14 <rr, dog> <=bark>     | 7:        EXACT <=>
  15 <rr, dog=> <bark>     | 9:        OPEN2
  15 <rr, dog=> <bark>     | 11:       PLUS
                          ALNUM can match 4 times out of 32767...
  Setting an EVAL scope, savestack=3
  19 <rr, dog=bark> <>     | 13:       CLOSE2
  19 <rr, dog=bark> <>     | 15:       END
Match successful!
Freeing REx: `(\w+)=(\w+)'
```

If you use the `debugcolor` option instead of `debug`, you'll get some form of highlighting or coloring in the output that'll make it prettier, if not more understandable.

Chapter 10

Increasing Maintainability (Prophylaxis)

Tara King, on seeing Steed playing with a toy airplane: "Aren't you a little old for that sort of thing?" Steed: "It's a present for my nephew's tenth birthday." Tara: "When's that?" Steed: "Three years ago. The instructions are very hard to follow."

— Patrick Macnee and Linda Thorson in *The Avengers*

Having taken charge of a program and made it your own, the last thing you want is for it to turn into the same kind of albatross that you got saddled with in the first place. So it falls to you to make it as maintainable as you can.

10.1 Making It Robust

The more robust a program is, the less likely it is to attract attention to itself and invite maintenance. Here are some modules that can help with that task.

10.1.1 Params::Validate

People who have programmed in other procedural languages like C, Java, and Pascal often wonder where the real subroutine prototypes are in Perl. They have this nagging feeling that subroutines just aren't safe until all their arguments have been validated just as strictly as those other languages do. Params::Validate does exactly what they want, and a lot more.[1]

If you're going to get strict about subroutine parameter checking, you might as well name your parameters. This is a good practice anyway whenever you create a subroutine that takes (or can take) more than about three arguments (that's the point at which I get the itch to stop using positional parameters).

Say you're writing a subroutine to search text for repeated phrases. You might want to specify options such as what to do with line breaks, whether capitalization matters, or what punctuation characters to ignore. Calling this subroutine with positional parameters:

```
@phrases = repeated_phrases($text, 0, 1, [qw(" ' ; , !)]);
```

is just going to be confusing, and using symbolic constants:

---

1. Albeit at run time, not compile time. Sorry. Perl 6 will have complete compile-time parameter checking.

```
@phrases = repeated_phrases($text,
                            IGNORE_LINE_BREAKS,
                            RESPECT_CAPITALIZATION,
                            [qw(" ' ; , !)]);
```

is not much better: You won't be told if you got the parameter order wrong, and you have to look it up each time you want to use the subroutine. Instead, write the subroutine to expect a hash of options, so you can call it like this:

```
@phrases = repeated_phrases($text, capitalization => 1,
                            ignore_punc => [qw(" ' ; , !)]);
```

Just a moment—what happened to the specification for line breaks? We no longer need it, because ignoring them is a sensible thing to do by default, and so we say so in the documentation for `repeated_phrases()`. Because ignoring is the default, we just made the parameter name `capitalization` instead of `respect_capitalization`. Now we no longer need to remember the order in which these parameters must be specified, either.

The next step up the evolutionary chain from named parameters is Params::Validate, by Dave Rolsky, and a giant step it is. The subroutine writer calls the `validate()` function (exported by Params::Validate) at or near the beginning of a subroutine, and passes the subroutine parameters along with a template specifying what arguments are valid.

By default `validate()` will throw an exception when the subroutine is called with a parameter that isn't specified in the template, but you can make parameters optional and specify defaults. The result of a successful call to `validate()` is the hash of parameter names and values that was input. You have complete control over what sort of validation is done; the standard options allow you to permit additional parameters or allow case-insensitive parameters or parameters with leading minus signs. Here's how to use Params::Validate on the `repeated_phrases()` subroutine:

```
use Params::Validate qw(:all);

my $text = join "", <>;
```

```
my @phrases = repeated_phrases(text            => $text,
                               capitalization => 1,
                               ignore_punc  => [qw(" ' ; , !)]
                               );

sub repeated_phrases
{
  my %param = validate(@_, {
        text           => { type => SCALAR },
        capitalization => { type => SCALAR, optional   => 1 },
        ignore_punc    => { type => ARRAYREF, optional => 1 },
        line_breaks    => { type => SCALAR, optional   => 1 }
                            });
  # ... Go on to look for repeated phrases, secure in the
  # knowledge that our parameter list is squeaky clean
}
```

Params::Validate can also validate positional parameters, via the exported `validate_pos()` function. You can deal with partially positional and partially named argument lists if you're clever enough to shift off the positional ones first. A simple case of this is an object or class method call; first you have to shift off the object or class before you can call `validate()` on the rest of `@_`.

There is far more that Params::Validate can do. See the module's documentation for full details.

10.1.2 Carp::Assert

A kissing cousin of Params::Validate is Carp::Assert, which enables you to make general assertions about the state of your program. (Okay, make that a kissing cousin twice removed . . . but they are still related.) Assertions are a venerable feature of "grown-up" languages and are like training wheels; you enable them for development, but turn them off in production environments where speed is an issue.

An assertion will cause an exception if a given condition is false. If you ever wrote something like:

```
die "This shouldn't happen!!!" if ...
```

then it would be more recognizable as an assertion. Carp::Assert gives you several ways of doing that:

```
use Carp::Assert;

sub yes_we_have_no_bananas
{
  my $bananas = shift;
  assert($bananas == 0) if DEBUG;
  print "Yes, we have no bananas\n";
}
```

Carp::Assert doesn't print "This shouldn't happen!!!" though. (Assertions are too staid for that sort of language.) Instead it prints "Assertion failed!" and a stack trace. If you'd like it to print out a message of your own, you can give a second argument:

```
assert($bananas == 0, "We DO have bananas!") if DEBUG;
```

and then the first line of an exception is "Assertion (We DO have bananas!) failed!"

What's the `if DEBUG` for? That's for improving performance when you want to disable that assertion and all the others in your code easily. Carp::Assert exports a constant, DEBUG, set to a true value. If you are satisfied that you have expunged from your code all the bugs that could fire an assertion, and you want it to be as efficient as possible in production, then you don't want Perl to spend time compiling and executing assertions.

You can prevent Perl from executing assertions by changing one word: instead of use Carp::Assert, you say no Carp::Assert. Now the assert() function becomes a function that returns immediately without doing anything. But that's still a subroutine call; if you're serious about performance you don't want even that. The purpose of saying if DEBUG is that Perl will not compile code that it can tell at compile time will never be executed, and because constants like DEBUG are defined at compile time, if DEBUG is false, then Perl won't compile the assert() statement.

Obviously, assert() is simply syntactic sugar for code that raises an exception if some condition is false. You could get the same effect with

```
use Carp;
use constant DEBUG => 1;
# ...
if (DEBUG)
{
  confess "We DO have bananas!" unless $bananas == 0;
}
```

but the verbosity of that construction is far more intrusive, and you want assertions to be as lightweight as possible.

10.1.3 Class::Contract

Damian Conway's Class::Contract (http://search.cpan.org/dist/Class-Contract/), now maintained by C. Garrett Goebel, implements the Design by Contract approach that originated in the Eiffel world [EIFFEL03]. Successfully using this approach requires high degrees of expertise in designing and discipline in implementing object classes; the payoff is a sturdy safety net.

Design by Contract is like assertions that have been pumped full of object-oriented steroids. It says that:

• Every method in the class shall define at least one *precondition,* which is a test of conditions that the method requires to be satisfied in order to do its job. Class::Contract will take care of running the precondition test every time the method is invoked before it actually does anything, and if the test fails, an exception will be thrown.

- Every method in the class shall define at least one *postcondition,* which is a test of what the method is supposed to guarantee to its caller. Class::Contract will take care of running the precondition test every time the method is invoked just before it returns to its caller, and if the test fails, an exception will be thrown.

- The class shall specify a global test or *invariant,* which is another test that will be run at the end of each method call and that tests that the method has not violated the integrity of the class.

As you might be able to tell, coming up with proper conditions might require considerable expertise. Class::Contract provides these capabilities and many more (e.g., conditions associated with object attributes); to do this, Conway virtually reimplemented large parts of Perl's object-oriented system (e.g., inheritance). In Class::Contract, you specify methods, attributes, and inheritance differently from the native Perl way; you use Class::Contract's own language for doing so. Here's a working, if extremely naive, example to show you what that language looks like:[2]

Example 10.1 BankAccount.pm Example for Class::Contract

```perl
package BankAccount;
use strict;
use warnings;
use Class::Contract qw(old);

my $INIT_RESERVES = 10_000;  # Bailey Building & Loan

contract
{
  class attr 'reserves' => 'SCALAR';
  class ctor;
    impl { ${self->reserves} = $INIT_RESERVES };
  class method 'adjust_reserves';
    pre  { defined $_[0] };
      failmsg "No amount to adjust reserves by given";
    impl { ${self->reserves} += $_[0] };
```

---

2. Class::Contract is best for very large applications that won't fit in this book.

```
    invar { ${self->reserves} >= 0 };
        failmsg "We gone bankrupt, Maw!";
    ctor 'new';
        impl { ${self->balance} = $_[0] };
    attr balance => 'SCALAR';
    method 'get_balance';
        impl { ${self->balance} };
    method 'loan';
        pre  { defined $_[0] };
        impl { ${self->balance} += $_[0];
               self->adjust_reserves(-$_[0])
             };
        post { ${self->balance} == ${old->balance} + $_[0] };
    method 'invest';
        pre  { defined $_[0] };
        impl { ${self->balance} -= $_[0];
               self->adjust_reserves($_[0])
             };
        post { ${self->balance} == ${old->balance} - $_[0] };
};

1;
```

Example 10.2 Test Suite for BankAccount.pm Example for Class::Contract

```
#!/usr/bin/perl
use strict;
use warnings;
use BankAccount;

use Test::More tests => 7;
use Test::Exception;

BEGIN { use_ok('BankAccount') }
my $acct = BankAccount->new(1000);
is($acct->get_balance, 1000);
lives_ok { $acct->loan(5000) };
is($acct->get_balance, 6000);
dies_ok { $acct->loan };
dies_ok { $acct->invest };
throws_ok { $acct->loan(1E8) } qr/bankrupt/;
```

The kind of verbosity that Class::Contract results in might not be for everyone, but if you're writing that legendary air traffic control application in Perl, you'll want this kind of industrial-strength help.

10.1.4 Log::Log4perl

Michael Schilli's Log::Log4perl (`http://search.cpan.org/dist/Log-Log4perl/`) provides logging to multiple destinations from multiple places in a class hierarchy. Use this when you have an application that is highly object-oriented. You may have a primitive database class, for instance, for which you enable logging of its connections, and as you create subclasses that, say, know about SQL or transactions, you want to log the SQL or transaction errors, respectively.

Imagine an application using the fairly adventurous class hierarchy shown in Figure 10.1.

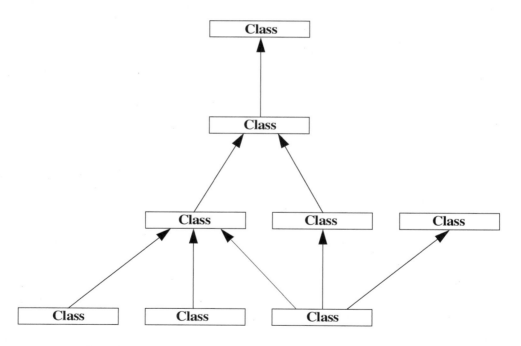

FIGURE 10.1 Log::Log4perl dispatch example class hierarchy.

Now suppose that an object in one of the leaf classes generates a logging message. Log::Log4perl allows you to attach zero or more *appenders* to each class; an appender is an object that is told to send log messages to a particular destination, such as a file or an e-mail recipient. Each appender is also configured to fire at a particular *severity level,* one of a series such as: DEBUG, INFO, WARNING, ERROR, FATAL. So if we had attached appenders at the leaf class and its ancestors, the message would percolate up through the class hierarchy of Log::Log4perl appenders, but only activating those appenders that were registered for the severity level of that message (or a lower level).

The activated appenders are denoted in bold in Figure 10.2.

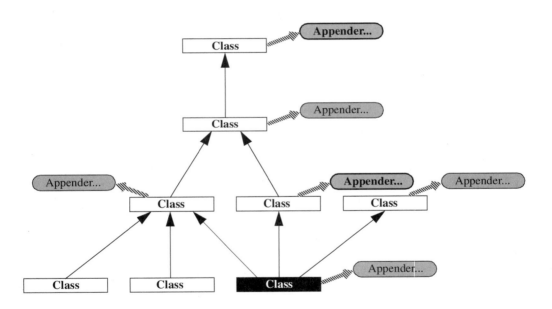

FIGURE 10.2 Log::Log4perl dispatch example appender firing.

10.1.5 Safe.pm

Taint checking for CGI programs or other programs that operate on possibly malicious user input can go only so far. Sometimes there just isn't a useful regular expression you can use that will capture what you wanted from the user input and still be guaranteed not to result in unsafe code.

For the ultimate in code protection, Safe.pm by Malcolm Beattie and Tim Bunce (in the Perl core since version 5.004) provides an environment in which you can execute Perl code in a private sandbox. That code will only be able to read data you specifically allow it to access, only perform operations you specifically enumerate, and can't affect anything outside its sandbox except to return a result for you to use. Safe.pm is not an easy module to use, but when security is paramount it may be your best option.

10.2 Advanced Brevity

Perl provides some sophisticated forms of syntactic sugaring (ways of making certain coding constructions briefer and more intuitive). Two of these techniques are *tieing* and *overloading*.

10.2.1 Tieing

We saw an example of tieing in Section 3.3. Tieing lets you take over the normal function of a variable. On the outside, it looks like a normal scalar, array, hash, or whatever. But underneath, whenever the variable is used, code you wrote gets called instead of what you'd expect to happen.

This looks on the face of it good mainly for practical jokes (and it certainly has that potential). However, it can also be used for making code more succinct and for gaining transparency.

Succinctness comes when you realize you are implementing functionality that behaves like a variable. For instance, if you have an electronic thermometer and code for reading the thermometer's value, you could certainly implement it with traditional procedural code:

```
use Thermometer;
$temp = Thermometer->read;
```

But a thermometer behaves just like a scalar variable (albeit a read-only scalar variable; changing the reading on a thermometer does not change the temperature it measures, unless you know how to break the laws of thermodynamics). How much cooler, then (so to speak), to say:

```
tie $current_temp, 'Thermometer';
```

and then whenever you read $current_temp, it is magically updated with the current temperature.

The module Themometer.pm can accomplish that quite easily through implementing methods TIESCALAR and FETCH according to the *perltie* documentation.

The semantics of the functionality you are implementing need to map onto the natural behavior of one of Perl's variable types for this to work. Our thermometer class is not a perfect match for a scalar (because it is meaningless to attempt to write it, and therefore we have to decide whether to implement and document any such attempt as either throwing an exception or having no effect), but it's certainly close enough to be worth the effort. We can associate attributes with each tied variable when we first tie it, so we might choose to declare:

```
tie $current_temp, 'Thermometer', 'Celsius';
```

to make sure we know what units the temperature will be in when we read it. This interface is now looking much better than the procedural equivalent:

```
$current_temp = Thermometer->read_celsius;
```

or even the object-oriented equivalent:

```
$current_temp = Thermometer->new(scale => 'Celsius');
print "Temperature: ", $current_temp->read;
```

And that's just for a simple scalar. When you discover functionality that maps onto a hash, for instance, you can make seriously succinct code. The most common tied interface for a hash is a database that stores the contents of the hash and makes them persistent. I was implementing a program once that had to store a lot of entries in a hash; eventually it overtaxed the virtual memory resources of the machine I had. In a classic trade-off of memory for speed, I could have hunted down every access to the hash and replaced it with a call to a database library's `fetch()` or `store()` method. But that's more work than I like to do, and fortunately others had been equally lazy before me and encapsulated the fruits of their laziness in a series of modules for tieing hashes to databases. All I had to do was add one line:

```
use DB_File;
```

and change the declaration of the hash from:

```
my %data;
```

to:

```
tie my %data, 'DB_File', $database, ...
```

(where the . . . arguments specified the file to use as a database and related information), and I had no need to change any other code. Thereafter, every access to the hash behaved just as it did before, only it took a bit longer but didn't use up memory. Into the bargain I got persistence, meaning that I could recover the values from a previous run, enabling functionality such as checkpoint/restart. The one caveat to remember when using databases tied to hashes is not to use any hash operation that returns a list from the whole hash if the hash is very large, because that reads the list from the database into memory, thus defeating one of the purposes of tieing the hash to begin with. What this boils down to is, don't use the `keys()` or `values()` functions, nor the name of the hash itself, in a list context; use the `each()` function instead. Gaining this persistence with such a small change demonstrates the transparency afforded by tieing.

In a stunning display of extreme laziness, Damian Conway simplified the use of a rather arcane Perl feature, attributes (added in Perl 5.6.0), by writing a module Attribute::Handlers (merged into the core with Perl 5.8.0) that can be used to make an interface as simple as:

```
my $current_temp : Thermometer;
```

or:

```
my $current_temp : Thermometer('Celsius');
```

10.2.2 Overloading

When you have created an object class for which you can reasonably impute behavior that ought to happen when instances of that class undergo basic operations such as arithmetic (`+ - * /`), string (`eq " "`), or another type, you have the option of making it behave that way. This is the same kind of operator overloading that C++ has and Java doesn't.

Of course, the object class has to have semantics that are amenable to this sort of intervention. If you had a Date class, addition of two members of the class would not make sense; on the other hand subtracting one from another could reasonably be interpreted as yielding a member of a class encapsulating duration; and the overloaded addition of a Duration object and a Date object could be interpreted as yielding another Date object.

Overloading is most often used for providing transparent stringification; this allows you to implement "dwimmery" for your own objects.[3] It's quite

---

3. Dwimmery is a term thrown around by Perl people as the adjectival noun for DWIM (Do what I mean). Now you can not only program like a Perl insider, but sound like one, too.

common for people to use an object in a string context either deliberately or by accident, and what they'll see printed ordinarily is something like "Foo=HASH(0x80fbb0c)". If you have defined an object class for which some kind of textual representation is natural, and you have found yourself implementing an instance method called, say `as_text()` or `as_string()`, then you can do your users a favor and overload stringification to call that method. This is as simple as inserting:

```
use overload '""' => \&as_text;
```

in your module. An example of a module that uses this to good effect is URI.pm (see Section 6.2.1), because the most common thing to want to do with a URI object is get at the textual form of the URI it represents. For more information, see the documentation for the `overload` pragma.

Yes, you can have tied variables that are also overloaded.

10.3 Documentation

In Chapter 3, I showed how you would develop tests for a module, including its documentation. Now I'll show you how to do the documentation itself.

Wake up in the back row, there! Yes, I know I said "documentation." That might have conjured up visions of Microsoft PowerPoint presentations, filling in sections with turgid headings like "Functional Requirements" and "Normative References," and formatting signature blocks. I'm not talking about that kind of documentation. I'm talking about documentation that tells another programmer what he or she needs to know about what you have done; the kind of documentation that you want to read when you take over someone else's code. Or the kind of documentation you want to read about your own code when you come back to it a year later and for the life of you can't remember how to use the object class whose interface you thought was "intuitively obvious."

10.3.1 Invasion of the POD People

Realizing that documentation is (a) painful and/or boring for programmers to write, and (b) essential for programmers to read, Larry Wall created a system to make it as easy as possible to create documentation. The system is prosaically called Plain Old Documentation (POD).

The first convenience of POD is that you can embed it right in the code it's describing; it's just a chunk of text marked off by special lines. You can choose to put the POD anywhere you want; any of the styles shown in Table 10-1 are acceptable and in common usage.

TABLE 10-1 POD Interspersion Styles

Code Before POD	POD Before Code	POD Within Code
Code	POD	Code
Code	POD	POD
Code	POD	Code
Code or __END__	POD	POD
POD	Code	Code
POD	Code	POD
POD	Code	Code
POD	Code	POD

So you can either put the POD all at the beginning, if you think it's the first thing a programmer should see, or all at the end, if you think the code is more important. A small optimization is available to you in the latter case; you can put the POD after a line consisting precisely of the text __END__ and when perl runs your program, it will stop compiling when it sees that line; so even the short time required to recognize and ignore POD will not be used.

The last style is "in line," and this is for when you want the documentation for each function to be embedded right next to that function. Obviously you could even carry it further and intersperse POD at smaller granularities, but bear in mind that anything that increases the amount of space a function requires to be viewed in an editor will make the code harder to read.

The second convenience is that POD is *simple*. Larry reasoned that to get people to write documentation, it had to be as easy as possible to create and edit, so there are only a handful of POD formatting directives to remember. You never have to worry about anything in your code being misinterpreted as POD—POD is only recognized between special lines that begin with an equal sign against the left margin and are followed by a word. Within POD you can cause any text to be output verbatim (nothing in it will be interpreted as formatting directives) simply by indenting it. So including POD with code looks as simple as this, for example:

```
sub quad_roots
{
  my ($a, $b, $c) = @_;
  my $disc = sqrt($b*$b - 4*$a*$c);
  return((-$b + $disc) / 2 / $a, (-$b - $disc) / 2 / $a);
}

=head2 ($root1, $root2) = quad_roots($a, $b, $c);

Return the two roots of a quadratic equation with
the given coefficients, but die if it has imaginary
roots (in which case, use L<Math::Complex>).
Calculated from the classic formula

    -b +/- sqrt(b**2 - 4ac)
    ---------------------
              2a

=cut
```

POD directive lines need to be between blank lines to be recognized. Within non-verbatim POD text, a few primitive markup tags are recognized. The one I used here, L< >, is used to format its contents as a *link;* when output to a format that supports the concept of hyperlinking, the text will be linked to the POD page for Math::Complex (assuming the formatter can find it; read on). Just be aware that it will render the output as "the <u>Math::Complex</u> manpage" unless I override the default text for links with something like:

```
use L<Math::Complex|the Math::Complex module>.
```

Remember, POD is for your users to see; notes intended to help maintenance programmers understand that nuances of implementation belong in in-line comments. At the other end of the scale, you might have pure documentation to create (embodying design, perhaps, or requirements, use cases, or customer stories). Go ahead and use POD for that also; there's no law that says it has to be in files that also contain Perl code.

10.3.2 POD Formatters

The main benefit of POD comes from extracting it into a form that contains only documentation. Just as we are used to reading documentation in many formats, POD can be converted to those many formats as well. The Perl core comes with programs for converting POD to text, LaTeX, HTsML, and UNIX *troff* manual page markup: they're all called pod2*something* and you'll find them in the directory where your distribution programs are installed, probably the same directory as *perl*. CPAN contains many more converters; search for "Pod::" in "Modules." For example, Matt Sergeant's *pod2xml* (http://search.cpan.org/dist/Pod-XML/).

10.4 Custom Warnings

Suppose you have written a module containing this method:

```
use Carp;
use Time::Local;

# Expect date in form MM/DD/YYYY
sub set_date
{
  my ($self, $date) = @_;
  my ($mon, $day, $year) = split m#/#, $date;
  length($year) == 2
    and carp "Y2K bug, year interpreted in"
            . " rolling century window";

  $self->{date} = timelocal(0, 0, 0, $day, $mon-1, $year);
}
```

You earn bonus points for using `carp()` instead of `warn()`(because `carp()` reports the error as occurring on the line of code that called this routine rather than the line of code containing the `carp()`; that's what you want to do in modules when you're warning of an error made by your user and not yourself). However, points are deducted for making the warning mandatory. We can do better, using lexical warnings:

```
1   use warnings;
2   use Time::Local;
3
4   # Expect date in form MM/DD/YYYY
5   sub set_date
6   {
7     my ($self, $date) = @_;
8     my ($mon, $day, $year) = split m#/#, $date;
9     if (length($year) == 2)
10    {
11      warnings::warnif("y2k", "Y2K bug, year interpreted in
   rolling century window");
12    }
13    $self->{date} = timelocal(0, 0, 0, $day, $mon-1, $year);
14  }
```

In line 1, we used the lexical warnings pragma (which should have been there anyway). That allowed us in line 11 to call the `warnings::warnif()` function, which issues the warning in its second parameter if the warning category in the first parameter is enabled.

The *perllexwarn* page told us that there is a hierarchy of warning categories, one of which is called "y2k", which looked appropriate, so we reused it. If the caller of this method does not want to see the warning, all they need to do is exclude it:

```
{
  no warnings 'y2k';
  $object->set_date('4/1/99');
}
```

If you want, you can define your own warning categories instead of being restricted to the standard ones; see *perllexwarn*.

If every module author used this method for issuing warnings, there'd be no need to ever use -w again.

10.5 *Version Control System Integration*

If you're using Revision Control System (RCS), you might like to have the RCS version number automatically be used as the version number of your code. The package variable $VERSION should be set in a module because various tools will look for it. However, you can't just say:

```
our $VERSION = '$Revision$';
```

because version numbers need to be numeric. What you need is an expression that incorporates the RCS Revision keyword and returns the numeric component of it. Here's one possibility:

```
our $VERSION = (qw$Revision: 3.42 $)[-1];
```

which cunningly uses the RCS $ keyword delimiter as the delimiter for the qw operator, extracting just the number 3.42 from the second space-separated component.

If you prefer more than two components to your version numbers, the ExtUtils::MakeMaker documentation shows an alternative approach:

```
our $VERSION = do { my @r = (q$Revision: 1.2.3 $ =~ /\d+/g); \
sprintf "%d"."%03d" x $#r, @r };
```

For MakeMaker to recognize this as a $VERSION assignment, all that code must be on one line.

Concurrent Versions System (CVS) uses the same keywords. Source Code Control Systems (SCCS) is used far less frequently than either RCS or CVS, but it would be trivial to do version numbering with it:

```
our $VERSION = "%I%";
```

Note the quotation marks: Perl has allowed *v-strings* for several versions (numbers that contain more than one period; they get turned into a binary form), but they were deprecated for versions of Perl after 5.8.1, so I conservatively stringified the version.

Because Subversion's version keyword is $Rev: $, you can just reuse the RCS suggestion for that product.

Chapter 11

A Case Study

"This cute mild curry uses 100% Japanese apple and cheerful hamster."

— Label on a package of Japanese Ham Monde curry, engrish.com

Let's put this book's lessons into practice with an example. I'll go over the phases of taking over a program that just landed in our In Bin. Space considerations—and not-boring-the-reader considerations—prevent me from covering a large program, so this example will be fairly small, and not egregiously bad to begin with. While it uses a capability—LDAP directory lookup—that you might have little use for, understanding LDAP is not important for understanding how this code is changed, and besides, LDAP is worth learning anyway.[1]

11.1 The Setup

Our program arrives in the form of a CGI program called dirsearch.cgi, and it is the target of a form that accepts inputs named *username, location,* and *hair-color.* It may help to understand what this program is doing if we look at the input form for this program and its response (see Figures 11.1 and 11.2):

FIGURE 11.1 Input form for dirsearch.cgi.

---

1. LDAP stands for "Lightweight Directory Access Protocol," and is getting more use every day.

FIGURE 11.2 Output from dirsearch.cgi.

Here is the code:

Example 11.1 dirsearch.cgi, Version 1

```perl
1   #!/usr/local/bin/duaperl
2
3   print "Content-type: text/html\n\n";
4
5   @values = split(/&/, $ENV{'QUERY_STRING'});
6   foreach $input (@values)
7   {
8     ($one, $two) = split(/=/,$input);
9     $filter && do_error("Cannot lookup by >1 attribute... pick
    one only");
10    $filter = "($one=$two)";
11  }
12  $filter || do_error("Need an attribute to search on");
13  &dua_settmout(10, 0);
14  unless (&dua_open("whitepages", 389, $dn, $pwd))
15  {
16    $msg = "Can't connect to whitepages: $dua_errstr";
17    do_email($msg);
18    do_error($msg);
19  }
20  $scope = 1;
21  $all = 0;
22  $rdn = '@dc=oz@dc=city@dc=emerald@dc=wp@ou=People';
23  %list = &dua_find($rdn, $filter, $scope, $all);
24  if ($dua_errstr)
```

```
25  {
26    do_email($dua_errstr);
27    do_error($dua_errstr);
28  }
29  unless (%list)
30  {
31    print "<HTML><HEAD><TITLE>Error</TITLE></HEAD><BODY>\n";
32    print "<H1>Error</H1><P>No match for $filter</P>\n";
33    print "</BODY></HTML>\n";
34    exit;
35  }
36  print "<HTML><HEAD><TITLE>Search Results</TITLE></HEAD>\n";
37  print "<BODY><H1>Results of search for $filter</H1>\n";
38  print "<TABLE BORDER=\"1\">\n";
39  print <<HEADER;
40  <TR><TH>username</TH>
41  <TH>location</TH>
42  <TH>haircolor</TH>
43  <TH>telephone</TH>
44  <TH>email</TH>
45  <TH>fax</TH>
46  <TH>name</TH></TR>
47  HEADER
48  foreach $i (sort { $a <=> $b } keys %list)
49  {
50    $dn = "\@". join("\@", reverse(split(/,\s*/, $list{$i})));
51    %attr = &dua_show($dn);
52    $username = $attr{'username'};
53    $location = $attr{'location'};
54    $haircolor = $attr{'haircolor'};
55    $telephone = $attr{'telephone'};
56    $email = $attr{'email'};
57    $fax = $attr{'fax'};
58    $name = $attr{'name'};
59    print "<TR><TD>$username</TD><TD>$location</TD>";
60    print "<TD>$haircolor</TD><TD>$telephone</TD>";
61    print "<TD>$email</TD><TD>$fax</TD><TD>$name</TD></TR>\n";
62  }
63  print "</TABLE></BODY></HTML>\n";
64
65  &dua_close();
66
```

```
67  sub do_error
68  {
69    local $mess = shift;
70    return unless $mess;
71    print "<HTML><HEAD><TITLE>Error</TITLE></HEAD><BODY>\n";
72    print "<H1>Error</H1><P>$mess</P>\n";
73    print "</BODY></HTML>\n";
74    exit;
75  }
76
77  sub do_email
78  {
79    local $mess = shift;
80    open MAIL, "|/usr/lib/sendmail -oi -t";
81    print MAIL "To: me\@here\n";
82    print MAIL "Subject: $0: LDAP lookup problem\n";
83    print MAIL "\n";
84    print MAIL "Error in LDAP processing in $0:\n\n";
85    print MAIL "$mess\n";
86    close MAIL;
87  }
```

11.2 Triage

After a brief pause to vent our frustration, we check to see if the program is still working in any environment we have access to. If so, we can construct a test that will tell us at any point whether our revised versions of the program are still working:

Example 11.2 Test for dirsearch.cgi, Version 1

```
#!/usr/bin/perl
use strict;
use warnings;

use Test::More tests => 6;
use WWW::Mechanize;
```

```
my $URL = "http://www.city.oz/oldcode/dirsearch.cgi";
my %SEARCH = (username  => "dorothy",
              location  => "Kansas",
              haircolor => "red");
my $ua = WWW::Mechanize->new;

for my $attr (keys %SEARCH)
{
  ok($ua->get("$URL?$attr=$SEARCH{$attr}")->is_success,
     "Submit okay");
  like($ua->content, qr/Dorothy Gale/, "Result okay");
}
```

The URL points to the location of the latest version of dirsearch.cgi as we edit it. Each different query should produce a page that contains directory search results containing at least the one person that all the query attributes are drawn from, including her full name.

Now we inspect the program for signs of its age. No need to look at its teeth this time; while the absence of use or my and the presence of local are strong hints, the dead giveaway is the duaperl in the first line. That dates it positively as Perl 4 code. The lack of warnings checking (there was no strict pragma in Perl 4), along with the fact that they did use hashes appropriately, means the programmer was about level 4.

En route to making this program maintainable, there are many problems with it that we should fix:

- There are many constants, configurable data, and magic numbers spread throughout the code.
- The HTML output is interwoven into the code instead of being easily viewed and edited.
- There are several hidden dependencies and other fragilities in the code.
- The code makes no attempt to secure itself against malicious inputs.

We will attack these problems through a process of successive refinement called *refactoring* (see [CHROMATIC03] for a concise discussion of this term and [FOWLER99] for a complete exposition). At each stage we will be applying more advanced techniques to gain greater advantages of maintainability; in practice, you might not carry a project as far as this one goes, depending on how much time and expertise you have at your disposal.

Let's get started by using line editing to compress the program to make it easier to read. Along the way, we'll make the executive decision that we can change the HTML output if we want as long as it still looks the same in a browser. So insignificant white space, in particular line breaks, don't have to match the original output. (Anyone who is depending on the formatting of white space in HTML deserves to have their cage rattled, anyway.)

Lines 32–35 are identical to the function of the do_error() subroutine, so we can call that routine instead. A couple of places call do_error() and do_email() in succession with the same message, so we can make a subroutine just for that purpose. The repetition in lines 40–46, 52–58, and 59–61 can be removed with map().

Example 11.3 dirsearch.cgi, Version 2

```
1   #!/usr/local/bin/duaperl
2
3   print "Content-type: text/html\n\n";
4
5   @values = split(/&/, $ENV{'QUERY_STRING'});
6   foreach $input (@values)
7   {
8     ($one, $two) = split(/=/,$input);
9     $filter && do_error("Cannot lookup by >1 attribute... pick
    one only");
10    $filter = "($one=$two)";
11  }
12  $filter || do_error("Need an attribute to search on");
13  &dua_settmout(10, 0);
14  unless (&dua_open("whitepages", 389, $dn, $pwd))
15  {
```

```
16    $msg = "Can't connect to whitepages: $dua_errstr";
17    do_email_error($msg);
18  }
19  $scope = 1;
20  $all = 0;
21  $rdn = '@dc=oz@dc=city@dc=emerald@dc=wp@ou=People';
22  %list = &dua_find($rdn, $filter, $scope, $all);
23  if ($dua_errstr)
24  {
25    do_email_error($dua_errstr);
26  }
27  unless (%list)
28  {
29    do_error("No match for $filter");
30  }
31  print "<HTML><HEAD><TITLE>Search Results</TITLE></HEAD>\n";
32  print "<BODY><H1>Results of search for $filter</H1>\n";
33  print "<TABLE BORDER=\"1\"><TR>\n";
34  my @attrs = qw(username location haircolor
35                 telephone email fax name);
36  print map "<TH>$_</TH>", @attrs;
37  print "</TR>\n";
38  foreach $i (sort { $a <=> $b } keys %list)
39  {
40    $dn = "\@". join("\@", reverse(split(/,\s*/, $list{$i})));
41    %attr = &dua_show($dn);
42    print "<TR>", map "<TD>$attr{$_}</TD>", @attrs;
43  }
44  print "</TR></TABLE></BODY></HTML>\n";
45
46  &dua_close();
47
48  sub do_email_error
49  {
50    my $mess = shift;
51    do_email($mess);
52    do_error($mess);
53  }
```

The do_error() and do_email() routines are as yet unchanged and therefore are not shown.

11.3 Desperately Seeking Sanity

We can't run this code yet for the simple reason that we're in the process of upgrading it to Perl 5 and we've already used Perl 5-isms such as map() and my to make the code more concise. In order to get it working we will have to get the LDAP code working. If we can get Dua.pm built—and that's a big "if," because I could only get it to build for Perl 5.004—we can do a nearly straight-forward replacement of &dua_ with $dua-> after creating a new Dua object. Errors are reported via a method instead of an exported variable, that's all:

Example 11.4 dirsearch.cgi, Version 3

```
1   #!/usr/bin/perl
2   use Dua;
3   print "Content-type: text/html\n\n";
4
5   @values = split(/&/, $ENV{'QUERY_STRING'});
6   foreach $input (@values)
7   {
8     ($one, $two) = split(/=/,$input);
9     $filter && do_error("Cannot lookup by >1 attribute... pick
    one only");
10    $filter = "($one=$two)";
11  }
12  $filter || do_error("Need an attribute to search on");
13  my $dua = Dua->new;
14  $dua->settmout(10, 0);
15  unless ($dua->open("whitepages", 389, $dn, $pwd))
16  {
17    $msg = "Can't connect to whitepages: " . $dua->error";
18    do_email_error($msg);
19  }
20  $scope = 1;
21  $all = 0;
22  $rdn = '@dc=oz@dc=city@dc=emerald@dc=wp@ou=People';
23  %list = $dua->find($rdn, $filter, $scope, $all);
24  if ($dua->error)
25  {
26    do_email_error($dua->error);
```

```
27  }
28  unless (%list)
29  {
30    do_error("No match for $filter");
31  }
32  print "<HTML><HEAD><TITLE>Search Results</TITLE></HEAD>\n";
33  print "<BODY><H1>Results of search for $filter</H1>\n";
34  print "<TABLE BORDER=\"1\"><TR>\n";
35  my @attrs = qw(username location haircolor
36         telephone email fax name);
37  print map "<TH>$_</TH>", @attrs;
38  print "</TR>\n";
39  foreach $i (sort { $a <=> $b } keys %list)
40  {
41    $dn = "\@". join("\@", reverse(split(/,\s*/, $list{$i})));
42    %attr = $dua->show($dn);
43    print "<TR>", map "<TD>$attr{$_}</TD>", @attrs;
44  }
45  print "</TR></TABLE></BODY></HTML>\n";
46
47  $dua->close;
```

Again I have omitted the unchanged subroutines. This is a major milestone in that we have it working on Perl 5, so now we can impose strictness and warnings on it. There is no need to invoke it via a web browser, because running it at the command line after inserting use strict and use warnings (in this case, -w if we're stuck with Perl 5.004 because that's the only perl we can build Dua.pm on) tells us all we need to know:

```
Global symbol "values" requires explicit package name at dirsearch.cgi line 8.
Global symbol "input" requires explicit package name at dirsearch.cgi line 9.
Global symbol "one" requires explicit package name at dirsearch.cgi line 11.
Global symbol "two" requires explicit package name at dirsearch.cgi line 11.
Global symbol "filter" requires explicit package name at dirsearch.cgi line 12.
Global symbol "dua" requires explicit package name at dirsearch.cgi line 16.
Global symbol "dn" requires explicit package name at dirsearch.cgi line 18.
Global symbol "pwd" requires explicit package name at dirsearch.cgi line 18.
Global symbol "msg" requires explicit package name at dirsearch.cgi line 20.
Global symbol "scope" requires explicit package name at dirsearch.cgi line 23.
Global symbol "all" requires explicit package name at dirsearch.cgi line 24.
Global symbol "rdn" requires explicit package name at dirsearch.cgi line 25.
Global symbol "list" requires explicit package name at dirsearch.cgi line 26.
Global symbol "i" requires explicit package name at dirsearch.cgi line 41.
```

```
Global symbol "attr" requires explicit package name at dirsearch.cgi line 45.
Global symbol "mess" requires explicit package name at dirsearch.cgi line 61.
Execution of dirsearch.cgi aborted due to compilation errors.
```

In the process of inserting enough my statements to fix these problems we find out that the $dn and $pwd in line 15 of Example 11.4 were never set to anything, are therefore undefined, and so might as well be left out of the subroutine call anyway since unspecified values are the same as undefined ones nearly always. The code now looks like this:

Example 11.5 dirsearch.cgi, Version 4

```perl
1    #!/usr/bin/perl -w
2    use strict;
3    use Dua;
4    print "Content-type: text/html\n\n";
5
6    my @values = split(/&/, $ENV{'QUERY_STRING'});
7    my $filter;
8    foreach my $input (@values)
9    {
10     my ($one, $two) = split(/=/,$input);
11     $filter && do_error("Cannot lookup by >1 attribute... pick
     one only");
12     $filter = "($one=$two)";
13   }
14   $filter || do_error("Need an attribute to search on");
15   my $dua = Dua->new;
16   $dua->settmout(10, 0);
17   unless ($dua->open("whitepages", 389, $dn, $pwd))
18   {
19     my $msg = "Can't connect to whitepages: " . $dua->error";
20     do_email_error($msg);
21   }
22   my ($scope, $all) = (1, 0);
23   my $rdn = '@dc=oz@dc=city@dc=emerald@dc=wp@ou=People';
24   my %list = $dua->find($rdn, $filter, $scope, $all);
25   if ($dua->error)
26   {
27     do_email_error($dua->error);
28   }
```

```
29  unless (%list)
30  {
31    do_error("No match for $filter");
32  }
33  print "<HTML><HEAD><TITLE>Search Results</TITLE></HEAD>\n";
34  print "<BODY><H1>Results of search for $filter</H1>\n";
35  print "<TABLE BORDER=\"1\"><TR>\n";
36  my @attrs = qw(username location haircolor
37                 telephone email fax name);
38  print map "<TH>$_</TH>", @attrs;
39  print "</TR>\n";
40  foreach my $i (sort { $a <=> $b } keys %list)
41  {
42    my $dn = "\@". join("\@", reverse(split(/,\s*/,
      $list{$i})));
43    my %attr = $dua->show($dn);
44    print "<TR>", map "<TD>$attr{$_}</TD>", @attrs;
45  }
46  print "</TR></TABLE></BODY></HTML>\n";
47
48  $dua->close;
49
50  sub do_email_error
51  {
52    my $mess = shift;
53    do_email($mess);
54    do_error($mess);
55  }
56
57  sub do_error
58  {
59    my $mess = shift;
60    return unless $mess;
61    print "<HTML><HEAD><TITLE>Error</TITLE></HEAD><BODY>\n";
62    print "<H1>Error</H1><P>$mess</P>\n";
63    print "</BODY></HTML>\n";
64    exit;
65  }
66
67  sub do_email
68  {
69    my $mess = shift;
```

```
70   open MAIL, "|/usr/lib/sendmail -oi -t";
71   print MAIL "To: me\@here\n";
72   print MAIL "Subject: $0: LDAP lookup problem\n";
73   print MAIL "\n";
74   print MAIL "Error in LDAP processing in $0:\n\n";
75   print MAIL "$mess\n";
76   close MAIL;
77 }
```

11.4 Coming into the 21st Century

Now we can no longer ignore the fact that we are using an ancient, unsupported module (Dua.pm) for LDAP operations, and we look up the documentation for Net::LDAP. Line by line we replace Dua.pm calls with Net::LDAP calls. This requires us to learn Net::LDAP if we don't already know it, but doing so will pay handsome dividends. Here are the changes we have to make:

- The timeout is now specified in the `new()` constructor.

- If the constructor fails it returns `undef` and puts the error in `$@`.

- The login to the server (called *binding* in LDAP terminology) is a separate method call, even though we are making an anonymous connection.

- Searching is done by the `search()` method, which returns a result object in the Net::LDAP::Search class.

- The `bind()` and `search()` methods return objects that have a `code()` method that returns true on error, and an `error()` method that returns the error text.

- The Net::LDAP::Search class has a method, `count()`, which returns the number of results found, and another method, `entries()`, which returns all the results as a list of Net::LDAP::Entry objects.

- Each Net::LDAP::Entry object has a `get_value()` method that will return the value of a named attribute.

• The base distinguished name (DN) of the search can now be specified in the natural order instead of the reversed order with @ separators that duaperl perversely required. We move it to the head of the program to get a head start on moving all magic constants there.

In the process, we discover that the magic number 389 in the Dua::open() method is actually the default port number for LDAP connections, so we can leave it out altogether. These changes bring us to:

Example 11.6 dirsearch.cgi, Version 5

```perl
1   #!/usr/bin/perl
2   use strict;
3   use warnings;
4   use Net::LDAP;
5
6   print "Content-type: text/html\n\n";
7   my $rdn = 'ou=People, dc=wp, dc=emerald, dc=city, dc=oz';
8
9   my @values = split(/&/, $ENV{'QUERY_STRING'});
10  my $filter;
11  foreach my $input (@values)
12  {
13    my ($one, $two) = split(/=/,$input);
14    $filter && do_error("Cannot lookup by >1 attribute... pick
    one only");
15    $filter = "($one=$two)";
16  }
17  $filter || do_error("Need an attribute to search on");
18  my $ldap = Net::LDAP->new("whitepages", timeout => 10)
19    or do_email_error("Can't connect to whitepages: $@");
20  my $mesg = $ldap->bind;
21  $mesg->code and do_email_error("Bind error: "
22                                  . $mesg->error);
23  my $res = $ldap->search(base => $rdn, filter => $filter,
    scope => 'sub');
24  $res->code and do_email_error("Search failure: "
25                                  . $res->error);
26
```

```
27  $res->count or do_error("No match for $filter");
28
29  print "<HTML><HEAD><TITLE>Search Results</TITLE></HEAD>\n";
30  print "<BODY><H1>Results of search for $filter</H1>\n";
31  print "<TABLE BORDER=\"1\"><TR>\n";
32  my @attrs = qw(username location haircolor
33          telephone email fax name);
34  print map "<TH>$_</TH>", @attrs;
35  print "</TR>\n";
36  foreach my $ent ($res->entries)
37  {
38    print "<TR>", map "<TD>" . $ent->get_value($_)
39                            . "</TD>", @attrs;
40  }
41  print "</TR></TABLE></BODY></HTML>\n";
42
43  $ldap->unbind;
```

Again, the later subroutines are as yet unchanged (but fear not, their day is coming). Now we have a program that uses only modern modules and runs on our latest perl. Are we done? Hardly. First, let's get rid of that festering sore of $ENV{QUERY_STRING} parsing. The problems with this approach start with the fact that it only works for forms submitted via the GET method and rapidly get far worse. Using CGI.pm will also allow us to test the program from the command line easily:

```
% ./dirsearch.cgi username=dorothy
```

and therefore we can make our test program run much faster by changing it to follow suit:

Example 11.7 Test for dirsearch.cgi, Version 2

```
#!/usr/bin/perl
use strict;
use warnings;

use Test::More tests => 3;
```

```
my %SEARCH = (username  => "dorothy",
              location  => "kansas",
              haircolor => "red");

for my $attr (keys %SEARCH)
{
  like(`./dirsearch.cgi $attr=$SEARCH{$attr}`,
       qr/Dorothy Gale/,
       "Result okay");
}
```

11.5 Incorporating Modules Effectively, Part 1

Let's break out CGI.pm and while we have it, we'll use its header() method in place of the hand-carved string that's been there so far.

While we're editing those lines we'll change the Perl 4-only || and && operators to their more natural or and and cousins, which look better where the intent is to change the flow of control. These changes only affect the first few lines of the program, which now look like this:

```
use CGI qw(param header);
use Net::LDAP;

print header;
my $rdn = 'ou=People, dc=wp, dc=emerald, dc=city, dc=oz';

my $filter;
foreach my $input (param)
{
  my $value = param($input);
  $filter and do_error("Cannot lookup by >1 attribute... pick
one only");
  $filter = "($input=$value)";
}
$filter or do_error("Need an attribute to search on");
```

Now let's do some serious cleaning up and move as many constant values as possible into named symbols at the head of the program. The main program now looks like this:

Example 11.8 dirsearch.cgi, Version 6

```
1   #!/usr/bin/perl
2   use strict;
3   use warnings;
4
5   use CGI qw(param header);
6   use Net::LDAP;
7
8   print header;
9   my %SEARCH_OPTS =
10      (base  => 'ou=People, dc=wp, dc=emerald, dc=city, dc=oz',
11       scope => 'sub');
12  my $LDAP_SERVER = "whitepages";
13  my @LDAP_OPTS = ($LDAP_SERVER, timeout => 10);
14  my @ATTRS = qw(username location haircolor
15                 telephone email fax name);
16
17  my $filter;
18  foreach my $input (param)
19  {
20    my $value = param($input);
21    $filter and do_error("Cannot lookup by >1 attribute...
    pick one only");
22    $filter = "($input=$value)";
23  }
24  $filter or do_error("Need an attribute to search on");
25
26  my $ldap = Net::LDAP->new(@LDAP_OPTS)
27    or do_email_error("Can't connect to $LDAP_SERVER: $@");
28  my $mesg = $ldap->bind;
29  $mesg->code and do_email_error("Bind error: "
30                                  . $mesg->error);
31  my $res = $ldap->search(%SEARCH_OPTS, filter => $filter);
32  $res->code and do_email_error("Search failure: "
33                                  . $res->error);
34
```

```
35  $res->count or do_error("No match for $filter");
36
37  print "<HTML><HEAD><TITLE>Search Results</TITLE></HEAD>\n";
38  print "<BODY><H1>Results of search for $filter</H1>\n";
39  print "<TABLE BORDER=\"1\"><TR>\n";
40  print map "<TH>$_</TH>", @ATTRS;
41  print "</TR>\n";
42  foreach my $ent ($res->entries)
43  {
44    print "<TR>", map "<TD>" . $ent->get_value($_)
45                              . "</TD>", @ATTRS;
46  }
47  print "</TR></TABLE></BODY></HTML>\n";
48
49  $ldap->unbind;
50
51  sub do_email_error
52  {
53    my $mess = shift;
54    do_email($mess);
55    do_error($mess);
56  }
57
58  sub do_error
59  {
60    my $mess = shift;
61    return unless $mess;
62    print "<HTML><HEAD><TITLE>Error</TITLE></HEAD><BODY>\n";
63    print "<H1>Error</H1><P>$mess</P>\n";
64    print "</BODY></HTML>\n";
65    exit;
66  }
67
68  sub do_email
69  {
70    my $mess = shift;
71    open MAIL, "|/usr/lib/sendmail -oi -t";
72    print MAIL "To: me\@here\n";
73    print MAIL "Subject: $0: LDAP lookup problem\n";
74    print MAIL "\n";
75    print MAIL "Error in LDAP processing in $0:\n\n";
76    print MAIL "$mess\n";
```

```
77    close MAIL;
78  }
```

11.6 Incorporating Modules Effectively, Part 2

However, this version feels dissatisfyingly inadequate. All that HTML text also looks like several large constant values; can we do the same with it?

Yes, we can, with HTML::Template. We can break the HTML out into its own files (one for normal output, one for error output) and those files will now contain just HTML. This will achieve separation of code and data—usually a good thing in its own right—and also allow us to pawn off—er, delegate—the job of HTML editing to someone else. Let's transfer the normal result HTML output to a file called output.tmpl:

Example 11.9 output.tmpl, Version 1

```
<HTML><HEAD><TITLE></TITLE></HEAD>
 <BODY>
  <H1>Results of search for <TMPL_VAR NAME=filter></H1>
  <TABLE BORDER="1">
   <TR>
    <TH>username</TH>
    <TH>location</TH>
    <TH>haircolor</TH>
    <TH>telephone</TH>
    <TH>email</TH>
    <TH>fax</TH>
    <TH>name</TH>
   </TR>
   <TMPL_LOOP NAME="results">
    <TR>
     <TD><TMPL_VAR NAME="username"></TD>
     <TD><TMPL_VAR NAME="location"></TD>
     <TD><TMPL_VAR NAME="haircolor"></TD>
     <TD><TMPL_VAR NAME="telephone"></TD>
     <TD><TMPL_VAR NAME="email"></TD>
```

```
   <TD><TMPL_VAR NAME="fax"></TD>
   <TD><TMPL_VAR NAME="name"></TD>
  </TR>
 </TMPL_LOOP>
 </TABLE>
</BODY>
</HTML>
```

The error text goes in a template called error.tmpl:

Example 11.10 error.tmpl, Version 1

```
<HTML><HEAD><TITLE>Error</TITLE></HEAD>
 <BODY>
  <H1>Error</H1>
   <P><TMPL_VAR NAME="reason"></P>
 </BODY>
</HTML>
```

In order to use these templates, we must bundle all our data up with the param() method of HTML::Template and output it in one go with the output() method. The full program (except for the do_email() subroutine, which isn't changing—yet) is now:

Example 11.11 dirsearch.cgi, Version 7

```
1   #!/usr/bin/perl
2   use strict;
3   use warnings;
4
5   use CGI qw(param header);
6   use Net::LDAP;
7   use HTML::Template;
8
9   my %SEARCH_OPTS =
10     (base  => 'ou=People, dc=wp, dc=emerald, dc=city, dc=oz',
11      scope => 'sub');
12  my $LDAP_SERVER = "whitepages";
13  my @LDAP_OPTS = ($LDAP_SERVER, timeout => 10);
```

```perl
14 my @ATTRS = qw(username location haircolor
15        telephone email fax name);
16
17 my $filter;
18 foreach my $input (param)
19 {
20   my $value = param($input);
21   $filter and do_error("Cannot lookup by >1 attribute...
   pick one only");
22   $filter = "($input=$value)";
23 }
24 $filter or do_error("Need an attribute to search on");
25
26 my $ldap = Net::LDAP->new(@LDAP_OPTS)
27   or do_email_error("Can't connect to $LDAP_SERVER: $@");
28 my $mesg = $ldap->bind;
29 $mesg->code and do_email_error("Bind error: "
30                                 . $mesg->error);
31 my $res = $ldap->search(%SEARCH_OPTS, filter => $filter);
32 $res->code and do_email_error("Search failure: "
33                                 . $res->error);
34
35 $res->count or do_error("No match for $filter");
36
37 my $tem = HTML::Template->new(filename => "output.tmpl");
38 my @results;
39 foreach my $ent ($res->entries)
40 {
41   push @results,
42     { map { $_ => $ent->get_value($_) } @ATTRS };
43 }
44 $tem->param(filter => $filter, results => \@results);
45 print header, $tem->output;
46
47 $ldap->unbind;
48
49 sub do_email_error
50 {
51   my $mess = shift;
52   do_email($mess);
53   do_error($mess);
54 }
```

```
55
56  sub do_error
57  {
58    my $mess = shift;
59    my $tem = HTML::Template->new(filename => "error.tmpl");
60    $tem->param(reason => $mess);
61    exit;
62  }
```

In line 41 we are pushing onto @results a reference to an anonymous hash, the contents of which are the result of applying the map() function to the @ATTRS array. The map() block evaluates to the two-element list of attribute name (from @ATTRS), and attribute value (from the Net::LDAP::Entry object), thus giving us the key-value pair for the hash. In do_error(), we realized that the original and rather warped logic behind the return unless $mess line (line 60 in version 4) doesn't apply . . . and apparently never did, in any version of the program we have seen. Expect to find vestigial code such as this in your own inherited programs; it might once have made sense, but as soon as you are sure that it has no place in your program, get rid of it. It's your program now, and you need to know why every line of code is there.

11.7 Making It Mature, Part 1

Are we satisfied yet? No! This program is still fragile because of duplication of information: The template contains the list of attributes, twice, and so does our program, and they all have to be in the same order. If the list of attributes changes, we'll have to update three places. Furthermore, our CGI parameter-parsing loop blindly accepts the first parameter it sees and assumes it is a search term. A future change to the input might pass in some other kind of parameter and then we'd pick up the wrong one. That change could happen by accident: Someone might be using an HTML editor that gives a NAME attribute to the submit button and then we'd receive an input parameter for the button click.

Let's get the template to use the list of attributes in the program, and at the same time, specify which attributes are search parameters. The results template now needs a loop wherever it had a list of attributes and becomes:

Example 11.12 output.tmpl, Version 2

```
<HTML><HEAD><TITLE>Search Results</TITLE></HEAD>
 <BODY>
  <H1>Results of search for <TMPL_VAR NAME=filter></H1>
  <TABLE BORDER="1">
   <TR>
    <TMPL_LOOP NAME="attributes">
     <TH><TMPL_VAR NAME="attribute"></TH>
    </TMPL_LOOP>
   </TR>
   <TMPL_LOOP NAME="results">
    <TR>
     <TMPL_LOOP NAME="attributes">
     <TD><TMPL_VAR NAME="attribute"></TD>
     </TMPL_LOOP>
    </TR>
   </TMPL_LOOP>
  </TABLE>
 </BODY>
</HTML>
```

While we're at it, this program has gone too long without taint checking, so we add the -T command-line flag to the shebang line. That requires that we untaint inputs that might be used in potentially dangerous operations like opening files. These inputs will only be used in LDAP searches, however, so they don't need untainting for the program to run; but this line of inquiry has put us in a cautious state of mind; could there be any kind of malicious or accidental input that could cause an LDAP search to fail?

It's apparent from looking at the way a filter (LDAP terminology for "search query") is constructed that a value that contained a right parenthesis would cause problems because it would appear that the filter ended at that point and contained extraneous characters. That is enough to make us wonder what other characters might cause a problem, and we browse the Net::LDAP documentation to find out. Finding the module Net::LDAP::Filter in a list, we see its documentation referring to the authoritative reference on the subject, a Request for Comments (RFC): `http://www.ietf.org/rfc/ rfc2254.txt`. That tells us that these characters must be escaped in filter values via hexadecimal encoding: (,), *, \, NUL.

Before we reach for the substitution operator, however, we should be lazy and see if someone else has done the work for us . . . and indeed they ("they" being Graham Barr) have, in Net::LDAP::Filter, the documentation for which states ". . . lets you directly manipulate LDAP filters without worrying about the string representation and all the associated escaping mechanisms." And the documentation for the `search()` method of Net::LDAP—which we read assiduously before using it, right?—says that the filter parameter can be text, or a Net::LDAP::Filter object. So all we have to do is wrap the filter text inside a Net::LDAP::Filter constructor, and the resulting object can be used in lieu of the filter text, without having to worry about escaping naughty characters.

All this documentation reading has revealed something else to us: The Net::LDAP class supports an option called *onerror,* which affects what happens when a Net::LDAP function has a problem. The code as it stands laboriously checks to see whether the `code()` method of the Net::LDAP object returns a nonzero value, indicating error, after every method call. Or does it? Isn't the `entries()` method a potential point of failure given that it involves a round trip to the server?

Well, why bother checking when we can just use *onerror* to ensure that any problem will be reported to the police; in this case, the "police" will be an exception handler:

Example 11.13 dirsearch.cgi, Version 8

```
1  #!/usr/bin/perl -T
2  use strict;
3  use warnings;
4
```

```perl
5   use CGI qw(param header);
6   use Net::LDAP;
7   use Net::LDAP::Filter;
8   use HTML::Template;
9
10  my %SEARCH_OPTS =
11     (base  => 'ou=People, dc=wp, dc=emerald, dc=city, dc=oz',
12      scope => 'sub');
13  my $LDAP_SERVER = "whitepages";
14  my @LDAP_OPTS = ($LDAP_SERVER, timeout => 10, onerror =>
    'die');
15  my @OUTPUT_ATTRS = qw(username location haircolor
16                        telephone email fax name);
17  my %SEARCH_ATTR = map { ($_ => 1) }
18                        qw(username location haircolor);
19
20  my $filter;
21  foreach my $input (param)
22  {
23    next unless $SEARCH_ATTR{$input};
24    my ($value) = param($input);
25    $filter and do_error("Cannot lookup by >1 attribute...
    pick one only");
26    $filter = "($input=$value)";
27  }
28  $filter or do_error("Need an attribute to search on");
29
30  my $ldap = Net::LDAP->new(@LDAP_OPTS)
31    or do_email_error("Can't connect to $LDAP_SERVER: $@");
32  eval
33  {
34    $ldap->bind;
35    my $res = $ldap->search(%SEARCH_OPTS,
36              filter => Net::LDAP::Filter->new($filter));
37
38    $res->count or do_error("No match for $filter");
39
40    my $tem = HTML::Template->new(filename => "output.tmpl");
41    my @results;
42    foreach my $ent ($res->entries)
43    {
44      push @results, { attributes =>
```

```
45                    [ map +{ attribute => $ent->get_value($_) } =>
46                          @OUTPUT_ATTRS ] };
47    }
48    $tem->param(filter    => $filter,
49                   attributes => [ map +{ (attribute => $_) } =>
      @OUTPUT_ATTRS ]
50                   results    => \@results);
51      print header, $tem->output;
52    };              # Remember the semicolon here!
53
54    do_email_error($@) if $@;
```

Once again, the remaining subroutines have not changed. We removed the unbind() method call because it is superfluous at the end of the program—the connection will be unbound automatically on program exit. Note that we still handle the case of no matches differently; that is one of the normal possible outcomes of the program, we don't need e-mail sent to us about it. Unfortunately, Net::LDAP::new() does not throw an exception if it fails, it returns undef and sets $@ instead.

11.8 Making It Mature, Part 2

Now we're on a roll! Why are we sending e-mail by talking to *sendmail* directly, when every other part of the code is portable to platforms that don't use *sendmail* for sending mail? Another trip to CPAN gives us Mail::Send, from Tim Bunce and Graham Barr, maintained by Mark Overmeer. At the same time, we'll move the mail addressing information up to the beginning of the program for configurability:

```
my %ERR_MAIL_ARGS = (Subject => "$0: LDAP lookup problem",
                     To      => 'me@here');
.
.
.
sub send_email
{
  require Mail::Send;
```

```
  my $sender = Mail::Send->new(%ERR_MAIL_ARGS);
  my $fh = $sender->open;
  print $fh <<"EOM";
Error in LDAP processing in $0:

  @_
EOM
  $fh->close;
}
```

We `require` Mail::Send in order to load it at run time because there's no point in loading the module every time with `use` if it's only going to be needed in extraordinary circumstances. We also gave the subroutine a name that's more appropriate than `do_email()` was.

Can we do better? Of course! (You don't think I'd be asking otherwise, do you?) Let's take those error messages and move them up to the front of the program so they also can become easily configurable by a maintenance programmer; and so we have all the possible failure messages listed in one place (this will help with documentation). Because some of them have variable components, we'll need to insert placeholders and use `sprintf()` to fill in the values.

As long as we're making the program more maintainable, how about considering the quite likely possibility that in the future it will have to deal with multiple search terms combined with some boolean operators? So, we can read in all input terms and for now, insist that the hash contain exactly one name-value pair. (We should also add tests for these errors; I'll leave those as an exercise for the reader at this point.)

We need to consider the possibility that the value of one of the attributes in the directory might be unset, so we want to avoid a warning about the use of an uninitialized value. Finally, because we're being cautious, let's get the NET::LDAP::Entry objects out one at a time via `shift_entry()`, just so we don't have to form the list of all those objects in memory at once. It won't take up any more code.

Example 11.14 dirsearch.cgi, Version 9

```perl
1   #!/usr/bin/perl -T
2   use strict;
3   use warnings;
4
5   use CGI qw(header param);
6   use HTML::Template;
7   use Net::LDAP;
8   use Net::LDAP::Filter;
9
10  my @OUTPUT_ATTRS = qw(username location haircolor
11                        telephone email fax name);
12  my %SEARCH_ATTRS = map { ($_ => 1) }
13                        qw(username location haircolor);
14  my $OUTPUT_TEMPLATE = "output.tmpl";
15  my $ERROR_TEMPLATE  = "error.tmpl";
16
17  my $LDAP_SERVER = "whitepages";
18  my @LDAP_OPTS = ($LDAP_SERVER, onerror => 'die', timeout =>
    10);
19
20  my %ERROR = (
21    TOOMANY => "Cannot lookup by >1 attribute... pick one only",
22    TOOFEW  => "Need an attribute to search on",
23    LDAPCON => "Can't connect to %s: %s",
24    LDAPERR => "LDAP error: %s",
25    NOMATCH => "No match for %s",
26               );
27  my %ERR_MAIL_ARGS = (Subject => "$0: LDAP lookup problem",
28                       To      => 'me@here');
29  my %SEARCH_OPTS =
30    (base  => "ou=People, dc=wp, dc=emerald, dc=city, dc=oz",
31     scope => "sub", attrs => \@OUTPUT_ATTRS);
32
33  my %query = map  { ($_ => param($_) }
34             grep { defined(param($_) } keys %SEARCH_ATTRS;
35  keys %query > 1 and error('TOOMANY');
36  keys %query     or error('TOOFEW');
37
38  my $ldap = Net::LDAP->new(@LDAP_OPTIONS)
```

```
39    or do_email_error(LDAPCON => $LDAP_SERVER, $@);
40
41  eval
42  {
43    $ldap->bind;
44    my ($filter) = map "$_=$query{$_}" => keys %query;
45    my $res = $ldap->search(%SEARCH_OPTS, filter =>
46                        Net::LDAP::Filter->new("($filter)"));
47    $res->count or error(NOMATCH => $filter);
48
49    my $tem = HTML::Template->new(filename =>
50                                  $OUTPUT_TEMPLATE);
51    my @results;
52    while (my $entry = $res->shift_entry)
53    {
54      my @data;
55      for my $attr (@OUTPUT_ATTRS)
56      {
57        my $val = $entry->get_value($attr);
58        push @data, { attribute => defined($val) ? $val : '' };
59      }
60      push @results, { attributes => \@data };
61    }
62    $tem->param(results    => \@results,
63                filter     => $filter,
64                attributes => [ map +{ (attribute => $_) } =>
    @OUTPUT_ATTRS ]
65        );
66    print header, $tem->output;
67  };
68  do_email_error(LDAPERR => $@) if $@;
69
70  sub do_email_error
71  {
72    my $fmt = shift;
73    send_email(@_);
74    error($fmt, @_);
75  }
76
77  sub error
78  {
79    my $fmt = $ERROR{+shift};
```

```
80    my $tem = HTML::Template->new(filename =>
81                                  $ERROR_TEMPLATE);
82    $tem->param(reason => sprintf $fmt, @_);
83    print header, $tem->output;
84    exit;
85  }
```

The `send_email()` subroutine is unchanged.

11.9 Making It Mature, Part 3

The next step consists of removing two lines of code. Specifically, lines 25 and 47. Why? Because they handle a normal case of user error, and we'd prefer that those error messages be under the control of the person who's got the job of editing our output templates. By using the knowledge that a `<TMPL_IF>` tag that names a loop will evaluate as true only if there is at least one item in the loop, we can handle the same condition in output.tmpl:

Example 11.15 output.tmpl, Version 3

```
<HTML><HEAD>
 <TITLE>
  <TMPL_IF NAME="results">
   Search Results
  <TMPL_ELSE>
   Error
  </TMPL_IF>
 </TITLE>
</HEAD>
 <BODY>
  <TMPL_IF NAME="results">
   <H1>Results of search for <TMPL_VAR NAME="filter"></H1>
   <TABLE BORDER="1">
    <TR>
     <TMPL_LOOP NAME="attributes">
      <TH><TMPL_VAR NAME="attribute"></TH>
     </TMPL_LOOP>
```

```
   </TR>
   <TMPL_LOOP NAME="results">
    <TR>
     <TMPL_LOOP NAME="attributes">
     <TD><TMPL_VAR NAME="attribute"></TD>
     </TMPL_LOOP>
    </TR>
   </TMPL_LOOP>
   </TABLE>
  <TMPL_ELSE>
   <H1>Error: No match for <TMPL_VAR NAME="filter"></H1>
  </TMPL_IF>
 </BODY>
</HTML>
```

11.10 Advanced Modification

Are we done yet? We *could* rest on our laurels . . . but something about this code is still unsatisfying. The advanced features we have added obscure what is really going on. We should make it easier to understand even at the expense of adding a few lines of code.

This will involve radical surgery. We will abstract as much as possible of the specialized LDAP code into its own module. We'll leave the handling of templates and e-mail messages to the program itself. We'll make our module a convenience wrapper around Net::LDAP; it will work like a Net::LDAP object, but with a few extra methods. We'll combine the constructor and bind() methods into one, which we'll call connect() to avoid confusion with the behavior of the Net::LDAP::new() method.

Everything to do with the attributes of an entry will go into this module, which we'll call OzLDAP. Because we still need to know the attributes, we'll provide a method attrs() to get them back, which will do double duty: Without any arguments, it will return the list of output attributes, but when handed a Net::LDAP::Entry object, it will return the list of values for the output attributes of that object. The main program now looks like this:

Example 11.16 dirsearch.cgi, Version 10

```perl
1   #!/usr/bin/perl -T
2   use strict;
3   use warnings;
4
5   use CGI qw(header param);
6   use HTML::Template;
7   use lib qw(.);
8   use OzLDAP;
9
10  my $OUTPUT_TEMPLATE = "output.tmpl";
11  my $ERROR_TEMPLATE  = "error.tmpl";
12
13  my %ERR_MAIL_ARGS = (Subject => "$0: LDAP lookup problem",
14                       To      => 'me@here');
15
16  eval
17  {
18    my $ldap = OzLDAP->connect(user_error => \&error);
19    my $res = $ldap->query(map { $_ => param($_) } param);
20
21    my $tem = HTML::Template->new(filename =>
22                                  $OUTPUT_TEMPLATE);
23
24    my @results;
25    while (my $entry = $res->shift_entry)
26    {
27      my @data = map +{ attribute => $_ }
28                  => $ldap->attrs($entry);
29      push @results, { attributes => \@data };
30    }
31    $tem->param(results    => \@results,
32                filter     => $ldap->filter,
33                attributes => [ map +{ (attribute => $_) }
34                                 => $ldap->attrs ]
35               );
36    print header, $tem->output;
37  };
38  if (my $exception = $@)
39  {
```

```
40    send_email($exception);
41    error($exception);
42  }
43
44  sub error
45  {
46    my $message = shift;
47    my $tem = HTML::Template->new(filename =>
48                                  $ERROR_TEMPLATE);
49    $tem->param(reason => $message);
50    print header, $tem->output;
51    exit;
52  }
```

The send_email() subroutine is unchanged. However, notice how in line 18 we passed a callback to the error() subroutine as the user_error parameter to our new object constructor. The purpose of that is for handling user errors; we want any mistake made by a user to be handled by our error() routine without OzLDAP.pm having to know anything about the way we chose to do that. Speaking of which, here's that module:

Example 11.17 OzLDAP.pm

```
1   package OzLDAP;
2   use strict;
3   use warnings;
4
5   use Carp;
6   use Net::LDAP;
7   use Net::LDAP::Filter;
8
9   my @OUTPUT_ATTRS = qw(username location haircolor
10                        telephone email fax name);
11  my %SEARCH_ATTR = map { ($_ => 1) } qw(username location
    haircolor);
12  my %ERROR = (
13   TOOMANY => "Cannot lookup by >1 attribute... pick one only",
14   TOOFEW  => "Need an attribute to search on",
15   LDAPERR => "LDAP error: %s",
16   LDAPCON => "Can't connect to %s: %s"
```

```
17                    );
18  my $LDAP_SERVER = "whitepages";
19  my @LDAP_OPTS = ($LDAP_SERVER, onerror => 'die',
20                       timeout => 10);
21  my %SEARCH_OPTS = (base  => "ou=People, dc=wp, dc=emerald,
    dc=city, dc=oz",
22                         scope => "sub", attrs => \@OUTPUT_ATTRS);
23  sub connect
24  {
25    my ($class, %opt) = @_;
26    my $error_handler = delete $opt{user_error};
27    my $self = bless { error_handler => $error_handler },
    $class;
28    my $ldap = Net::LDAP->new(@LDAP_OPTS, %opt)
29      or croak _error_message(LDAPCON => $LDAP_SERVER, $@);
30    $self->{ldap} = $ldap;
31    $ldap->bind;
32    $self;
33  }
34
35  sub query
36  {
37    my ($self, %query) = @_;
38    $SEARCH_ATTR{$_} or delete $query{$_} for keys %query;
39
40    keys %query > 1 and $self->_error('TOOMANY');
41    keys %query       or $self->_error('TOOFEW');
42    my ($filter) = map "$_=$query{$_}" => keys %query;
43    $self->{filter} = $filter;
44    $self->{ldap}->search(%SEARCH_OPTS,
45          filter => Net::LDAP::Filter->new("($filter)"));
46  }
47
48  sub _error
49  {
50    my $self = shift;
51    return unless my $error_handler = $self->{error_handler};
52    $error_handler->(_error_message(@_));
53  }
54
55  sub attrs
56  {
```

```
57    my ($self, $entry) = @_;
58    $entry or return @OUTPUT_ATTRS;
59    map defined($entry->get_value($_))
60          ? $entry->get_value($_) : ''
61          => @OUTPUT_ATTRS;
62  }
63
64  sub _error_message
65  {
66    my $fmt = $ERROR{+shift};
67    sprintf $fmt, @_;
68  }
69
70  sub filter
71  {
72    my $self = shift;
73    $self->{filter};
74  }
75
76  sub AUTOLOAD
77  {
78    my $self = shift;
79    our $AUTOLOAD =~ s/.*:://;
80    return if $AUTOLOAD eq 'DESTROY';
81    $self->{ldap}->$AUTOLOAD; (@_);
82  }
83
84  1;
```

Some notable features of this module are:

- The `_error_message()` private subroutine for formatting error messages; it is used by both our private `_error()` method and in the event of a problem in `connect()`.

- The `filter()` method for getting back the text version of the filter the way we like it (without the external parentheses).

- The `query()` method accepts a hash of names and values and uses only the ones that are valid search parameters; if later on we have reason to use a boolean combination of multiple search terms we only need to change this routine.

- The `AUTOLOAD()` routine intercepts any method calls we haven't defined and delegates them to the Net::LDAP object ensconced within our OzLDAP object.

11.10.1 What Next?

At this point, many other possible changes might suggest themselves to you; there are certainly more methods we could add to OzLDAP, for instance. However, in the absence of a need for them it's not clear that the effort would be worth it.

You'd be entitled to point out at this stage that the current version of the program is not only longer than the original, but more complicated. Fair enough. But readability depends on other factors besides length, and we are more expert in Perl than the author of the original program. And in addition to cleaning up unclear and buggy code, we've added many features. We've produced a full-fledged module that both provides a foundation for code reuse (if it takes an LDAP directory to track the denizens of Oz, there are quite likely to be other uses for OzLDAP.pm) and enables us to modify our test script to test the essential search functionality independently of the CGI front end. We might easily have been justified in stopping several revisions ago.

So let's declare success at this point before getting carried away even further. Remember to add POD documentation to the program and the module!

Chapter 12

Conclusion (Prognosis)

"I don't know why I did it, I don't know why I enjoyed it, and I don't know why I'll do it again . . ."

— Bart Simpson in *The Simpsons*

Everything ends, although for a long time this book looked like it was going to be an exception. Let's just say that when I started writing, the original reason given in the Preface for Bill's sudden departure from the company was that his stock options had matured . . .

12.1 In Conclusion

There are many reasons why I use and prefer Perl to other languages; having recently returned from the Open Source Conference and its embedded annual Perl Conference, I am reminded once again of an important one; namely, the quality of the people involved in the development and promotion of Perl. You don't need to attend a conference to experience the pleasure of interacting with these people (although it's certainly the most direct way of doing so); there are various online methods, some of which I will enumerate. A complete list would fill a book in its own right.

12.1.1 Mailing Lists

See `http://lists.perl.org/` for a list far too lengthy and dynamic to reproduce here. Worthy of mention is the beginners list, whose charter is to answer questions from Perl beginners without flaming.

12.1.2 Newsgroups

The main Usenet newsgroups for Perl are the following:

- comp.lang.perl.misc: The main newsgroup for Perl postings, sees about a couple of hundred postings a day, including not a few heated discussions. Many Perl experts hang out here.
- comp.lang.perl.moderated: A low-traffic group (fewer than a dozen postings a day) with a high signal-to-noise ratio. Postings need to be coherent and not asking FAQs in order to be approved.

- comp.lang.perl.modules: Low-traffic group for questions and answers about using and writing Perl modules.

- comp.lang.perl.announce: Very low-traffic moderated group for announcements about some new module releases and other significant events.

- comp.lang.perl.tk: Just for users of PerlTk, the graphical user interface.

- alt.perl: Fewer than a dozen postings a day, but very few experts compared with comp.lang.perl.misc.

- At least 20 regional groups.

In addition, every mailing list hosted on perl.org is also bidirectionally gatewayed to a newsgroup on nntp.perl.org, which is how I prefer to access the lists.

12.1.3 Portals Allowing User Content Creation

- `use.perl.org`: This site is based on Slashdot code and hosts lots of up-to-date news and reactions thereto. This is the best place to post news stories (which will be moderated). A free daily mailing list is also available.

- `www.perlmonks.org`: This site has lots of visitors, and features Q&A discussions and real-time chat. It is an excellent place to get help fast and hone your skills at helping others. The rapid exchanges on topics of new interest mean that Perlmonks threads are often cited elsewhere.

- `www.perlguru.com`: Jasmine Merced's site offers many useful forums for all kinds of Perl questions, including job searches.

12.1.4 Other Web Sites

- `www.perl.com`: O'Reilly's gateway to numerous current and archived articles about Perl and their voluminous book catalog. Free mailing list.

- `www.perl.org`: The community's portal to all things Perl; useful as a "Perl Home Page."

- `www.perldoc.com`: Easy interface to every piece of documentation that came with the current and previous versions of the Perl core back to 5.004.

- `jobs.perl.org`: Worth calling out explicitly from among the many `perl.org` specialized sites, this one is for people looking for work and people looking for workers.

- `learn.perl.org`: Also worth noting explicitly, this site is designed to help people learn Perl.

- `www.stonehenge.com/merlyn/columns.html`: Randal Schwartz has written hundreds of articles for magazine columns and placed them online here; this site is a treasure trove of valuable and interesting examples.

- `perl.plover.com`: Mark-Jason Dominus is incredibly prolific and has placed hundreds of informative articles online. Some (e.g., "Coping with Scoping") have become the de facto citations for answering certain common questions.

- `www.perlmedic.com`: The web site for this book.

Look for Wiki sites to spring up now that Brian Ingerson has made them so easy to create with CGI::Kwiki. A list of Kwikis is maintained at `http://www.kwiki.org/index.cgi?KwikiSites`.

12.1.5 Chat Channels

On just about any Internet Relay Chat (IRC) network, #perl will be populated by Perl people and usually also purl, a "bot" or program (the appropriate term is *agent*) capable of answering various questions, learning from the conversation, and interjecting ad hoc comments. If you're wondering what language it's written in, you haven't been paying attention.

12.1.6 User Groups

There is a worldwide Perl user group society known as the Perl Mongers, based at http://www.pm.org. Quite likely there is a group within a reasonable distance of you, and if not, you can easily start one, as I did. Publishers and other vendors have special deals for Perl Mongers, and there is also a natty line of clothing. pm.org provides web servers and mailing lists for groups on demand.

12.1.7 Periodicals

Two periodicals devoted exclusively to Perl are both available online:

- The Perl Journal, http://www.tpj.com/. Monthly PDF download; $12 for a one-year subscription.
- The Perl Review, http://www.theperlreview.com/. Free PDF download; donations accepted.

12.1.8 Conferences

- In 1997 the first Perl Conference was produced by O'Reilly and Associates in San José, California.[1] In 1999 the rest of the open source world caught up and the conference was expanded to include them. Now the annual Open Source Conference includes—as its largest component—The Perl Conference, and is held every summer on the west coast of North America. See http://conferences.oreillynet.com/oscon/.

- In 1999 some Perl Mongers decided they wanted a low-cost alternative, and held the first Yet Another Perl Conference (YAPC; http://www.yapc.org) at Carnegie-Mellon University. Since then YAPC has expanded to conferences in Europe (http://www.yapc.org/Europe/), and 2003 saw the first

---

1. At the time it was referred to as the "zeroth" Perl Conference because computer people like to start counting from zero. Later on this was recognized to be too confusing and the conference was retroactively renumbered to number 1.

YAPC in Israel (`http://www.perl.org.il/YAPC/`) and the first truly Canadian YAPC (`http://www.yapc.ca/`). The home page of the original North American YAPC is `http://www.yapc.org/America/`.

12.1.9 The Perl Foundation

The nonprofit organization called Yet Another Society (YAS; `http://www.yetanother.org/`) promotes, among other projects, the YAPC events. A YAS affiliate is the Perl Foundation (`http://www.perl-foundation.org/`), which exists to collect donations and fund worthy projects. Current and past benefactors include Larry Wall and Damian Conway. If you're looking to donate money to advancing the progress of Perl, this is the place to send it.

12.2 Perl People

One of the key qualities of Perl people is how much fun they have with the language. I think this is a synergistic and symbiotic relationship between the language and those people; they create a language that is fun to use, which attracts people who like to have fun and then they put more fun into the language. (Don't think this means that the language isn't suited to serious, important work. Perl people believe that you can get more work done by having fun at the same time. Here's hoping that more managers will catch on to that idea.) Attending a Perl conference is a direct way of finding out what Perl people are like.

12.2.1 How to Ask Questions That Get Answered

Perl people, like any computer experts, thrive on accurate and complete information. (They have to be able to think like a computer works.) They also enjoy helping other people. The best way you can ensure that they answer your question is to make it possible and easy for them to do so. Questions that are vague about what is wanted or don't supply enough information to figure out an answer frustrate the people who are reading them, because they are unable to help. They also see that help as a collaboration between themselves and the questioner; when answering questions for free, they want to promote a "pay it forward" model whereby the questioner becomes empowered to help others himself or herself. That goal is frustrated if the questioner doesn't appear willing to make an equal effort to learn.

Knowing these things about how Perl people think allows us to craft questions that get answered. (Here I am talking only about posting to the various online resources previously listed requesting free help; if you are paying a Perl consultant for help you're entitled to get it under whatever terms you agree upon.) Follow these principles:

- Sound coherent. This does not mean that postings by people who are not fluent in the language they are posting in are disparaged; I have seen many postings in halting English that were perfectly clear about their intention. You need to sound like you have enough intelligence to understand the answer, and your words are the only guide readers have for making that evaluation. You must distinguish yourself from the legions of people posting on the Internet who for all intents and purposes sound like infants who have discovered their parents' keyboard.

- Be clear about what you want. Do you want someone to write a piece of code for you, to tell you what's wrong with something you've written, or to explain a concept to you?

- Be humble. Or at least appear that way. Show that you understand that anyone helping you is doing it out of generosity; don't give the impression that you believe you're entitled to an answer.

- Be clear about what happened. If you experienced a problem, report what you did, what the computer's response was, and what you expected it should have been. Don't make assumptions about what the cause was unless you really know, in which case you're not assuming.

- Give all the information needed to solve the problem. If Perl did something you think was wrong, at a minimum you should report the version of Perl and the platform you were running it on (the output of `perl -V` is designed for this purpose).

- Be succinct. If you have a 1,000-line program that generated an error, no one is likely to read the whole thing for free. Condense the problem to the smallest piece of code that demonstrates your issue. Often this process will reveal the answer to you. Code of fewer than 50 lines has a good chance of being read.

- Show that you want to learn. Say where you have already looked in the documentation for help. Did you try a Google search? See in particular `http://groups.google.com/` where you can look to see if someone else has already asked the same question.

- If you've found something wrong with someone else's code and you think you know how to fix it, send them the fix (preferably in `diff -u` format). Such an act takes you out of the category of questioner and puts you into the developer camp, where you will be warmly welcomed (especially if your patch works).

An excellent example of such a question was forwarded to me while I was writing this chapter, and I include it here because there's a twist to it. First, the question:

> I'm working on two slide shows—one on my personal page with photos of my college reunion. This one is working just fine. Take a look: [URL deleted]
>
> I'm using a free perl package from [URL].
>
> When I try the same code on [other Web site] it hangs up with no error message. [hosting service] is the provider for both pages, but they do have different security for personal pages than for business web sites, and they really don't encourage people writing their own perl code, so I'm posing the question to you first.

Here's the code and output for the subroutine it hangs in.

First, here's the output:

[Debugging output mostly deleted. It referred to variables called 'this' and 'that']
this is ...., that is   <--doesn't paste into this message.
"this" is 4 of those square boxes, then an N with ~ over it and an upside down ? next to it followed by 9 more square boxes. "that" is similar with a P before the funny N and an s after the next square box. You can view it yourself at: [URL]

And here's the subroutine: Note I've peppered it with print statements.

[code deleted]

Notice how the questioner provides complete information as to what she's doing, where her code came from, URLs for working and nonworking examples, what the output is (with particular attention to unusual characters she doesn't understand that might not show up the same way for the reader), and the code snippet (not shown) where the problem occurs.

The twist is that the questioner, Mary Byrne, was the 71-year-old mother of a friend of mine. Clearly, age is no barrier to learning how to frame questions properly. Or to learning Perl.

12.3 A Final Thought

One day your code, too, will be inherited by someone else. We all leave behind reminders of our presence wherever we go: some pleasant, some otherwise. Code is one such reminder, admittedly a minor one in the grand scheme of things. However, it can be argued that no act is small, and that you can be judged as accurately from your code as anything else you create. I tell my students that there are three mental prerequisites for a successful programming project (in addition to the expertise that they must acquire anyway):

- You must believe you can do it.
- You must want to make it as good as possible.
- You must have fun doing it.

My best wishes for the success of your own endeavors.

Appendix: Source Code

Tie::Array::Bounded

```perl
package Tie::Array::Bounded;
use strict;
use warnings;
use Carp;

use base qw(Tie::Array);

our $VERSION = '0.01';

sub TIEARRAY
{
  my ($class, %arg) = @_;
  my ($upper, $lower) = delete @arg{qw(upper lower)};
  croak "Illegal arguments in tie" if %arg;
  $lower ||= 0;
  croak "No upper bound for array" unless $upper;
  /\D/ and croak "Array bound must be integer"
    for ($upper, $lower);
  croak "Upper bound < lower bound" if $upper < $lower;
  return bless { upper => $upper,
                 lower => $lower,
                 array => []
               }, $class;
}

sub _bound_check
{
  my ($self, $index) = @_;
  my ($upper, $lower) = @{$self}{qw(upper lower)};
  croak "Index $index out of range [$lower, $upper]"
```

```perl
    if $index < $lower || $index > $upper;
}

sub STORE
{
  my ($self, $index, $value) = @_;
  $self->_bound_check($index);
  $self->{array}[$index] = $value;
}

sub FETCH
{
  my ($self, $index) = @_;
  $self->_bound_check($index);
  $self->{array}[$index];
}

sub FETCHSIZE
{
  my $self = shift;
  scalar @{$self->{array}};
}

sub STORESIZE
{
  my ($self, $size) = @_;
  $self->_bound_check($size-1);
  $#{$self->{array}} = $size - 1;
}

1;

__END__

=head1 NAME

Tie::Array::Bounded - Bounded arrays

=head1 SYNOPSIS

  use Tie::Array::Bounded;
  tie @array, "Tie::Array::Bounded", upper => 100;

=head1 DESCRIPTION

C<Tie::Array::Bounded> is a subclass of L<Tie::Array> that
```

allows you to create arrays which perform bounds checking
upon their indices. A fatal exception will be thrown upon
an attempt to go outside specified bounds.

Usage:

```
tie @array, "Tie::Array::Bounded",
            upper => $upper_limit [, lower => $lower_limit]
```

A mandatory upper limit is specified with the C<upper> keyword.
An optional lower limit is specified with the C<lower> keyword;
the default is 0. Each specifies the limit of array indices
that may be used. Any attempt to exceed them results in the
fatal exception "index <index> out of range [<lower>, <upper>]".

=head1 AUTHOR

Peter Scott, C<Peter@PSDT.com>

=head1 SEE ALSO

L<perltie>, L<Tie::Array>.

=cut

Benchmark::TimeTick

```perl
package Benchmark::TimeTick;

use 5.006;
use strict;
use warnings;
use Exporter;
use File::Basename;

our @ISA       = qw(Exporter);
our @EXPORT_OK = qw(timetick);
our $VERSION   = '0.01';

my @Tix;             # Where we keep the time ticks
our %Opt;            # Global option setting interface
my $Epoch = $^T;     # Point from which times are measured
```

```perl
sub import
{
  my $class = $_[0];

  eval { require Time::HiRes };
  $Epoch = _current_time() if $Opt{reset_start};

  unless ($Opt{suppress_initial})
  {
    my $prog = basename($0);
    timetick("Timeticker for $prog starting");
  }

  $class->export_to_level(1, @_);
}

sub timetick
{
  my $tag = pop;
  $Opt{format_tick_tag} and $tag = $Opt{format_tick_tag}->($tag);
  push @Tix, [ _current_time() - $Epoch, $tag ];
}

sub _current_time
{
  exists &Time::HiRes::time ? Time::HiRes::time() : time;
}

sub report
{
  unless ($Opt{suppress_report})
  {
    &{ $Opt{format_report} || \&_format_report }(@Tix);
  }

  @Tix = ();
}

sub _format_report
{
  printf("%7.4f %s\n", @$_) for @_;
}

sub end
{
  unless ($Opt{suppress_final})
```

```
{
  my $prog = basename($0);
  timetick("Timeticker for $prog finishing");
}

report();
}

END { end() }

1;

__END__
```

=head1 NAME

Benchmark::TimeTick - Keep a tally of times at different places in your
program

=head1 SYNOPSIS

```
use Benchmark::TimeTick qw(timetick);
# Your code...
timetick("Starting phase three");
# More of your code...
```

=head1 DESCRIPTION

C<Benchmark::TimeTick> provides a quick and convenient way of
instrumenting a program to find out how long it took to reach various
points. Just use the module and call the C<timetick()> method whenever
you want to mark the time at a point in your program. When the
program ends, a report will be output giving the times at which each
point was reached.

The times will be recorded using C<Time::HiRes::time()> if
L<Time::HiRes> is available, otherwise C<time()> will be used. (Since
C<time()> has one-second granularity this is unlikely to be useful.)

=head1 CONFIGURATION

You can customize the action of L<Benchmark::TimeTick> via
the package hash C<%Benchmark::TimeTick::Opt>. Recognized keys are:

=over 4

```
=item suppress_initial
```

If true, do not put an initial entry in the report when the
module is loaded.

```
=item suppress_final
```

If true, do not put a final entry in the report when the
program terminates.

```
=item reset_start
```

If true, report all times relative to the time that C<Benchmark::Time-
Tick> was loaded rather than the actual start of the program.

```
=item format_tick_tag
```

If set, should be a reference to a subroutine that will take as
input a C<$tag> passed to C<timetick()> and return the actual tag
to be used. Can be helpful for applying a lengthy transformation
to every tag while keeping the calling code short.

```
=item format_report
```

If set, should be a reference to a subroutine that will take as
input a list of time ticks for reporting. Each list element will be
a reference to an array containing the time and the tag respectively.
The default C<format_report> callback is:

```
  sub { printf("%7.4f %s\n", @$_) for @_ }
```

```
=item suppress_report
```

If true, do not output a report when C<report()> is called; just
reset the time tick list instead.

```
=back
```

For either C<suppress_initial> or C<reset_start> to be effective,
they must be set in C<BEGIN> blocks before this module is C<use>d.

```
=head1 METHODS
```

```
=over 4
```

```
=item Benchmark::TimeTick::timetick($tag)
```

Record the time at this point of the program and label it with
the string C<$tag>.

=item Benchmark::TimeTick::report()

Output a report (unless C<suppress_report> is set) and reset
the time tick list.

=item Benchmark::TimeTick::end()

Add a final time tick (unless C<suppress_final> is set), and output a
report. Called by default when the program finishes.

=back

=head2 Optional Exports

C<Benchmark::TimeTick::timetick()> will be exported on demand.
This is recommended for the sake of brevity.

=head1 EXAMPLE

```
  BEGIN { $Benchmark::TimeTick::Opt{suppress_initial} = 1 }
  use Benchmark::TimeTick qw(timetick);
  # ... time passes
  timetick("Phase 2");
  # ... more time passes, program ends
```

Output from L<Benchmark::TimeTick>:

```
  0.7524 Phase 2
  0.8328 Timeticker for testprog finishing
```

=head1 AUTHOR

Peter Scott, E<lt>PerlMedic@PSDT.comE<gt>

=head1 SEE ALSO

L<Benchmark::Timer>, L<Time::HiRes>.

=head1 COPYRIGHT

Copyright (c) 2004 Peter Scott.

This library is free software; you can redistribute it and/or modify
it under the same terms as Perl itself.

=cut

smallprofpp

```perl
#!/usr/bin/perl
use strict;
use warnings;

use Getopt::Std;
my $USAGE = "Usage: $0 [-c|-w] [profile]\n";
my $MAXLEN = 80;

getopts('cw', \my %opt) or die $USAGE;

my $profile = shift || 'smallprof.out';
open my $fh, '<', $profile
  or die "Can't open profile: $!\n";

my ($header, $filename, @to_sort);
while (<$fh>)
{
  $header = $_, next if /^\s+count/;
  $filename = $1, next if /^\s+Profile of (.*?\S)\s+Page/;
  /^\s+(\d+)\s+([\d.]+)\s+([\d.]+)\s+\d+:/
    and $1 and push @to_sort, [ $_, $2, $3, $filename ];
}
my $which = $opt{c} ? 2 : 1;        # Default: wall clock time
my $other = $which == 1 ? 2 : 1;    # The other time
print $header,
      map  { (my $line = $_->[0]) =~ s/\b\s+(\d+):.*/ /s;
             my $fileline = "$_->[3]:$1";
             if (length($fileline) + length($line) > $MAXLEN)
             {
               substr($fileline,
                      0,
                      length($fileline)+length($line)-$MAXLEN+3,
                      '...');
             }
             "$line$fileline\n";
           }
      sort {    $b->[$which] <=> $a->[$which]
```

```
          || $b->[$other] <=> $a->[$other]
        } @to_sort;
```

```
__END__
```

=head1 NAME

smallprofpp - sort profile data from Devel::SmallProf

=head1 SYNOPSIS

smallprofpp [B<-c>|B<-w>] [profile]

=head1 DESCRIPTION

The I<smallprofpp> command sorts and outputs the named file
(default C<smallprof.out>) produced by Devel::SmallProf. Page
headings are removed and only one header line will be printed;
no lines will be printed for source code lines that were never
called (you can prevent Devel::SmallProf from outputting them
in the first place with the statement

```
  $DB::drop_zeros = 1
```

which may be placed in a C<.smallprof> file; see
Devel::SmallProf). Lines will be sorted in descending order
of either cpu time or wall clock time; ties will be sorted by
the other time.

=head1 OPTIONS

=over 4

=item B<-c>

Sort first by cpu time, second by wall clock time.

=item B<-w>

Sort first by wall clock time, second by cpu time. This is the
default.

=back

=head1 SEE ALSO

L<Devel::SmallProf>.

Bibliography

- **AHO74**: Aho, Alfred V., Hopcroft, John E., and Ullman, Jeffrey D., *The Design and Analysis of Computer Algorithms,* Addison-Wesley (1974). ISBN: 0-201-00029-6.

- **AHO83**: Aho, Alfred V., Ullman, Jeffrey D., and Hopcroft, John E., *Data Structures and Algorithms,* Addison-Wesley (1983). ISBN: 0-201-00023-7.

- **BECK00**: Beck, Kent, *Extreme Programming Explained,* Addison-Wesley (2000). ISBN: 0-201-61641-6.

- **BEKMAN03**: Bekman, Stas and Cholet, Eric, *Practical mod_perl,* O'Reilly & Associates (2003). ISBN: 0-596-00227-0.

- **BENTLEY82**: Bentley, Jon, *Writing Efficient Programs,* Prentice Hall (1982). ISBN: 0-139-70244-X.

- **BOLINGER95**: Bolinger, Don and Bronson, Tan, *Applying RCS and SCCS,* O'Reilly & Associates (1995). ISBN: 1-56592-117-8.

- **BROWN98**: Brown, William J., Malveau, Raphael C., McCormick III, Hays W., and Mowbray, Thomas J., *AntiPatterns,* Wiley (1998). ISBN: 0-471-19713-0.

- **BURKE02**: Burke, Sean M., *Perl & LWP,* O'Reilly & Associates (2002). ISBN: 0-59600-178-9.

- **CHAPMAN98**: Chapman, Nigel, *Perl: The Programmer's Companion,* Wiley (1998). ISBN: 0-471-97563-X.

- **CHRISTIANSEN98**: Christiansen, Tom, at `http://groups.google.com/groups?selm=6bt80h%24req%241%40csnews.cs.colorado.edu`.

- **CHROMATIC03**: chromatic, *Extreme Programming Pocket Guide,* O'Reilly & Associates (2003). ISBN: 0-596-00485-0.

- **CMU03**: `http://www.sei.cmu.edu/cmm/cmm.html`.

- **DESCARTES00**: Descartes, Alligator and Bunce, Tim, *Programming the Perl DBI,* O'Reilly & Associates (2000). ISBN: 1-56592-699-4.

- **DOMINUS98**: Dominus, Mark Jason, at `http://perl.plover.com/FAQs/Namespaces.html`.

- **EIFFEL03**: `http://archive.eiffel.com/doc/manuals/technology/contract/`.

- **FOWLER99**: Fowler, Martin, *Refactoring: Improving the Design of Existing Code,* Addison-Wesley (1999). ISBN: 0-201-48567-2.

- **FRIEDL02**: Friedl, Jeffrey, *Mastering Regular Expressions,* 2nd Edition, O'Reilly & Associates (2002). ISBN: 0-596-00289-0.

- **GAMMA95**: Gamma, Erich, Helm, Richard, Johnson, Ralph, and Vlissides, John. *Design Patterns,* Addison-Wesley (1995). ISBN: 0-201-63361-2.

- **GLOBE99**: `http://www.boston.com/allstar99/news/all_hack_070799.htm`.

- **GUTTMAN98**: Guttman, Uri, at `http://www.sysarch.com/perl/tutorials/hash_slices.txt`.

- **HALL98**: Hall, Joseph N., *Effective Perl Programming,* Addison-Wesley (1998). ISBN: 0-201-41975-0.

- **HOGABOOM03**: Hogaboom, Richard, "Perl and Air Traffic Control," *The Perl Journal*, September 2003.

- **HUMPHREY94**: Humphrey, Watts S., *A Discipline for Software Engineering,* Addison-Wesley (1994). ISBN: 0-201-54610-8.

- **HUNT00**: Hunt, Andrew and Thomas, David. *The Pragmatic Programmer,* Addison-Wesley (2000). ISBN: 0-201-61622-X.

- **JOHNSON99**: Johnson, Andrew L., *Elements of Programming with Perl,* Manning (1999). ISBN: 1-884777-80-5.

- **LEUF01**: Leuf, Bo and Cunningham, Ward, *The Wiki Way,* Addison-Wesley (2001). ISBN: 0-201-71499-X.

- **LIDIE02**: Lidie, Stephen O. and Walsh, Nancy, *Mastering Perl/Tk,* O'Reilly & Associates (2002). ISBN: 1-56592-716-8.

- **OREILLY99**: `http://perl.oreilly.com/news/success_stories.html`.

- **ORWANT99**: Orwant, Jon, Hietaniemi, Jarkko, and Macdonald, John, *Mastering Algorithms with Perl,* O'Reilly & Associates (1999). ISBN: 1-56592-398-7.

- **PEPPLER02**: `http://www.mbay.net/~mpeppler/Sybperl/sybperl-faq.html`.

- **RANDAL03**: Randal, Allison, Sugalski, Dan, and Tötsch, Leopold, *Perl 6 Essentials,* O'Reilly & Associates (2003). ISBN: 0-596-00499-0.

- **RAY02**: Ray, Erik T., and McIntosh, Jason, *Perl & XML,* O'Reilly & Associates (2002). ISBN: 0-596-00205-X.

- **SCHWARTZ97**: Schwartz, Randal L. and Christiansen, Tom, *Learning Perl,* 2nd Edition, O'Reilly & Associates (1997). ISBN: 1-56592-284-0.

- **SCHWARTZ01**: Schwartz, Randal L. and Phoenix, Tom, *Learning Perl,* 3rd Edition, O'Reilly & Associates (2001). ISBN: 0-596-00132-0.

- **SCHWARTZ03a**: Schwartz, Randal L. and Phoenix, Tom, *Learning Perl Objects, References and Modules,* O'Reilly & Associates (2003). ISBN: 0-596-00478-8.

- **SCHWARTZ03b**: Schwartz, Randal L., "Perl of Wisdom," *Linux Magazine*, June 2003.

- **SCOTT01**: Scott, Peter J. and Wright, Ed, *Perl Debugged,* Addison-Wesley (2001). ISBN: 0-201-70054-9.

- **STEIN00**: Stein, Lincoln D., *Network Programming with Perl,* Addison-Wesley (2000). ISBN: 0-201-61571-1.

- **STLAURENT01**: St. Laurent, Simon, Johnston, Joe, and Dumbill, Edd, *Programming Web Services with XML-RPC,* O'Reilly & Associates (2001). ISBN: 0-596-00119-3.

- **SWIFT47**: Swift, Jonathan, *Gulliver's Travels,* Deluxe Edition, Price Stern Sloan (1947). ISBN: 0-44806-010-8.

- **TAYLOR02**: Taylor, Richard, "Order in Pollock's Chaos," *Scientific American,* December 2002.

- **TREGAR02**: Tregar, Sam, *Writing Perl Modules for CPAN,* Apress (2002). ISBN: 1-59059-018-X.

- **VESPERMAN03**: Vesperman, Jennifer, *Essential CVS,* O'Reilly & Associates (2003). ISBN: 0-596-00459-1.

- **WALL96**: Wall, Larry, Christiansen, Tom, and Schwartz, Randal L., *Programming Perl,* 2nd Edition, O'Reilly & Associates (1996). ISBN: 1-56592-149-6.

- **WALL00**: Wall, Larry, Christiansen, Tom, and Orwant, Jon, *Programming Perl,* 3rd Edition. O'Reilly & Associates (2000). ISBN: 0-596-00027-8.

Index

About the Author

PETER J. SCOTT runs Pacific Systems Design Technologies, providing Perl training, application development, and enterprise systems analysis. He was a speaker on the 2002 Perl Whirl cruise and at YAPC::Canada, and he founded his local Perl Monger group. A software developer since 1981 and a Perl developer since 1992, he has also created programs for NASA's Jet Propulsion Laboratory. Scott graduated from Cambridge University, England, with a Master of Arts Degree in Computer Science and now lives in the Pacific Northwest with his wife Grace, a cat, and a parrot, at least one of which also uses Perl. He is the lead author of *Perl Debugged*.

inform IT

YOUR GUIDE TO IT REFERENCE

Articles

Keep your edge with thousands of free articles, in-depth features, interviews, and IT reference recommendations – all written by experts you know and trust.

Online Books

Answers in an instant from **InformIT Online Book's** 600+ fully searchable on line books. Sign up now and get your first 14 days **free**.

POWERED BY

Safari

Catalog

Review online sample chapters, author biographies and customer rankings and choose exactly the right book from a selection of over 5,000 titles.